OPEN

ADMISSIONS

The Poetics and
Pedagogy of
Toni Cade Bambara,
June Jordan,
Audre Lorde, and
Adrienne Rich in the
Era of Free College

OPEN ADMISSIONS

DANICA SAVONICK

DUKE UNIVERSITY PRESS   DURHAM AND LONDON   2024

© 2024 Duke University Press
All rights reserved
Printed in the United States of America
on acid-free paper ∞
Project Editor: Ihsan Taylor
Designed by Aimee C. Harrison
Typeset in Minion Pro, Trade Gothic, and Space Grotesk
by Westchester Publishing Services

Library of Congress Cataloging-in-Publication Data
Names: Savonick, Danica, [date] author.
Title: Open admissions : the poetics and pedagogy of Toni Cade
Bambara, June Jordan, Audre Lorde, and Adrienne Rich in the era of
free college / Danica Savonick.
Description: Durham : Duke University Press, 2024. | Includes
bibliographical references and index.
Identifiers: LCCN 2023042689 (print)
LCCN 2023042690 (ebook)
ISBN 9781478030614 (paperback)
ISBN 9781478026372 (hardcover)
ISBN 9781478059639 (ebook)
Subjects: LCSH: Bambara, Toni Cade. | Jordan, June, 1936–2002.
| Lorde, Audre. | Rich, Adrienne, 1929–2012. | City University of
New York—History. | African Americans—Education (Higher)—New
York (State)—New York—20th century. | African American women in
higher education. | Feminist literary criticism. | BISAC: LITERARY CRITI-
CISM / Feminist | SOCIAL SCIENCE / Ethnic Studies / American / African
American & Black Studies
Classification: LCC LC2781 .S27 2024 (print) | LCC LC2781 (ebook) |
DDC 378.1/982996073—dc23/eng/20240125
LC record available at https://lccn.loc.gov/2023042689
LC ebook record available at https://lccn.loc.gov/2023042690

Cover art credit: (*Clockwise from top left*) June Jordan, circa
1960s, gelatin silver print, Brooklyn Daily Eagle photographs,
Brooklyn Public Library, Center for Brooklyn History; Toni Cade
Bambara, 1972, photo by LeRoy W. Henderson; Adrienne Rich,
circa 1970s, Library of Congress; Audre Lorde, photo by Robert
Giard, copyright estate of Robert Giard.

This book was supported by a subvention from the CUNY Graduate
Center.

For my mom, **Julie Barad,**

my first and most beloved teacher

CONTENTS

Preface: As Free as Air and Water ix
Acknowledgments xiii

Introduction: The Winds of Possibility 1

1   **Toni Cade Bambara**'s Community-Controlled and Multimodal Pedagogy 19

2   "This Class . . . Has Much to Teach America": **June Jordan**'s Public and Project-Based Pedagogy 60

3   Of Parallels and Intersections: **Adrienne Rich**'s Pedagogy of Location 99

4   Sharing the Illumination: **Audre Lorde**'s Pedagogies of Difference 139

Conclusion: An Education Worth Fighting For 177

Notes 183
Bibliography 215
Index 239

PREFACE

As Free as Air and Water

This book is about what free college makes possible.
    Like the writers and students you'll encounter in these pages, my life was changed by free higher education. As an undergraduate, I attended college gratis—something relatively uncommon among my generation. This was primarily due to the fact that my mom was an administrator at our state university, which had a tuition-remission program. Middle-class comfort and white privilege also significantly eased my path. Free from the question of "return on investment" that weighs so heavily on my generation, I took classes based on what I was interested in, who had a reputation for being a life-changing professor, and which courses were transforming my perspectives, and abandoned those (analytic philosophy!) that felt like irrelevant armchair exercises in erudition. In brilliantly themed literature courses like Experimental Lives, the novels we read served as sounding boards for many of us living away from home for the first time, figuring out how—and who—we wanted to be in the world. Classes on Marxism, feminist theory, and Black literature challenged what many of us had been taught about the United States as a nation of freedom and opportunity. Instead, they foregrounded systemic injustice, power disparities, and the uneven distribution of resources in society. Yet they also introduced us to the idea that things could be otherwise: that there are more desirable ways of organizing social life and that such worlds are worth fighting for. Realizing I still had much to learn, I parted ways with my career-bound peers and entered an English PhD program, despite being told there would be no jobs as a professor waiting

for me on the other end. When you don't have looming debt to pay off, such financially dubious but personally enriching choices feel more possible.

This book began in 2012. That year, student debt in the United States surpassed the one-trillion-dollar mark—a figure that now, ten years later, has nearly doubled. Wall Street executives rejoiced as their coffers expanded, while young people's futures slipped through their fingers. That fall, I joined the Free University of New York City, an offshoot of Occupy Wall Street that organized pop-up universities in parks throughout the city. We were a group of primarily twenty- and thirty-somethings, many of whom were pursuing graduate degrees. Though our stipends were meager, we had the attendant luxuries of flexible jobs, health care, and a bit of time with which to organize. What brought us together was a shared belief in education as a human right. We held as our maxim the words of Peter Cooper (founder of the working-class art and architecture school Cooper Union): that education should be "as free as air and water."[1] That fall, we organized outdoor universities where anyone could drop in and take—or teach—a class.

These free universities boiled learning down to its essence: just teachers, students, a schedule, and a hand-drawn map. Notably absent were expensive textbooks, fancy equipment, grades, and, of course, tuition. Some courses were taught by professors who moved their regularly scheduled classes to the park, others by local artists and activists. With no set curriculum, courses reflected topics that were important to us and that we imagined would be interesting and useful to others, too. Many of them—like The Carceral State; 1930s Labor Movements; Jews, the Bronx, and Whiteness; Agrarian Struggles in Latin America; and Hydrofracking and Why It Matters—addressed the material conditions in which our lives were unfolding. Others, like workshops on yoga and puppetry, Dating in NYC, and Fermenting Dissent: Sauerkraut and Quick Pickling, aimed to expand participants' capacities to experience joy and live more fully in the world. Not only did these pop-up universities give rise to new ideas about what might be a suitable subject for education, they also allowed us to experiment with less hierarchical teaching methods. In these outdoor classes, where you might be facilitating a conversation in one moment and taking notes the next, rigid binaries like "student" and "teacher" gave way to a more fluid sense of learning. Many were run using practices developed in Occupy, such as taking "stack" to ensure a fair distribution of speaking time, and according to principles that came to be known as "horizontal pedagogy."[2] That fall, in a crisp week in September, we demonstrated what learning could look like if liberated from the fetters of tuition.

The second major experience that forms the bedrock of this book was teaching English at Queens College, part of the City University of New York (CUNY), during some of the most racially charged years in recent history. CUNY serves a large percentage of students who are working class, immigrants, people of color, and the first in their families to attend college, owing in part to comparatively low tuition costs. Students at CUNY pay around $3,000 per year for tuition (after financial aid), a not-insignificant expense for individuals who are often working their way through college but a far cry from figures of $50,000 and more that we see at other institutions. At the time I began teaching, the Black Lives Matter movement pulsed like a heartbeat through the city. While the movement focused on police brutality, it also raised questions about how schools help to maintain a racist society. At CUNY I was part of a community of educators who wanted to address this. Together, we interrogated every facet of our work—curriculum, assignments, classroom practices, evaluation methods—to determine which aspects upheld white supremacy and how these might be reimagined. As a new professor, I wanted to address injustice and empower my students, but I had more questions than answers about exactly how to do so. What had my education taught me that would be useful to them? How could I create classrooms they would look forward to attending? Was helping them to organize their ideas in writing a way of enforcing white, bourgeois, middle-class norms on working-class students of color, or a way of preparing them for the careers they desired? Though I didn't know it at the time, nearly fifty years earlier, four of the twentieth century's most important authors had found themselves in the same university system, asking remarkably similar questions.

This book was born beneath the leafy canopies of Madison Square Park, in the fluorescent classrooms of Klapper Hall, and on the city's streets, where our insistence that "Black Lives Matter" echoed off of Manhattan's skyscrapers, those glittering monuments to capitalist accumulation. It is the product of a moment in which we were living and breathing Peter Cooper's vision: that education should be "as free as air and water." And yet, as the mere mention of Flint, Michigan, makes all too clear, neither water nor air is free. Someone has to pay for professors, classrooms, desks, and textbooks. Thus, this book explores what happens when a society decides to invest in free college, not just for affluent students, but for everyone. As we will see, the benefits of such policies extend far beyond the individuals who choose to attend college. They lead to a more just, equitable, and beautiful world.

ACKNOWLEDGMENTS

Open Admissions *reflects the collective wisdom of the many people whom I have had the great pleasure of thinking with.*

This book's insistence that teaching can change lives was shaped by the educators who transformed mine. Thank you to Kandice Chuh, Cathy Davidson, and Richard Dienst, who showed me how learning can illuminate unseen paths and ways of being in the world.

This project has also been supported in immeasurable ways by Kati Ahern, Liz Ahl, Alica Andrzejewski, Molly Appel, Hilarie Ashton, Alexander Baldassano, Faith Barter, Heather Bartlett, Lynne Beckenstein, Andrew Belton, Shanna Greene Benjamin, Roya Biggie, Teagan Bradway, Jaime Shearn Coan, Lou Cornum, Elizabeth Maddock Dillon, LeiLani Dowell, Christopher Eng, Duncan Faherty, Michelle Fine, Rebecca Fullan, Marcos Gonsalez, Sean X. Goudie, Timothy Griffiths, Andy Hines, David Hollingshead, Kristina Huang, Renee Hudson, Christina Katopodis, Amanda Licastro, Eric Lott, Justin Mann, Cori McKenzie, Kristin Moriah, Britt Munro, Paul Nadal, Chris Newfield, Andrew Newman, Melissa Phruksachart, Sonya Posmentier, Dan Radus, Robert Reid-Pharr, Katina Rogers, Ana Schwartz, Jesse Schwartz, Talia Shalev, Holly Smith, Lisa Tagliaferri, Frances Tran, Sharon Tran, Priscilla Wald, Kassandra Ware, Kalle Westerling, Elizabeth Weybright, everyone involved with the Free University of NYC, my colleagues at the City University of New York (CUNY) and in the State University of New York (SUNY) Cortland English Department, and, of course, my students, especially those in our spring 2020 seminar on Audre Lorde. I couldn't have done this without you.

Thank you to Elizabeth Ault, Ken Wissoker, the anonymous peer reviewers, and the entire Duke University Press team.

This research was supported by a Mellon / American Council of Learned Societies (ACLS) Dissertation Completion Grant, an Institute for Citizens and Scholars Women's Studies Fellowship, a Nuala McGann Drescher Leave, an ACLS Faculty Fellowship, and generous gifts from SUNY Cortland President Erik Bitterbaum, William L. Haines, and the Provost's Office.

I'm so grateful for Nicole Barbuto, Leah Delaney, Selena Drobnick, Allison Howard, Michele McCaffrey, Amy Orr, Marie Pace, Annemarie Rodriguez, Giselle Silvestrini, Arielle Urman, and Sarah Verbil, who have been tireless cheerleaders for this project throughout the decade it took to complete.

To my family—both biological and chosen, and especially Nikhil Gajwani—I love you.

Introduction
The Winds of Possibility

A writer by definition is a teacher.
—**AUDRE LORDE**, "POET AS TEACHER—
HUMAN AS POET—TEACHER AS HUMAN"

In the summer of 1968, author Toni Cade Bambara made a bold, unprecedented decision that likely would have scandalized her more conservative professional colleagues, had they been privy to the situation. That summer, she was teaching a remedial writing course in a hot room in Harlem's Alamac Hotel, which had recently been repurposed as a dormitory. By now a seasoned educator, she knew that in such summer courses "attendance was spotty, weather singularly lousy, classrooms unbearable, and attention not always rapt."[1] To make matters worse, she and her students would be confined to a classroom as people took to the streets to protest the recent assassination of Martin Luther King Jr. and the seemingly endless war in Vietnam. Were they really expected to review the rules of sentence construction while antiwar activists and the Poor People's Campaign staged rallies and die-ins outside their classroom windows? That summer, in these less-than-inspiring conditions, in classrooms equipped with minimal resources, Bambara made a radical decision to turn the "content, direction, and goals of the course" over to her students.² These so-called remedial students would now be in charge of deciding not only what but also how they would learn, and on what terms they would participate in the course.

Earlier that year, Bambara had taken a break from lesson planning to walk the newly hired poet and journalist June Jordan through the Gothic halls of the City College of New York and to her first classroom, calming the new instructor's nerves by assuring her, "Anything you have to give, just give it to them.... They'll be grateful for it."³ Quietly, to herself, Jordan was still marveling at her good fortune to have found a writing program "experimental enough to allow instruction by a college dropout."⁴ While Jordan was initially relieved that this new position would help pay rent and support her young son, the experience of teaching quickly began "to alter ... the way [she] approached things as a writer."⁵ The two authors were soon joined by Audre Lorde, whose brief stint as a visiting poet at Tougaloo College had left her hungry for more teaching opportunities. That same year, as critiques of educational racism swept through the city, poet Adrienne Rich made a "political decision to use [her] energies in work with 'disadvantaged' (Black and Puerto Rican) students."⁶ She packed up her desk at prestigious, exclusive, and predominantly white Columbia University and traveled fifteen blocks north to teach, instead, at City College. Thus, while each arrived by their own path, by the tumultuous year of 1968, four of the twentieth century's most important authors were teaching down the hall from one another at Harlem's City College. Though they didn't know it at the time, these years would soon come to be known as some of the most controversial and revolutionary in educational history.

While Bambara, Jordan, Lorde, and Rich are best known for their literature, this book recovers the untold stories of their classrooms. Like many authors, these women spent their lives teaching at universities throughout the country. Yet relatively little has been said about this aspect of their work. Often, it is tacitly understood that writers undertake teaching positions merely for financial purposes, to pay the bills and support the more important work of writing. And in the case of some authors, this is certainly true. Vladimir Nabokov, for example, saw teaching as a "material necessity" that impinged on his "real life as an artist."⁷ Nabokov took little interest in his Cornell University students, delivering the same lectures year after year. In a letter to fellow writer Edmund Wilson, he whined about this burden: "I am sick of teaching, I am sick of teaching, I am sick of teaching."⁸ But the archives of these teacher-poets tell a different story. Though they, too, relied on their university paychecks, they saw teaching not as an ancillary obligation but as a meaningful form of creative, political, and intellectual work, deeply related to their writing.

Open Admissions focuses on these writers' overlapping experiences teaching at the City College of New York—the founding institution of the City University of New York (CUNY)—in the late 1960s and early 1970s. Like the majority of educators today, these women were not teaching wealthy or even middle-class students at elite universities with ample resources. Rather, they were teaching working-class students and students of color at a massive, urban, public university. What brought them together was not merely fate but the college's new policies that expanded access to higher education. They were hired to teach in a landmark educational opportunity program known as SEEK, established in 1965 to bring Black and Puerto Rican students into the historically white City College. By 1970 this initiative led to an open admissions policy that guaranteed every graduate of the city's high schools a seat at one of its public colleges, free of tuition. I call this "the era of open admissions" (1965–76): a period that spans both the years leading up to CUNY's policy of free college for all (1965–69) and its official implementation (1970–76). At a time when journalists and faculty were accusing these democratizing initiatives of killing higher education, these writers understood free college as crucial to the flourishing of marginalized communities. And it was in these public college classrooms—not the ivy-clad towers of Harvard or Yale—that these four women became part of a teaching community that would forever alter their lives and the course of literary and educational history.

This book looks in two directions at once. It recovers the pedagogical legacy of these renowned writers and illustrates how that legacy shaped their literary works. As their archival syllabi, lesson plans, and assignments indicate, these authors were also transformative teachers who developed creative methods of teaching students to advocate for social change. And at the same time that they were developing social justice pedagogies and fighting for open admissions, they were simultaneously writing poems, short stories, young adult novels, and essays inspired by their experiences. We will see how these classrooms gave rise to new literary forms, what I call "the genres of open admissions," as well as many insights associated with intersectional feminism. *Open Admissions* thus reveals how teaching at CUNY transformed their writing and, with it, the course of American literature, learning, and feminist criticism.

* * *

Education has historically been a site of contested power struggle, where debates over what gets taught, who gets taught, how they are instructed, and who will pay for learning index broader questions about the kind of society we wish to inhabit. In Pierre Bourdieu and Jean-Claude Passeron's terms, education is a form of social reproduction: the means by which a society passes its knowledge, skills, and values—as well as its social hierarchies—on to the next generation.[9] It is also a means by which the state enacts its political projects. Throughout US history, classrooms have been used to dispossess Native Americans, assimilate immigrants, and protect American hearts and minds against the incursions of communism. Yet activist educators have also turned these sites of reproduction into sites of interruption and instead bent the future's arc toward a more just, equitable, and pleasurable world.

Bambara's, Jordan's, Lorde's, and Rich's work builds on a long history of *transgressive teaching*, a term, borrowed from bell hooks, for learning that prepares students both to navigate the world and to change it.[10] Indeed, for as long as education has been used as an instrument of oppression, it has also been used to inspire, empower, liberate, and transform. In the United States, this tradition extends back at least to the nineteenth century. Throughout the Jim Crow era, as Black students were often subjected to what Carter Woodson called "mis-education," learning that serves the interests of white people, Black educators developed what Jarvis R. Givens calls "fugitive pedagogies" that taught students about the social, economic, and political conditions of oppression in order to resist and change them. Black K–12 teachers, Givens writes, "appropriated schooling to work in service of their freedom dreams," often while under surveillance, scrutiny, and the threat of violent repercussions.[11] Among these subversive educators were women like Anna Julia Cooper, Mary McLeod Bethune, Fanny Jackson Coppin, and Lucy Laney, all of whom, according to Stephanie Y. Evans, developed innovative educational philosophies grounded in applied learning, recognition of cultural and social differences, critiques of American ideals, and a sense of communal responsibility.[12] Like the activist educators who preceded (and succeeded) them, Bambara, Jordan, Lorde, and Rich taught students to interrogate the status quo and imagine far beyond it.

Open Admissions revisits the 1960s and 1970s, a critical flash point in the history of transgressive teaching. Perhaps the best-known educator of this era is Paulo Freire, a figure whose work was read, utilized, and occasionally challenged by the women in this book. In *Pedagogy of the Oppressed*, first translated into English in 1970, Freire argued that traditional, hierarchical teaching methods—lecturing students, then testing their comprehension—constitute a "banking" model of education, which trains them to be passive, obedient members of society. Such methods, he contended, should be replaced with more empowering "problem-posing" and "consciousness-raising" techniques.[13] While Freire's focus was on adult literacy programs in Brazil, this period also saw the emergence of liberatory pedagogies in the United States. There, activists in the era's social movements both criticized mainstream education as a tool of white supremacy, patriarchy, and imperialism and used learning to challenge these practices of domination. As scholars have demonstrated, much of this transgressive teaching took place outside of formal academic institutions: in sites like communist labor schools (Andy Hines), the Citizenship and Freedom Schools of the civil rights movement (Jon N. Hale), and the Pan-African and Black Liberation Schools of the Black Power movement (Russell Rickford, Donna Jean Murch).[14] But it also occurred within universities: in new departments of Black, ethnic, and women's studies and, as this book illustrates, in CUNY's basic writing classrooms.[15] In fact, the same year that Freire was writing *Pedagogy of the Oppressed*, these authors and their coconspirators were developing a range of creative and consciousness-raising teaching methods—approaches that we can learn from and build on today.

A Quiet Revolution

Our story takes place at Harlem's City College, the first tuition-free public university in the United States. America's earliest universities were the province of the upper echelon: they trained the sons of wealthy white men to become the next generation of ministers, doctors, lawyers, and leaders of industry. City College, then the Free Academy, was established in 1847 "to provide children of immigrants and the poor access to free higher education based on academic merit" rather than inherited generational wealth.[16] According to its first president, Horace Webster, the new college was a democratic "experiment ... [in] whether the children of the people, the children of the whole people, can be educated; and whether an institution of the highest grade can be successfully controlled by the popular will, not by the privileged few."[17] Since then, many have felt as if "the future of higher education in the United States was bound up with the fate of ... City College."[18]

Though City College now serves many students of color (it's one of the most diverse institutions in the country), this wasn't always the case. In the late nineteenth and early twentieth centuries, its professors proudly provided an Ivy League education—in terms of both curriculum and rigor—to those who couldn't afford one, earning the school a reputation as the "Harvard of the Proletariat." Yet throughout its early history, demand far outstripped the limited number of students the college could admit, and administrators relied on increasingly strict admissions requirements, such as an 85 percent high school average (3.0 GPA), to determine who would gain access to these coveted seats. As the city's Black and Puerto Rican population increased, these steep requirements combined with entrenched conditions of educational racism within K–12 schools effectively excluded them from the university.[19] Thus, the majority of City College students were high-achieving young Jewish men who were barred by anti-Semitic quotas from schools like Harvard, Yale, and Columbia.[20]

In the 1960s, the hypocrisy of this college for the working class, located in Harlem, but full of white students, became even more apparent. Nationwide, college enrollments were skyrocketing—everywhere, that is, except at City College.[21] In fact, Harlem's public university was actually shrinking, admitting ever smaller and more selective fractions of the city's high school graduates.[22] And despite its reputation as a hotbed of political radicalism, faculty and administrators resisted opportunities to increase enrollments and desegregate the college. Instead, they clung to their exclusive admissions criteria in an effort to preserve their elite reputation. As a result, while CUNY was funded by collective taxpayer dollars, paid by all New York City residents, regardless of race or creed, between 94 and 97 percent of the students educated by those funds were white.[23] What was supposed to be the "Harvard of the Proletariat" looked more like a "white citadel" and "white colony" towering over its Harlem hill.[24]

In 1964 activists came together to challenge this racial exclusion. Amid protests over the city's failed integration efforts, members of the Congress of Racial Equality (CORE) joined with Black and Puerto Rican students, parents, politicians, activists, educators, and progressive administrators to hold City College accountable to its historical mandate to educate "the children of the whole people."[25] Among their efforts was a Midnight March, organized by Shirley Chisholm and Percy Sutton, to demand that City College accept more students of color. According to New York City's former mayor David Dinkins, "That night the SEEK program was born."[26]

In 1965 City College established the Search for Education, Elevation, and Knowledge (SEEK) program, the nation's first state-mandated educational opportunity program.[27] SEEK recruited "economically and educationally disadvantaged" students from the surrounding Harlem neighborhood who didn't meet the college's entrance requirements but showed academic promise. Supported by a federal antipoverty grant, the program waived their enrollment fees, provided book and travel stipends, and prepared them to matriculate at City College through remedial coursework and specialized tutoring and counseling.[28] Though historically Black colleges and universities (HBCUs) had been educating Black students for over a century, SEEK was one of the first initiatives that prepared entire cohorts of working-class students—90 percent of whom were students of color—for entrance to a predominantly white institution.[29] While SEEK would eventually expand throughout the CUNY system and become a model for similar programs nationwide, when these authors were initially hired, its success was much less certain.[30]

Despite the historic grounds SEEK broke, many professors wanted little to do with it. Among faculty, sentiments ranged from skepticism about whether such students could handle the rigorous curriculum to outright hostility toward a new program that they believed might tarnish the college's reputation. English professors, in particular, did not want to teach the remedial and introductory writing courses these students would need to matriculate. These "tweedy, Anglophile," white men were "steeped in the traditional ideals of connoisseurship ... concern[ed] with parsing and preserving the classics of English and American writing."[31] They viewed writing courses merely as skills training and preparation for "real" courses on literature—entrenched biases that are still familiar today. While the old guard was uninterested, a number of up-and-coming authors were lining up at the door to teach in this exciting new program. They included Bambara, Lorde, Jordan, and Rich as well as poets David Henderson and Raymond Patterson, African American literature scholars Barbara Christian and Addison Gayle, and Mina Shaughnessy, whose work at City College became foundational to the field of basic writing. Together, they formed a creative community committed to empowering their educationally disenfranchised students.

As Alexis Pauline Gumbs observes, SEEK instructors were hired, at least on paper, to perform the cultural work of assimilation. The government agreed to fund such initiatives in hopes that access to college would quell social unrest and pacify "unruly" minorities who were disrupting the city through strikes and protests. And this labor to "institutionally manage a post-civil rights diasporic population" fell squarely on the shoulders of writing instructors. Officially, these authors and their colleagues were supposed "to teach students to compose coherent essays ... memos and reports" and, by extension, to be "composed, contained, and conformist."[32] However, as Gumbs acknowledges, this is not what transpired. Instead of issuing, in Fred Moten and Stefano Harney's terms, "the call to order," they transformed their classrooms into sites of social change.[33] Beginning in their basic writing classes, and for many years to come, SEEK educators helped students deepen their analyses of injustice, sharpen their tools for advocacy, and prepare for lifelong learning.

Though the stories of all SEEK instructors deserve to be told, *Open Admissions* focuses on four women whose experiences in the program shaped their development as major authors of American literature and feminist criticism. Unlike authors who teach advanced creative writing seminars to a select handful of affluent students, these women all taught introductory and remedial writing courses to students whose underfunded schools had failed to prepare them for college—a fact that was not incidental to their literature. Indeed, during the same period in which they were writing the short stories, poems, and essays that would eventually make them famous, they were also exchanging syllabi, adapting each other's assignments, reading radical education philosophies, and sitting in on each other's classes to take notes on how students responded to different teaching methods. Immersed in the creative community of the SEEK program, they became activist teacher-poets: writers who saw their work with words as connected to their work with students and who understood both as forms of political action.[34]

SEEK began as what Addison Gayle called a "quiet revolution" stealthily redistributing educational resources, but it did not remain quiet for long.[35] In the spring of 1969, inspired by both nationwide Black student movements and, as this book argues, the transgressive teaching they encountered in classrooms, SEEK students and their allies staged what political scientist Conrad Dyer refers to as "one of the largest and longest student occupations of an American University campus."[36] They halted regular classes and went on strike for two weeks, demanding a more racially just curriculum and more equitable admissions policies. The result was a historic victory: an open admissions policy that expanded SEEK's commitment to access and equity throughout the CUNY system.

Though CUNY was not the first university to adopt an open admissions policy—that honor, writes Carmen Kynard, belongs to HBCUs—its version was historic in several regards.[37] CUNY's policy constituted a dramatic departure from the college's highly selective admissions requirements. It defined "educational opportunity" in terms of not only access but also student outcomes and success. It was also implemented with unprecedented speed. And it captured the era's broader national sense that public institutions should be doing more to reduce poverty and increase opportunities for minorities.[38]

Today SEEK and open admissions are remembered for their dramatic socioeconomic benefits.[39] Through these initiatives, thousands of working-class students, students of color, and women gained access to college.[40]

Shirley Chisholm, the first African American woman in Congress, saw SEEK as one of her greatest political contributions.[41] At the behest of a Democratic-majority Congress, Ronald Reagan declared December 11, 1986, to be National SEEK and College Discovery Day (even as he eviscerated the funding structures that would make such initiatives possible).[42] Today nearly every public university in the United States has some kind of opportunity program, many of which are modeled on SEEK. And though open admissions lasted only six years (1970–76), it led to the growth of a college-educated class in New York City's Black and Latinx communities, higher incomes within those communities, and greater levels of college attainment for many generations to come.[43]

But open admissions was more than an engine of social mobility. It was also what Lorde called "a wind of possibility" that swept across the CUNY campuses inspiring new ideas about learning, literature, and power and rustling many feathers with its squalls.[44] In these pages, we'll travel into Jordan's, Lorde's, Bambara's, and Rich's classrooms, where the era's debates surrounding educational access lit a fire in the imaginations of both professors and students. There, in their classrooms-turned-canvases, they questioned prevailing assumptions about learning: that teachers should determine what is taught, that students are the passive recipients of wisdom, that intellectual work should be painful, torturous, and disciplinary. If redesigned to serve the will of the people, what could learning look like? What might it become? And if an institution as historically exclusive as universities could be democratized, what other hierarchies might be toppled? As we will see, this spirit of creativity, experimentation, and imaginative possibility spilled out of the classroom and into the writing of these authors and their students.

The Archives of Activist Teaching

Open Admissions centers pedagogy: both theoretical and philosophical orientations toward teaching and learning, and actual classroom practices. Pedagogy is about how we discover and share ideas, skills, frameworks, methods, and ways of being and knowing. Although teaching has historically been one of the few professions available to women, pedagogy has been a strangely white, male-dominated field. With the exception of bell hooks, women and people of color are often sidelined in these discussions. Evans and Olivia N. Perlow and colleagues have observed that Black women, in particular, are often recognized as teachers and activists but not as educational philosophers, researchers, or pedagogical theorists.[45] One reason for this critical neglect stems from how narrowly we tend to define what counts as pedagogical theory. Academic conversations on the subject often privilege peer-reviewed articles and academic books over actual everyday teaching materials. It's not unusual to see journals calling for papers for a special issue on pedagogy (teaching is almost always relegated to the occasional special issue) while explicitly stating that they do *not* want submissions of mere teaching materials, which are considered less valuable ephemera. This limited understanding privileges those with the time and resources to formalize their teaching philosophies in such labor-intensive formats. Within the tiered economy of higher education, the authors of such materials are more likely to be wealthy, white, tenured, male professors at elite institutions, who have the greatest access to research time, while women, people of color, and people who are working class perform the majority of our nation's teaching and service.[46] A narrow focus on books and peer-reviewed articles therefore reinforces a raced, classed, and gendered distinction between theory and practice, in which affluent white men are associated with the development of innovative teaching philosophies, which are then implemented by everyone else.

Drawing inspiration from Barbara Christian's notion that Black women have historically produced theoretical work in a range of forms, including those that are not recognized within academia, this book explores two different forms through which historically marginalized educators have produced pedagogical theory.[47] The first is archival teaching materials including syllabi, lesson plans, assignments, lecture notes, and student work. It is through such everyday materials, and the classroom practices they index, that many women, people of color, and working-class educators have engaged in transgressive teaching. Moreover, the creation of such materials, like a new assignment, involves extensive research into existing methods, multiple drafts, peer review with other instructors, and revision based on student feedback—intellectual labor rarely valued by the academy. Thus, we should understand teaching materials as sources of pedagogical knowledge: the means by which educators theorize through practice. Though these teacher-poets may not have published tomes like John Dewey's *Democracy and Education* (1916) or Freire's *Pedagogy of the Oppressed* ([1968] 1970), their archives reveal nuanced philosophies of education that they revised and refined through their actual classroom work with students—what we now call *praxis*.

Most of the archival materials analyzed in this project are located at the Spelman College Archives and the Schlesinger Library at Radcliffe. This project would not be possible without the work of the archivists at both institutions. I owe a special debt of gratitude to Kassandra Ware and Holly Smith, who so generously assisted me in writing this book. To be able to hold such materials—to admire Rich's lesson plans, neatly preserved in violet mimeograph ink; to find Jordan's assignments, smudged with the stains of snacks smuggled between classes; to realize that Bambara also revised her essay prompts until the wording was just right; to encounter Lorde's grocery list ("sardines... green peppers... sandals... dust pan") wedged between her syllabi, or her grumbling in the margins of a student's poem submitted in ink so faint "I can hardly read this!"—is an immense privilege that many of their readers would cherish. With that in mind, I've quoted such materials liberally in hopes of sharing their actual words about teaching with readers, maybe even inspiring some to try something new or different in their own classrooms. For readers who want to learn more about their teaching, Lost and Found: The CUNY Poetics Documents Initiative has published excerpts of each author's archival teaching materials, with important introductory essays by Miriam Atkin, Iemanjá Brown, erica kaufman, Makeba Lavan, Conor Tomás Reed, and Talia Shalev. They can be purchased in chapbook form or viewed freely online, honoring these teacher-poets' commitments to learning from each other's teaching.[48]

The other materials I consider as sites of pedagogical knowledge are literary texts. Historically, literature has been a means by which marginalized people have shared knowledge beyond the walls of formal institutions that excluded them. While some educational insights emerge in the places we might expect, such as essays like Jordan's "Writing and Teaching" and Rich's "Teaching Language in Open Admissions," others are embedded in their poems, novels, short stories, and films that are not ostensibly about education. We will see how such texts theorize relations of power, knowledge, and learning, even through their treatments of other subjects: a backyard, a playground, a bombing, a healing. Feminist literature, with its attention to quotidian politics, the embodied nature of experience, resistance at multiple scales, modes of relationality, and the historicity of the present, constitutes an underexplored archive for pedagogical thought.

This story is constructed from archives that conceal as much as they reveal. These absences and omissions remind us how ephemeral teaching and learning are—how much occurs in the intimate spark of the encounter, the fleeting moment that will linger on only in the memories of the professors and students who were present, and might be remembered differently by each. Confronted with such silences, I try not to re-create these classrooms but to tell the stories in ways that are useful for our present. In some instances, I engage in small acts of what Saidiya Hartman calls "critical fabulation," "imagin[ing] what might have happened or might have been said or might have been done," while in other moments, I refuse "to fill in the gaps and to provide closure."[49] I don't pretend to construct the singular truth of a given class or assignment but to speculate in ways that are faithful to the lives and work of these monumental women and might illuminate possibilities for us today. Such an approach might be thought of, in Rich's terms, as an "educated guess," a key methodology for feminist historiography and the study of those whose lives are least documented.[50] Like all stories, those you will read here are filtered through the writer's perspectives and experiences—in my case, as a white, middle-class, Jewish, cisgender woman, a CUNY and SUNY professor. I hope this book will inspire others to engage with their archives and find other stories.

As their archival materials and published writing indicate, these authors taught students to make decisions about the structure of their courses; to conduct local research on poverty, housing, food, and education; to write and publish literature; and to become teachers in their classrooms and leaders in their communities. Two patterns are especially prominent across their work. First, as illustrated by the opening example of Bambara's cocreated course, they developed teaching methods that redistributed classroom power to students. Second, instead of merely transmitting preestablished wisdom, they facilitated student knowledge production. More precisely, they helped students generate the ideas and perspectives missing from mainstream media, journalism, and curricula, what I'm calling *insurgent knowledge*.[51] Often, this involved the publication of student writing. Though not all of these women engaged in these practices evenly, traces of them are evident throughout the archives of all four.

I am hardly the first person to write about these authors as teachers. Linda Janet Holmes and Abena Busia have analyzed Bambara's creative, activist teaching, and Valerie Kinloch and Kirsten Bartholomew Ortega have examined Jordan's community-engaged instruction methods. As Gumbs has demonstrated, Jordan and Lorde developed "counter-poetic" pedagogies that used classrooms to protest "the colonial project... with varying levels of success."[52] And Tomás Reed has illustrated how, in their CUNY classrooms, Bambara, Jordan, and Lorde contributed to the early development of Black women's studies.[53] Building on the work of these scholars, I explore the distinct pedagogies of each writer as well as the ways their teaching emerged through conversations among SEEK instructors and with educators across the country. Though we often think of teaching in individualized terms—one cites Freire's notion of "the banking model of education" or hooks's concept of "engaged pedagogy"—their archives highlight the collective networks of pedagogical exchange that go into producing the scene of teaching and learning. Indeed, nestled among each author's own archives are similar materials from other educators that they collected, adapted, and remixed. Through these documents, this book traces what I call *collaboration in the archives*: the ways teaching materials travel from one pair of hands to another, forming often-unacknowledged collaborations that transcend the walls of individual classrooms and institutions.

Many of the practices in this book—daily journals, student-led discussions, collaborative public projects—will be familiar to contemporary educators. They exemplify what's known as *student-centered* teaching: methods that involve students in decisions about their learning, emphasize inquiry and discovery, and connect course content to their ideas and experiences. The term emerged in the 1920s to name a paradigm shift away from memorization, discipline, and lecturing to instead prioritizing the interests and needs of individual learners. Though student-centered learning is often traced back to the Progressive Era, and the work of John Dewey, it also has long-standing roots in Black educational history.[54] In fact, Fanny Jackson Coppin's calls for active learning and Anna Julia Cooper's philosophies of relevant, applied, and practical education both predated Dewey's more famous philosophies (in Coppin's case, by a quarter of a century).[55]

Though student-centered teaching transformed many midcentury K–12 classrooms, especially in well-funded districts that could afford the personalized attention it required, its implementation in higher education was slower and more sporadic. According to Jonathan Zimmerman, the twentieth century's increasing college enrollments combined with lack of incentives for good university teaching meant that lectures and exams remained more common, despite research showing active and participatory methods to be more effective.[56] Exceptions could be found, however, in certain pockets of academia. Rachel Sagner Buurma and Laura Heffernan have shown that English professors in varied institutional settings, from junior colleges to extension schools, developed pedagogical practices that centered student inquiry and collaborative knowledge production.[57] Student-centered methods could also be found among practitioners of critical pedagogy, such as Henry Giroux, Peter McLaren, and Ira Shor, who adapted Freire's work to the context of American classrooms.[58] They were also present among professors involved with the era's social movements, some of whom taught in the new fields of Black, ethnic, and women's studies, while others, like the women in this book, taught basic writing. These educators recognized that they could not challenge practices of domination—racism, sexism, imperialism—through pedagogical paradigms predicated on the tyranny of instructors over students. Rather, challenging social hierarchies required remaking the classroom, too.

Bambara, Jordan, Rich, and Lorde were theorists and practitioners of both student-centered and feminist pedagogy. Feminist pedagogy is an approach to learning that addresses the uneven distribution of resources and opportunities along axes of race, class, gender, sexuality, and ability and attempts to democratize power in the classroom and in society. While I use the more general term *feminist pedagogy*, my definition is grounded in theories of "Black feminist" and "engaged" pedagogy developed by scholars including Barbara Omolade, Gloria Joseph, and bell hooks.[59] Black feminist pedagogy centers the histories, intellectual traditions, and experiences of Black women (Omolade) and "Third World" people (Joseph). It honors the experiential knowledge that students bring to the classroom and expands their intellectual, analytical, and imaginative horizons, especially their understanding of structural inequality.[60] Similarly, engaged pedagogy involves students in cocreating classrooms and sharing knowledge, facilitates personal and social transformation, emphasizes students' well-being, and links contemplation to action.

As practitioners of feminist pedagogy, these teacher-poets saw classrooms as sites in the broader struggle to bring about a better world: one in which everyone has access to health care, housing, food, education, decision-making power, and the time and resources to pursue what brings them joy. Among their many contributions to the field, perhaps the most exciting are their shared emphases on imagination and creativity, and their experiments with alternative worldmaking in the classroom. I hope that their teaching might help us engage contemporary questions of justice and equity in more meaningful, material ways, rather than merely paying lip service to diversity.

Though I went to their archives looking for teaching materials, what I found was evidence of educational activism that extended far beyond the classroom. As it turns out, not everyone agreed with this era's new vision of college for all. Like many efforts to expand education to working-class students and students of color, open admissions was met with vehement opposition. The *New York Times* ran articles with headlines like "50% of Freshmen to Come from Slums without Need to Qualify on Grades."[61] Journalists pathologized these "new students" as "deprived... drug addicts, unwed mothers, and fatherless, ghetto residents."⁶² And much of this rhetoric was echoed by the CUNY professoriate. In books like Louis G. Heller's *The Death of the American University: With Special Reference to the Collapse of the City College of New York* (1973) and Geoffrey Wagner's *End of Education* (1976), faculty argued that open admissions decreased academic standards and diluted the quality of a City College degree. Such policies, wrote Theodore L. Gross, chair of the City College English Department (and later dean of humanities), were "how to kill a college."⁶³

Unlike these elitist critics, Bambara, Jordan, Lorde, and Rich saw CUNY's democratic initiatives as a tremendous opportunity to reinvent higher education, making it more useful and relevant to marginalized communities. They wrote position papers in support of students' demands, advocated for free college at Board of Higher Education meetings, garnered support among faculty, and joined their students' protests. Reflecting on this moment, Jordan recalls that they were working "double overtime fighting for Open Admissions," inspired by the dream that they "could change public education in this country."⁶⁴ And what began at CUNY would inform, for each, a lifetime of educational activism.

The Classroom Contexts of Feminist Literature and Criticism

In addition to recovering these authors' pedagogies, *Open Admissions* explores the surprising and complex ways that their art, literature, and criticism were impacted by their classrooms. In recent years, scholars have begun to challenge the assumption that teaching is merely a way for artists, authors, and critics to support their creative and intellectual work. Lesley Wheeler and Chris Gavaler, for instance, have shown how Marianne Moore's experiences teaching at the Carlisle Indian School inspired her writing about the flexible nature of identity. Similarly, Andy Hines has demonstrated how the work of midcentury Black artists like Elizabeth Catlett and Oliver Killens was influenced by their teaching in progressive people's schools.⁶⁵ Other scholars, like Buurma and Heffernan and Matt Brim, have illustrated how literary criticism and queer theory have emerged from—and often reflected the politics and practices of—critics' classrooms.⁶⁶ Building on this research, this book illustrates how some of these authors' most important works were born in their CUNY classrooms. While Lorde has since become famous for speeches like "The Master's Tools Will Never Dismantle the Master's House," we will observe how that text drew on ideas about difference and creativity she first developed in courses like Race and the Urban Situation, and how Bambara's groundbreaking anthology *The Black Woman* was written, in part, by her City College students. In fact, we would not know nearly as much today about the overlapping experiences of race, class, gender, and sexuality, were it not for these CUNY classrooms.

This book also contributes to our knowledge of how education initiatives and policies impacted the literature of the 1960s and 1970s. Mark McGurl has recently labeled this period "the program era" to highlight the influence that creative writing MFA programs had on this work. The rise of such programs, McGurl writes, generated a "constellation of aesthetic problems" around the tensions between modernist aesthetic principles and the protocols of institutional life that many midcentury authors took up in their writing.[67] However, at the same time that these exclusive (and notoriously racist) programs were influencing writers like Thomas Pynchon, John Cheever, and Kurt Vonnegut, CUNY's democratic education initiatives were simultaneously giving rise to major works of feminist literature and criticism. If we focus not on the era's MFA programs but instead on CUNY's access-oriented classrooms, literary history looks a bit different. Unlike the "self-involved" and "self-referential" fiction that reflected the MFA program's obsession with "individuals and their individuality," Jordan's, Lorde's, Bambara's, and Rich's writing was shaped by the open admissions ethos: the idea that transformative learning should be available to anyone who wants it.[68] In addition, while the campus novel is the paradigmatic genre of the program era, open admissions inspired its own literary forms, what I call *the genres of open admissions*: the classroom lyric, the campus essay, and the anthology of student writing. Each of these offers unique insights into the era's debates over relevant learning, educational access, and the value of experiential knowledge.

As much as these authors were inspired by their classrooms, they were also impacted by each other. Bringing together these three venerated poets (Lorde, Rich, Jordan), three women associated with the Black Arts Movement (Bambara, Jordan, Lorde), and two foundational figures of lesbian feminism and queer theory (Lorde, Rich), in the context of their classrooms, illuminates new perspectives on their work. We will witness how Bambara's friendship with Jordan influenced her fiction, how Lorde and Rich introduced Jordan to women's poetry, how Lorde understood her work in dialogue with Bambara's, and the ways her Black women colleagues shaped Rich's writings about race. Indeed, these friendships first forged amid open admissions—in support of their students and the fight for free college—left an indelible mark on feminist literature and criticism.

The following chapters trace the reciprocal relations between teaching and writing in the work of each author, while also placing them in conversation and in context, as part of a broader movement that understood teaching methods, the humanities, and public education as crucial to social change. In addition, by following these figures beyond the open admissions era—as they went on to teach in other sites as distinct as Rutgers, Stanford, the Neighborhood Arts Center in Atlanta, and the Free University of Berlin—each chapter illustrates how their experiences at CUNY continued to impact their writing and teaching for many decades to come.

Chapter 1 explores how SEEK's earliest educators—Bambara, Christian, and Gayle—laid the groundwork for much of the transgressive and student-centered teaching that followed. Bambara, in particular, developed a community-controlled and multimodal pedagogy that involved students in making collective decisions about their learning, including what forms that learning would take. This chapter also recovers the classroom context of Bambara's anthology *The Black Woman* (1970) to highlight the key role that writing classrooms have played in the history of feminist criticism. Chapter 2 analyzes how—in her City College classrooms and weekend writing workshops—Jordan began developing a public and project-based pedagogy that encouraged students to use what they learned in the service of social change. It focuses on Jordan and Bambara's shared practice of publishing student writing and the products of that pedagogy, including nearly a dozen anthologies that they edited throughout their careers. Considered alongside their teaching archives, these anthologies demonstrate how classrooms have been central for not only the reception and dissemination of American literature but also its production.

The final two chapters focus on Rich and Lorde, both of whom arrived at City College in the fall of 1968. Chapter 3 shows how Rich's early experiences in SEEK inspired her pedagogy of location: ways of teaching students to use their lived experiences as points of entry into broader material conditions and questions of power. It also illustrates how her development as a radical feminist was influenced by her time at City College. Chapter 4 explores how Lorde's theories of difference emerged from, and were also shaped by, her

CUNY classrooms. It examines both her pedagogies of difference—how she helped students cultivate an activist consciousness—and the ways that teaching inspired some of her most influential writing.

Open Admissions thus illustrates how New York City's radical experiment in free college for all transformed twentieth-century poetics and pedagogy. But for contemporary readers, this era may feel like a distant dream. At present, the future of higher education seems more uncertain than ever. Since the 1970s, the right's defunding of public universities has resulted in widespread austerity and levels of student debt approaching the two-trillion-dollar mark. More recently, this assault has also included attacks on the study of race, class, gender, and sexuality. Yet research in fields such as Black and ethnic studies and abolitionist university studies has tended to focus more on the ways universities are complicit in (re)producing a racist, sexist, capitalist, and imperialist society.[69] These insights are invaluable, but they leave us with few reasons to organize against the dismantling of public higher education. The pages that follow reorient these conversations around four women who not only critiqued the neoliberalization of higher education but fought tirelessly to expand access to transformative learning, and whose lives were forever changed in the process. Together, they remind us of the multifaceted ways that educators can work toward a better world within our classrooms—and why such spaces are worth fighting for. It is my hope that this history will help us contest the privatization of knowledge and power that has come to dominate educational policy and practice.

Toni Cade Bambara's Community-Controlled & Multimodal Pedagogy

1

TONI CADE BAMBARA was a writer whose work centered African American communities, especially women, celebrating their long traditions of using storytelling to survive and flourish. Inspired by the Black Arts Movement's emphasis on Black art for Black audiences, not the white gaze, Bambara wrote in the Black vernacular and experimented with jazz aesthetics, as well as nonlinear, polyvocal storytelling. In short-story collections like *Gorilla, My Love* (1972) and *The Sea Birds Are Still Alive* (1977) and her novel *The Salt Eaters* (1980), readers meet characters at various stages of their personal and political journeys, who are finding their way amid the uneven playing field carved out by racism, sexism, imperialism, and capitalism. These stories of struggles large and small—filled with sharp insights into the machinations of power, punctuated by moments of belly-laugh-inducing humor—have earned her an enduring place in the history of American literature and Black feminism. Yet long before she received the American Book Award or was inducted into the Georgia Writers Hall of Fame, Bambara's life revolved around teaching. "For years," she recalls, "students ... [were] the center of my days and nights; writing of the pre-dawn in-betweens."[1]

Before she identified as a writer, Bambara saw herself as a teacher: someone who "equip[s] people to respect their rage and their power."[2] Her work as an educator began in 1965, when she was one of the first English professors hired to teach in City College's new SEEK program. This chapter explores how, as SEEK's earliest educators, Bambara and her colleagues Barbara Christian and Addison Gayle developed student-centered teaching methods as part of their efforts to empower educationally disenfranchised students. Among their many creative approaches, it focuses on two particular aspects of Bambara's teaching. First, it illustrates how she developed a community-controlled pedagogy that involved students in making collective decisions about their learning, including what they would read, what they would write, and how their learning would be evaluated. Second, it shows how she devised what we would now call a "multimodal" or "multimedia" pedagogy that taught students to compose in different media, genres, and forms. This chapter also revisits Bambara's anthology *The Black Woman*, which she edited while teaching in the SEEK program. While *The Black Woman* has been recognized as a foundational text of Black feminist criticism, this chapter highlights the classrooms that gave rise to it. The final section follows Bambara beyond the era of open admissions as she largely withdrew from academic institutions and shifted her focus to local community centers, where her teaching could more effectively reach Black communities. In sites like Philadelphia's Scribe Video Center and the occasional courses she taught at Duke University, Spelman College, the University of Delaware, and Carleton College, she continued developing the community-controlled and multimodal pedagogy she first explored at City College.

Harlem, I Hear You

As a curious child growing up in Harlem in the 1940s, Bambara was excited about the prospect of school. She imagined it as "a great hall filled with books and paper and clay and musical instruments and very knowledgeable people who loved children."[3] Like the plucky protagonists of her short stories, she was eager to have her "why this and how come that" questions answered: "I'd figured I'd just march in . . . [and] grab hold of someone . . . who'd teach me how to tell time, and how to cross the Drive without getting killed, and how to keep the dog upstairs from jumping on me."[4] What she wanted, even from an early age, was knowledge that would help her survive, gain independence, not have to rely so heavily on adults, and better understand the world. Instead, she encountered teachers who were more "concerned with getting that aviator cap off [her] head" than cultivating her imagination.[5] Her teachers in Harlem and later Jersey City and Queens all seemed to reserve the brightest crayons and highest grades for their white students and had only discipline and discrimination left over for Bambara. Her mother, however, "did not tolerate racial insults directed at her children."[6] Helen Cade taught her daughter, from a young age, that her creativity far outstripped the low expectations of her racist teachers and schools.

Growing up in the epicenter of African American and Latinx art, culture, and politics, Bambara couldn't help but notice how much was missing from her formal education. Jazz wafted through the Harlem hills of her childhood, blending with the opera her mother often played on the radio. Reflecting on her childhood at 125th Street and Seventh Avenue, she recalls that "Rastafarians, Muslims, trade unionists, communists, [and] Pan-Africanists" were her favorite teachers, and the subway, beauty parlors, the Apollo, and Speaker's Corner were her most enlightening classrooms.[7] Dangling her legs through fire escape grates, Bambara soaked up Harlem's lessons like a sponge: "While Grandma Dorothy was teaching me theory... the bebop musicians... were teaching me about pitch, structure, and beat, and the performers and audiences at the Apollo and the Harlem Opera House were teaching me about the community's high standards regarding expressive gifts."[8] Yet hardly any of her community's music, literature, art, and ideas appeared within her textbooks. When, in his poem "Theme for English B," Langston Hughes points out the discrepancy between the radiant art of the Harlem Renaissance and the ossified white curriculum at Columbia University, he could have just as easily been describing Bambara's own experiences.

In adolescence, Bambara briefly escaped the underfunded schools that New York City reserves for its working-class students of color. She attended the progressive Greer Academy, located in the lush and verdant Hudson Valley, where courses on the arts and gardening nurtured students' curiosity. She also enrolled in dance classes at the Katherine Dunham School, founded by the renowned African American dancer and choreographer, which blended arts education with instruction in the humanities, philosophy, drama, and languages. Together, this community-based education in Harlem combined with the holistic arts education of the Greer Academy and Dunham School convinced her that learning could nourish the mind, body, imagination, and spirit. For years to come, she maintained a vision of educational possibility that exceeded the irrelevant curricula and stultifying teaching methods she encountered in formal institutions.

For as long as she could remember, Bambara had "dreamed of college" as a place to continue what her biographer, Linda Janet Holmes, calls her "journey of self-discovery through the arts."[9] Bambara writes, "I wanted to major in ME. I had it all figured out—a year's apprenticeship with a yogi-fakir high priest type, a couple of courses in abnormal psychology, the complete core in anthro and philo, a sabbatical to a brain farm in Big Sur, a research course from Christ to Gurdieff, and for my mentor-counselor: a hypnotist (preferably an Aries or Leo type)."[10] While she fantasized about a holistic education that would teach her about different cultures, religions, and philosophies, such courses were few and far between at Queens College. The closest she could come were classes in writing, theater, and dance. Though disappointed by the white, Western curricula, she turned the campus into her own personal stage.[11] She might be spotted strutting across the suburban quad, flaunting a single gold hoop earring, chatting about existentialism at a hip campus café, or sewing sequins onto costumes for an upcoming production. Bambara's peers were enamored with her "encyclopedic knowledge" of jazz, passionate left-wing politics, and dazzling humor. But this exuberance belied a deeper isolation: she was sick of being the only Black person on the Queens College arts and politics scene. While she couldn't have known it at the time, she would soon find the creative and activist community she craved among her colleagues in the SEEK program.

Teaching in "Unfamiliar Country"

For Bambara, learning took place both within and beyond formal classrooms, and throughout her twenties, she moved between the two. After graduating from Queens College and spending several years as a social worker and occupational therapist, she used her earnings to travel to Europe. There she studied the ancient ruins and fragrant, open-air markets and took courses in theater, mime, and commedia dell'arte.[12] In 1964 the then twenty-five-year-old returned to Harlem to complete an MA in modern American literature at City College. Her master's thesis, "The American Adolescent Apprentice Novel," portended what would become a lifelong fascination with relationships of teaching and learning. Her next adventure was into the "unfamiliar country" at the front of the classroom.

In 1965, MA degree in hand, Bambara was hired to teach in the new SEEK program at her alma mater. The SEEK program had recently been established to recruit more students from the surrounding Black and Puerto Rican community. Because English faculty did not want to teach the introductory and remedial writing courses these students required, the college instead hired temporary lecturers. That fall, SEEK's first semester, Bambara and her colleague Anthony Penale taught English for all 113 students in the pilot cohort. They were soon joined by Addison Gayle, who was also a student in the

English MA program, and Barbara Christian, then a PhD student at nearby Columbia. While Gayle and Christian would go on to become renowned scholars of African American literature, at this time, their careers, like Bambara's, were just beginning.

As lecturers, their positions were in some ways similar to, but in important ways distinct from, such positions today. Like many of today's temporary instructors, SEEK lecturers had a demanding workload. Full-time lecturers like Bambara taught three basic writing courses per semester, with roughly nineteen students in each. Unlike the college's standard three-credit courses, these were hefty five-hour writing-intensive courses that required far more work. Lecturers were required to have individual conferences with their fifty to sixty students and to attend SEEK staff meetings; later, they would also have to work two hours per week in the writing center. And there was no guarantee they would be rehired the following year (a 1969–70 labor agreement would later change this). However, unlike today's adjuncts, SEEK's earliest educators were paid a living wage. Though compensated at a lower rate than the tenure-line professors in English, full-time lecturers earned around $10,000 per year.[13] This would amount, in 2023 dollars, to $95,000, three times the average annual salary of $28,000 that temporary instructors earn today.

At the outset, Bambara was told that SEEK students "do not do well in many courses" because "they have deficient skills or flabby motivation."[14] But the young people she met were inquisitive, sharp-witted, and incredibly bright. Many were activists involved in the civil rights and antiwar movements. Like all students, they wanted to learn about the world and to carve a place for themselves within it. They aspired to become doctors, lawyers, artists, authors, and journalists and effect change in their communities. The only thing "deficient" was the educational racism they had been subjected to. For many, school had meant "overcrowded classes in dilapidated buildings" bereft of even basic facilities like libraries and gyms.[15] There, they were assigned "obsolete books about the great wars, the great men, the great games, the great lies," which bore little relevance to their lives. Many had been taught "by a series of middle-class white teachers who come and go in turnstile nonchalance" and who were more interested in discipline than nurturing their intellect.[16] Bambara referred to this toxic combination of substandard conditions and racist textbooks, teaching methods, and instructors as "the criminality of education."[17]

With little to no formal training, Bambara took what she called a "stumble trial and error approach" to this new adventure.[18] The first question she confronted was, What should they read? Because SEEK instructors were helping students strengthen their reading and writing skills, rather than imparting knowledge about a specific subject, they were free to choose what students would read and write about. Bambara could assign a play by William Shakespeare or a *New York Times* article, a poem or an essay, an op-ed or a manifesto, or one of the apprentice novels she had researched for her thesis.

For students who had been subjected to a whitewashed curriculum, SEEK's earliest educators scoured local bookstores for works of Black and Puerto Rican literature that would excite them. Given the college's Harlem location, they did not have to look far. Just five blocks away, Amiri Baraka's Black Arts Repertory Theater/School was giving rise to the Black Arts Movement: the provocative artistic wing of the Black Power movement. Many of the books they assigned—works like Ralph Ellison's *Invisible Man* (1952) and poems by Nuyorican writer Victor Hernández Cruz—foregrounded the unequal power structures of racism, capitalism, and imperialism that shape daily life. One of the most popular was Amiri Baraka's (then LeRoi Jones's) essay collection *Home* (1965), which conveyed Black radical critiques of capitalism, white liberalism, and the vicissitudes of American racism.[19] In class, instructors solicited students' reactions to these texts. At the beginning of Bambara's courses, she or a student would "summarize the assigned readings, raise questions, [and] ask for parallels in their own experience(s)." They would then evaluate whether the author's claims were "valid, relevant, incidental, phony, half-baked or suspect." Even when assigning writers she deeply admired, like Frantz Fanon, she encouraged them to "question everything" and identify any argumentative "holes."[20]

Often, these works of literature were treated as models for student writing. In what I've come to think of as creative mimicry assignments, SEEK educators frequently paired readings with writing assignments that asked students to experiment with that author's ideas or method in their own writing. Unlike "themes" (similar to a book report) summarizing the assigned text, creative mimicry assignments challenged students to use the writer's interpretive framework or a particular rhetorical technique to perform their own analysis of a current event or something they had experienced. One example of this is Bambara's assignment, which began with Baraka's essay "Cuba Libre": an analysis of the "lies we are forced to abide by in a country with a powerful press."[21] After reading the essay, they discussed how rhetorical tricks such as "euphemism, distortions, censorship, [and] propaganda" shape daily discourse and the ways this "brainwashing" is perpetuated in schools. She then asked students to use Baraka's method to analyze "the lies they encountered growing up... brotherhood, melting pot, land of the free and the home of the brave."[22]

These creative mimicry assignments, versions of which will appear throughout this book, had many benefits. Practicing with the methods of more experienced authors sharpened students' reading and writing.[23] In addition, emulating the particular techniques of writers like Baraka, Ann Petry, Richard Wright, Alfred North Whitehead, and Virginia Woolf equipped them with a range of analytical frameworks that they could use for social critique (Bambara's assignment, for example, gave them a method to interrogate the lies of dominant discourse). And by inviting students to reflect on—and draw lessons from—their everyday lives, these assignments affirmed that their experiences were valid grounds from which to analyze the world, critique unjust institutions, and stake positions in political debates.

For many SEEK students, their former classrooms had been teacher- and textbook-centered spaces, where the instructor lectured from the front of the room, as the clock ticked mercilessly in the background, stubborn and slow. These classrooms, by contrast, centered students' ideas through discussions, debates, and presentations. They were often boisterous and loud with learning: Bambara shouting questions, students yelling answers, everyone learning from one another. She even stood along the side of the classroom, rather than at the front, to physically foreground their voices.[24] And students appreciated the different tenor of these classes. Former student Marvina White recalls that Christian's ability to offer engaged responses to their "specific ideas and thoughts" was something she "had never... experience[d] before."[25]

As Sean Molloy has shown, SEEK educators developed a student-centered approach to writing instruction that defied the college's official pedagogy.[26] Like many departments across the country, City College's English Department espoused what James A. Berlin calls the "current traditional approach" to writing instruction: an emphasis on grammatical correctness, evaluated through exams.[27] Yet this was the very paradigm that had convinced many of the Black and Puerto Rican SEEK students that they weren't good at writing. Its focus on grammatical correctness—according to upper-middle-class white standards of language use—meant that, by virtue of the dialects many grew up speaking at home, they were wrong from the moment they set foot inside a writing classroom. Thus, SEEK educators refused to administer the department's mandatory grammar exams. Instead, they focused on rhetorical techniques like argumentation and persuasion and pushed grammar, mechanics, and copyediting to the end of the writing process. They knew that once students cared about getting their point across, writing became far more interesting and exciting. This approach gave students like Francee Covington "the skills to lay out opinions of how things are and how things should be."[28] Covington also recalls constant positive feedback and many questions from instructors: about why she decided to structure a paper in a particular way, or what direction she planned to take an early draft. While the SEEK program would later become famous among scholars of composition and rhetoric as the site where Mina Shaughnessy pioneered key innovations in the field of basic writing, Molloy writes that it was actually Bambara, Gayle, and Christian who developed many of these methods, years before Shaughnessy ever set foot on campus.[29]

As SEEK instructors developed creative methods of empowering their students, business continued as usual in the English Department. Having recently received a master's degree from that department, Bambara was now a colleague of her former professors, though most wanted little to do with SEEK. Ever since the Great Depression, when literature PhDs were obligated to teach composition to meet the overwhelming demand, freshman writing had been looked down on as a dull, utilitarian service course and handmaiden of literature.[30] During SEEK's first two years, 1965–67, the department chair, Edmond Volpe, prohibited senior English faculty from teaching SEEK classes, even on a voluntary basis. This created a two-tiered department of tenured white, male faculty who were paid more to teach upper-level, and less labor-intensive, literature courses for the college's predominantly white students and a separate staff of primarily Black temporary professors who were paid less to teach more labor-intensive writing classes for the students of color in SEEK. SEEK professors were demeaned and marginalized—sometimes even physically so. When space was tight, they were assigned makeshift classrooms at the Alamac Hotel, sixty-five blocks away from campus. In 1971 Gayle accused the department of "minim[izing] contact between Blacks and whites in an educational setting" and thus promoting segregation.[31]

But being banished to the outskirts of the academy can sometimes have its upsides. Away from the surveilling eyes of the white institution, Bambara, Christian, and Gayle smuggled Black and Puerto Rican literature into a university with an otherwise lily-white curriculum. This literature explored racism, capitalism, and imperialism and modeled ways for students to analyze these in their own writing. And whereas the English Department provided, in Bambara's words, a "bourgeois training that promoted 'literaphilia' as a surrogate for political action and 'sensibility' as a substitute for social consciousness," SEEK educators used literature to raise questions about power, oppression, injustice, and resistance.[32] From the periphery, they replaced the department's error-centric writing pedagogy with a student-centered approach. For students who felt "jaded and fearful about mastering English," SEEK educators, counselors, and administrators created a rigorous, supportive intellectual environment where students sharpened their reading and writing skills and their political consciousness.[33]

Community Control in the Classroom

In the SEEK program, Bambara created the classrooms she had longed for, where learning was exciting, relevant, and driven by students' interests and the pursuit of answers to their most pressing questions. Often, their discussions of Black and Puerto Rican literature expanded to broader conversations about the ways school curricula erase "the role the African and Afro-American tradition plays in our history, our art, our culture."[34] And students were hungry for this missing information. They "began, on an individual slink-up-to-the-desk basis, to ask for books they should read that would offset their previous education, an antidote, a book that 'tells the truth.'"[35] But rather than simply answering their questions, Bambara taught students to locate these missing perspectives themselves.

While college courses typically progress toward eventual research projects, Bambara's students performed research from day one. Anytime they encountered an unfamiliar topic, such as "Senghor and the Negritude Movement" or "Pan-Africanism," she sent them out to find the information obscured by white-dominated curricula. They dug through the shelves at City College's Cohen Library, performed archival research at the Schomburg Center for Research in Black Culture, combed their neighborhoods for newspapers, and conducted oral histories with their friends, families, and community leaders. Other times they would venture further, such as to Newark to report on the Afrocentric teaching methods at the Chad School, an independent school formed by Black activists. Rather than cultivating what Roderick Ferguson calls a "will to institutionality," a kind of reverence for and attachment to the university as a privileged site of truth, these assignments highlight the knowledge located in places not valued by academic institutions.[36] They insist that a community organization or a local Harlem newspaper can be just as informative as a textbook. And as students ventured through the city, they "were not... boning up for some exam or other"; they were in hot pursuit of the knowledge that had been withheld from them and were developing reading, writing, and research skills along the way.[37]

These research projects were not solely for each student's own personal enrichment; instead, they were expected to report back and share what they had learned with the class. Each week, a full hour was devoted to student report-backs, skill shares, and student-led discussions. According to Bambara, this time was reserved for students

> who felt they had either acquired a skill which they wanted to demonstrate (the ability to persuade, refute, recruit, mobilize to action, cool out, dissuade), or had hit upon some salient material while working on the special reports in libraries of the city or foundations or other institutes, or had beaten their way toward a "position" and wished to use the group as a sounding board.[38]

Students thus used this hour to solicit the critiques, counterexamples, and rebuttals they could address to make their arguments more persuasive and to help each other interpret their research findings.

These student-led knowledge- and skill-sharing sessions drew on the community knowledge practices Bambara grew up with in Harlem. From subway preachers to the Speaker's Corner, Harlemites shared what they learned with each other. Such practices of communal literacy have roots in the nineteenth century, when Black communities circumvented antiliteracy laws by having those who were literate read aloud to others. This allowed, writes Jarvis R. Givens, for "collective engagement in the learning process."[39] Adapting these Black communal literacy practices, Bambara created opportunities for students to teach and learn from one another. The result was an early example of peer review: a classroom practice in which students provide feedback on each other's work. Though research would later reveal how dramatically peer review improves the quality of student writing, at the time, such practices challenged age-old assumptions that only expert teachers were capable of correcting their work. While Kenneth A. Bruffee has demonstrated how peer review arose during the era of open admissions, Bambara's work suggests that it was less "a harried, slipshod response" to overcrowded classes and more a deliberate pedagogical practice, grounded in her belief that students possess knowledge and skills worth sharing with one another.[40]

Of course, these student-led approaches occasionally went awry. At the end of one semester, a student chose to rap for "two hours" on "at least 80% of the themes" they had discussed, including "the criminality of education . . . [and] the freedom and limits of learning."[41] While clearly an impressive intellectual feat, this student had effectively hijacked the class. An unsuspecting observer stumbling into such a classroom might have asked the same question as the protagonist of Bambara's novel *The Salt Eaters*: "Well, what [is] this anyway, a healing or a jam session?"[42] "Both," Bambara might have replied, delighted at these metaphorical descriptions of her classroom.

As a final project, Bambara often asked students to "design a course that they would like, that would fulfill their needs," and submit a syllabus for this dream course.[43] This assignment encouraged them to reflect on what they had already learned, identify gaps in their knowledge, and research reliable sources that would help answer their questions. We can sense in this assignment Bambara's awareness of a future time (a few weeks or maybe months away) when she will not be with them and they will be responsible for teaching new material to themselves. Though finitude is constitutive of all classroom relationships, it was acutely felt in SEEK. As a new, experimental program that served low-income students of color, SEEK was in a precarious position. In white-dominated institutions like City College, such programs would likely be the first ones eliminated if purse strings tightened.[44] Should that happen, Bambara's assignment ensured that students would have a concrete plan to continue their learning independent of the era's educational politics.

At first glance, these research assignments, student-led discussions, and final projects resemble progressive pedagogy: an approach, dating back to the nineteenth century, that emphasizes active learning and critical thinking. However, Bambara, who had attended progressive schools, saw the shortcomings of such paradigms. She believed, writes Abena Busia, that such schools began from "a good premise—that children should be free."[45] However, like other Black educators such as Carter Woodson, she criticized their neglect of race, power, and social theory, which failed to provide students with a compass for societal change.[46] By contrast, she was inspired by the Afrocentric teaching methods implemented at Pan-African schools like the Chad School (Newark), the Nairobi Schools (East Palo Alto), the Freedom Library Day School (Philadelphia), and later the Oakland Community School. These schools, a product of the era's Black liberation movements, combined the progressive emphasis on hands-on, experiential learning with the Black Power movement's commitment to challenging systemic racism and empowering Black communities.[47] Bambara admired how these schools "start with the premise that children are responsible, competent, efficient, and principled ... kids are encouraged to raise questions. They're encouraged to take on responsibility, they're encouraged to critique everything they read, everything they see."[48]

Bambara's teaching was also inspired by the movement for community control of schools. In the late 1960s, parents in several predominantly Black and Puerto Rican school districts in New York City wrenched control of their local public schools from the white dominated Board of Education in order to change their racist, colonial, and paternalistic policies.[49] In the experimental school districts established in Harlem, the Lower East Side, and Ocean Hill–Brownsville, community governing boards gave parents a voice in educational decisions. There, as Stephen Brier writes, educators "abandoned... forced discipline and rote recitation" and "pioneered new curricula" focusing on "black history and African culture."[50] In 1970 Bambara reported on the movement for the readers of the popular women's magazine *Redbook*. Her article "The Children Who Got Cheated" described the movement as a "long-overdue reaction to the intellectual imperialism of white America, the white control and conditioning of Black minds."[51] This "intellectual imperialism" (elsewhere described as a form of "coloniality" and "criminality") was evident even in the SEEK program, where administrators and professors made decisions that would affect working-class students of color, often without their consent or involvement in decision-making processes. In fact, Bambara and her students had a term for this phenomenon: the "paternalism of the SEEK program."[52] By contrast, Bambara involved students in making the decisions that would affect them—what we might think of as community control within the classroom.[53]

Nowhere is this community-controlled teaching more apparent than in the 1968 SEEK summer course that Bambara taught for returning sophomores, juniors, and seniors. That June, when she arrived at the Alamac Hotel (repurposed as a SEEK dormitory), her syllabus was blank and her determination resolute. Rather than simply following instructions laid out by the professor, these students would determine the "content, direction, and goals of the course." This was not, however, a free-for-all. Bambara knew that one couldn't simply turn things over to students and expect them to successfully codesign a course. How could they, when nothing in their previous education would have prepared them for such a task? That Wednesday evening in early June, she handed out copies of students' descriptions of their dream courses (what they had submitted as final projects) to be used as inspiration. For several hours they discussed these materials and "mapped out their summer course."[54] Students proposed topics, instructors suggested books, and they debated their way toward a syllabus agreed on by all. Though Bambara may have been hired to prepare these students to assimilate into the existing curriculum, she instead gave them the tools to invent their own.

Given the opportunity to study anything in the world, these students developed the course Colonialism, Neocolonialism, and Liberation, which would let them learn more about subjects that had been conspicuously absent from their education.[55] They decided their course would focus on the recent liberations of African nations, the imperialist war in Vietnam, and what Black Power activists referred to as the "internal colonialism" of US racism. They would begin with Fanon's *The Wretched of the Earth* (an analysis of the damaging psychological effects of colonialism) and discuss its influence on radical movements, then proceed to Eldridge Cleaver's prison memoir *Soul on Ice*. They would also compare how colonialism was depicted in national and local newspapers.[56] Among the many "texts" they selected was Gillo Pontecorvo's film *The Battle of Algiers* (1966), one of the most popular films among Black student activists throughout the country. The film's depiction of the guerrilla tactics Algerians used to resist French occupation inspired many a campus protest.[57] As the following year would soon reveal, City College was no exception.

Though the course focused on geopolitical struggles, there was another form of colonialism they were challenging as well. Bambara called this the "colonial ... nature" of "the teacher-student relationship": the dangerous amount of "power given teachers over students' minds ... spirits ... [and] development."[58] Echoing Paulo Freire's famous critique of the "banking" model of education, Bambara similarly denounced how hierarchical student-teacher relationships nurture psychological dependence on those in positions of authority. This, in turn, can serve the interests of the ruling class by teaching students to accept what those in power tell them to be true. Instead, she sought to "equip" each student "with the skills so that he can sever ties with the teacher quickly and teach himself."[59]

Bambara's commitment to students' collective decision-making extended even to those moments when their desires and choices conflicted with her own. That summer, after several weeks devoted to nonfiction, the class transitioned to reading novels including André Malraux's *Man's Fate* (about a communist insurrection) and Alan Paton's *Cry, the Beloved Country* (about apartheid). But when they did, their conversations lost momentum and became "sluggish." As a fiction writer, Bambara wondered what was up. "I'm tired of living through fiction," one student explained, as the class nodded vigorously in agreement.[60] That evening, Bambara received a phone call from another student who felt like the class was losing its urgency. "Identifying with heroes in books is like masturbating," he told her.[61] Students felt like the novels, despite their revolutionary themes, pulled them out of contemporary events and politics when they wanted to dig deeper. While some were "wary" of their daily struggles and found "sanctuary in literature," the majority felt "guilty with living vicariously" through fictional characters "in these times that demand vital and total participation." Rather than trying to convert them to her own belief in "the emancipatory impulse" of fiction, Bambara agreed to "abandon the lesson on the short story that had been planned" and continue, instead, their conversations about "brainwashing."[62]

In some cases, this community-controlled pedagogy extended even to grading. The syllabus for one of her later courses states that students' "Grade" would be "based on continued productivity and usefulness to group development. Can be negotiated within the group."[63] As this statement suggests, Bambara saw learning in collective, rather than individualized, terms and encouraged students to become accountable to one another. While we can only speculate, it's easy to imagine them discussing the various potential aims of grading. Are grades assigned to reward, motivate, punish, or instruct? Do they inform students of whether they are satisfactorily meeting course requirements, or do they signal something about a student's abilities to an external audience, like an employer? By what metrics should learning be evaluated? Effort? Improvement? Quality of work? Mastery of a subject? Creativity? How does one quantify something so amorphous and idiosyncratic?

The SEEK students would have had something to say about this. For many, grading had been a weapon white teachers wielded against them, returning their papers with racist comments or unexplained low marks. Reflecting on one of Bambara's later classes, Holmes recalls that students presented the grade they felt they deserved for debate, negotiation, bargaining, compromise, and collective agreement.[64] Bambara thus turned what is often a tool of oppression into a learning opportunity, in which students must define what constitutes good work, evaluate whether they have adhered to those criteria, persuade others to share their view, and practice collective decision-making. And as any professor who has tried such methods will tell you, involving students in the evaluation process inevitably increases the quality of their work. When students know that their work will be evaluated not just by their professor but also by their peers, they're more willing to revise, rewrite, and refine. And students are often far tougher on themselves and each other than professors are, especially if they must provide evidence to support each grade.

In recent years, efforts to involve students in the grading process have become more common. Since the publication of Asao B. Inoue's *Antiracist Writing Assessment Ecologies* (2015), which argues that community-based assessment practices are essential to more socially just pedagogy, there has been an uptick in practices like contract grading, labor-based grading, and formative assessment methods like minimal grading, process letters, and portfolios—what some scholars call *ungrading*.[65] As Bambara's work indicates, these practices have a much longer history, one that is entangled with the Black Power movement's emphasis on community control: that is, Black people's right to make decisions that will affect their lives and communities.[66]

Whether or not Bambara's community-controlled course was a success depends on how you measure. At the summer's end, one group of students began collaborating with the Experimental College, a campus organization that was conducting courses on abortion, guerrilla warfare, and the radical press.[67] Another group drafted a proposal for a course on community organizing, which they planned to submit to the Sociology Department. A third was establishing a journal for literary, critical, and political work. And a fourth was invited to teach a course on African and Afro-American history at a local dorm. If the goal is empowering students to advocate for change, then Colonialism, Neocolonialism, and Liberation succeeded.

Following their six-week course, Bambara was required to submit a report on the summer seminar to SEEK administrators. What could have been a dry bureaucratic document is instead an explosive manifesto for her pedagogy of social change. The document contains what we might read as her teaching philosophy. Yet so distinct is it from contemporary statements of teaching philosophy—formulaic documents in which professors dutifully recite their commitments to student-centered learning—that it is worth quoting at length. She writes:

> The aim of my stumble trial and error approach, then, is to make the classroom unsafe, to bomb the hiding student out of his corner, to blast the insulating walls down, to nimbly take the most rash and contradictory positions so that students do not feel they have to preach the party line to pass the course, to demand that each student participate in the content, direction, and goals of the course, and to provide the kind of relationship in which the student will always feel free to terminate or to change, to walk out of the room to work [on] his project, to do advance work on material he feels more important than what is offered in the classroom.[68]

These images of bombs and an "unsafe" classroom illustrate just how deeply racist and imperial violence shaped Bambara's thinking about pedagogy. If conventional classrooms are "insulating," nurseries protected from the world's brutality, she reimagines them as training grounds where students learn to navigate and transform the unjust war zone beyond its walls. And this is no gentle wakeup call—it's time to report for duty.

Bambara was the first to admit that teaching such a community-controlled course was not easy. Quite the opposite: it was "often agonizing... the most difficult kind of course to 'teach' for there can be no 'control' in the usual pedagogic sense."[69] Rather than preparing lectures or assignments in advance, decisions would be made with the students. Much of her actual teaching occurred in those difficult-to-plan-for moments when she connected the ideas that surfaced in their discussions to the broader themes and questions of the course. (Fortunately, like the jazz musicians who were her closest friends, Bambara was a skilled improviser.) She believed that this, although difficult, was "the most worthwhile kind of educational adventure."[70] Students left her courses cognizant of the gaps in dominant, institutional knowledges and mainstream narratives; able to do research and seek out missing perspectives; aware that authority is not synonymous with knowledge and not always legitimate; and with the power to tell stories rather than be told by them. We are left with little doubt that, faced with a whitewashed syllabus or dull assignments, these students would challenge the teacher, propose alternatives, or "walk out of the room" to work on more important material.[71] And, in the spring of 1969, this is exactly what happened.

When Bambara was first hired at City College, she had been recognized for her writing as an undergraduate and had successfully placed a short story in the *Massachusetts Review*, but she was far from the widely celebrated author that we know her as today. In fact, it wasn't until she began teaching in SEEK that she started "writing in a serious way."[72] During her time at City College, Bambara wrote many of her most influential short stories. Several of these were inspired by her students and took up questions of educational power and authority.[73] For example, "The Lesson" (1972), one of her most frequently anthologized stories, follows a teacher, Miss Moore, who returns home from college to educate the youth in her neighborhood. Rather than lecturing them on society's unequal allocation of resources, she takes them on a field trip to an expensive toy store, reminiscent of FAO Schwarz. Confronted with the extravagant toys, the narrator wonders, "Who are these people that spend that much for performing clowns and $1000 for toy sailboats? What kinda work they do and how they live and how come we ain't in on it?"[74] The expensive sailboat prompts her to ask Miss Moore "how much a real boat costs?" Instead of answering, Miss Moore challenges her to "check that out... and report back to the group," just as Bambara did with her own students. As the children begin to feel shame and anger, Miss Moore helps them connect this experience to broader social structures: "Imagine for a minute what kind of society it is in which some people can spend on a toy what it would cost to feed a family of six or seven. What you think?"[75] The narrator's cousin, Sugar, responds "that this is not much of a democracy if you ask me. Equal chance to pursue happiness means an equal crack at the dough, don't it?"[76] After discussing their reactions, Miss Moore delivers a short lecture on the idea that "where we are is who we are.... But it don't necessarily have to be that way."[77] "The Lesson" can thus be read as an adventure in student-centered and consciousness-raising learning, in which an educator helps these young people to draw their own conclusions.

"The Lesson" is just one example of how Bambara's teaching impacted her writing.[78] As Busia and Holmes have shown, many of her stories either are about learning or are themselves intended to teach readers a lesson—sometimes both. Thabiti Lewis describes them as "liberation lessons, tutelage in how to go about the business of... cultivating consciousness."[79] According to Busia, it is often Bambara's bold young protagonists and narrators who have "something to learn" or unlearn, allowing readers to do so alongside them. The result is a pedagogy that is "light, oblique, and experiential rather than didactic."[80] "Bambara taught us through her stories," Busia writes, with a "delicacy of touch" and the same "sensitivity to learning situations" evident in her classrooms.[81] And according to Toni Morrison (Bambara's editor), she was keenly aware of her fiction's "pedagogy" and "its use."[82] Bambara herself described her stories as a way to "dramatize lessons learned."[83]

But it wasn't only Bambara's students who inspired her writing, it was her colleagues as well. As the SEEK program grew, Bambara, Gayle, and Christian were joined by up-and-coming writers like David Henderson and Raymond Patterson, as well as June Jordan, Adrienne Rich, and Audre Lorde. "In the camaraderie of progressive writers who were activists, new cutting-edge feminists, and leading voices in the Black Arts Movement," writes Holmes, "Bambara experienced a new sense of herself as a writer."[84] She and Jordan formed a friendship that would eventually alter her writing practice, and she and Lorde became advocates of each other's work. While the extent of Bambara and Rich's actual conversations is difficult to discern, Rich cited how Bambara's writing shaped her thinking about race and adapted Bambara's assignments for her classrooms. In fact, some of Bambara's teaching materials are located not in her own archives but in Rich's. This rather astonishing fact, that to understand Bambara's teaching requires digging in the unlikely archives of a Jewish, lesbian, feminist poet with whom she is rarely associated, reminds us that these four women are all part of a larger story knitted together by the classroom.

* * *

When SEEK students completed their remedial coursework and entered the college's mainstream curriculum, many were disappointed by the predominantly white students, faculty, and curriculum they encountered. In contrast to SEEK, where they read Baraka and Fanon and codesigned courses like Colonialism, Neocolonialism, and Liberation, City College courses, quite literally, paled by comparison. There, Black and Puerto Rican history and culture were treated as nonexistent. And unlike the supportive faculty mentors in SEEK, many of the college's professors could not be trusted. They accused SEEK students of cheating, deliberately lowered their grades, and would publicly berate, insult, and humiliate them.[85]

In 1969 students' outrage with the college's recalcitrant racism reached a boiling point. By then, the SEEK program, now four years in existence, had enrolled a small but critical mass of students of color. That February, at the height of the nationwide Black campus movement, Black and Puerto Rican students delivered five demands to the City College administration. They demanded more equitable admissions policies, greater resources for Black and Puerto Rican Studies, curricular changes so that all education majors would study the Spanish language and Black and Puerto Rican history, a separate orientation for students of color, and the involvement of SEEK students in governance decisions about their program.[86] These students, whom Bambara had given control over the "content, methods, and goals of the course," now demanded "a determining voice in setting the guidelines" for the program and managing its operation.[87]

As students awaited a response, an essay by Bambara appeared in the campus newspaper. "Realizing the Dream of a Black University" (1969) argued that the college could address students' demands by creating a Center for Black and Hispanic Studies. The essay whets (or intensifies!) readers' appetites for change by vividly describing the courses such a center might offer. In courses like Nutrition, students would explore "soul food of Black and Latin people from a nutritional, geographical, historical, cultural point of view," focusing, for instance, on "how the African staples introduced in slave areas (U.S., South America, Caribbean, etc.), helped to stabilize the [local] economy and ... diet," and perform fieldwork in restaurants (what we might now call *experiential learning*).[88] In what she called a "root course," "part workshop or studio dance ... part lecture-demonstration," a team of instructors would teach students about the historical significance of dance moves such as the "locked leg and the body pivoting around it," found in Nigerian, Haitian, and Brazilian dance. In the course she imagines on "Revolution," students would read "the empire novels of Conrad, Dostoevsky, [and] Kipling" alongside Vietnamese poetry, Chinua Achebe's novels, and works by guerrilla historians like Che Guevara to consider how literature has both bolstered and challenged imperialism. Instructors would not necessarily possess advanced degrees; they would include "whoever happens to have the knowledge and expertise we desire": activists, Black Panthers, lawyers, members of the NAACP, SEEK instructors, chefs from soul food restaurants, grandmothers, dieticians, students, and dancers. As Makeba Lavan and Conor Tomás Reed write, Bambara's vision of a Black university was a "more expansive intellectual project than simply adding Black students, teachers, and courses. It meant disrupting disciplinary boundaries, identifying knowledge bases outside of the university that flourished inside poor multi-ethnic neighborhoods," and committing to "collective" rather than individualized modes of learning.[89]

"Realizing the Dream" is a campus essay, one of the genres of open admissions. While universities can often feel intransigent and monolithic, campus essays convey the alternative visions of higher education that bubble up in moments of tectonic shift, like the 1960s and 1970s, or amid Occupy Wall Street, the two distinct moments that form a constellation in this book. Though utopian dreaming has long been a component of Black liberation and Black feminism, the social movements of the 1960s and 1970s prompted a wave of visionary thinking about what higher education could look like.[90] At HBCUs, for example, students were demanding the transformation of their bourgeois "Negro Universities" into "Black Universities" that would, in Ibram X. Kendi's words, "connect students to African American culture, imbue them with a social responsibility," and prepare them "to aid the black masses."[91] The same year that Bambara wrote her essay, students in the Lumumba-Zapata movement at the University of California San Diego demanded the formation of a people's college that would aid them in their liberation struggles. In addition to the student-authored demand statements that are, themselves, a major genre of this era, campus essays were means by which faculty used their positions of relative power to bolster students' demands and expand our imagination of what universities could do.

"Realizing the Dream" carried different messages for the distinct audiences who might be reading the college newspaper. On the one hand, Bambara situates students' demands within the college's longer history of educating the working class—a history that faculty and administrators took great pride in. She reminds her colleagues that educating non-elite students has always produced changes to the curriculum. When previous generations of "non-upper-class, non Anglo stock students" came to City College, they brought "a wide range of skills, needs, ambitions, demands" that challenged curricular orthodoxies.[92] They wanted to study new subjects like Romance languages and science, not Latin, as tradition had dictated. They "played havoc with the traditional education, but not enough" for the current students (and faculty), who saw how much was still missing: "Enter the hippie, the yippie, the radical, the militant, the underclass, the overlooked, and further fissures in the surface appear."[93] She also cautions her colleagues that if they fail to act, City College could go the way of San Francisco State, where a student strike that had begun three months earlier continued on with no end in sight. "An explosion" she writes, "is imminent."[94]

The essay's primary audience, however, is students. "Realizing the Dream" was published on Valentine's Day, and it is, in a way, a love letter to them. In it, she assigns them homework, the love language of professors everywhere:

> What remains is work from you, students. It will do none of us any good if the Center is run by faculty, if curriculum is designed wholly by faculty, if staff is hired merely by faculty.... The job of setting up a curriculum, of establishing priorities, of putting into operation what is necessary... that job has got to be done cooperatively, with the major work on your shoulders, the thrust and demand coming from you.[95]

This is followed by suggestions for concrete actions they should take, including designing courses, coordinating various student groups, and joining with the citywide Black Student Union. She also recommends holding a daylong conference to "map out the areas that need to be covered" and decide such logistical matters as "which course to offer first" (the same process they used to codesign Colonialism, Neocolonialism, and Liberation, though at a larger scale). Her words are thus a blueprint not only for a Black university but for a student-centered one as well. Addressing students directly, she urges them not to hang their hats on decisions made by university administrators and city officials but to get organized and start creating the better education they desired: "To obtain a relevant, real education, we shall have to either topple the university or set up our own."[96] And on April 22, 1969, that's just what they did.

That spring, as students awaited a response to their demands, Governor Nelson Rockefeller announced that New York's state budget for 1969–70 would include drastic cuts to the SEEK program and other reductions in higher education funding—the opposite of what the activists had petitioned for.[97] In response, more than two hundred Black and Puerto Rican students and their allies went on strike to pressure the administration to meet their demands. They occupied the campus and established Harlem University, a pop-up university with political education classes, tutorials, nightly community meetings, a walk-in clinic, free breakfast, and day care for neighborhood children.[98] There, students modeled the kind of free, open, accessible, and community-responsive institution they wanted City College to be. Two weeks later, CUNY agreed to implement an open admissions policy that would guarantee every New York City high school graduate a tuition-free college education.

Scholars have described some of the ways that the SEEK program led to these now-famous protests.[99] In addition to enrolling students of color, SEEK put what education scholar David E. Lavin calls "a minority consciousness into the university" and helped students realize their collective power.[100] As poet, essayist, and SEEK graduate Louis Reyes Rivera recalls, SEEK bolstered students' understanding that higher education was a right that had been collectively denied to African Americans and Puerto Ricans. Many felt they had "an obligation to open doors so that more could come in."[101] As former SEEK director Allen B. Ballard states, the program "transformed higher education. It made it from something that was exclusionary, kind of property of whites primarily to something that was to be shared."[102] By examining archival teaching materials, we can see how revolution was also nurtured in SEEK classrooms like Bambara's.

Senior English faculty had figured that what happened in SEEK classrooms was of little significance. But they were wrong. Like many of the freshman composition courses of the 1960s and 1970s, these classrooms were incubators of student activism.[103] There, SEEK educators taught students to analyze power structures, make decisions about their learning, hold institutions accountable, and demand what they desired. And instructors' experiments with community control in the classroom led to an occupation in which students demanded community control of the campus.[104] The result was an open admissions policy that historian Martha Biondi has called "the biggest structural shift in opportunity during the long civil-rights era."[105] Neither

City College nor the rest of American higher education would ever look the same again.

"Dancing Is Her Way to Learn Now"

During the open admissions era, English professors like Theodore L. Gross and Geoffrey Wagner increasingly found themselves teaching "new" more racially, ethnically, and economically diverse students, who seemed to them comparatively "plebeian."[106] Among their complaints, Gross and Wagner disliked that these students seemed to prefer radio and television to the literature they assigned. In his jeremiad against open admissions, "How to Kill a College," Gross lambasted the fact that "the Blacks and Puerto Ricans and Asians [who] arrive[d] at the City College came from working-class families in which television and radio were the exclusive sources of information and in which there was no tradition of learning."[107] His description of them as "illiterate" and "chronic nonreader(s)" overlooks the different kinds of knowledge, skills, histories, cultures, perspectives, and traditions of art and learning they brought to the classroom: stories and myths passed down around kitchen tables, survival strategies woven into patchwork quilts, lyrics reverberating over airwaves, usable histories left simmering on the stove. Their knowledge simply didn't take a form recognized by Gross, such as appreciation for white, Western "classics" or argument-driven essays. And even if they did prefer radio and television to Gross's syllabi filled with Geoffrey Chaucer and William Wordsworth, who could blame them? There, they were far more likely to encounter people who looked like them and spoke about issues related to their lives in the language of their everyday experiences.

While conservative professors like Gross feared that television, radio, and film would destroy the American intellect, Bambara saw in these newer media political possibilities for empowering students and engaging diverse audiences. Although she is most famous for her writing, she frequently undertook creative work in a range of forms including theater, mime, dance, radio, film, and television. In fact, she identified as a "cultural worker" and saw all of these (as well as teaching and mothering), in Holmes's words, "as instruments of self-renewal and transformation."[108] In Bambara's eyes, an obsession with the written word over other forms of knowing was one way universities reproduced whiteness. She writes, "The white community reveres the written word. Ours is a singing strength; we spring from and have maintained an oral tradition. Our manner of communication is largely auditory, kinesthetic, and visual."[109]

Though Bambara was hired to teach students to write in Standard English (according to criteria determined by upper-middle-class white folks), she instead encouraged them to make their own decisions about the forms their learning would take. Students rapped in her writing classes, recorded oral histories and interviews with local activists, and used documentaries like *The Battle of Algiers* to plan their own occupation of City College. Rather than trying to eradicate her students' preferred modes of expression, she looked beyond the era's narrowly text-based paradigms and embraced multiple ways of knowing. Indeed, she developed what we would now call a "multimodal" pedagogy that taught students to compose, not just with words, but also with images, movement, and sound.

This multimodal pedagogy is especially evident in Bambara's final projects. Instead of papers, she assigned open-ended projects in which students had to find or invent a form that would share something they had learned with an audience beyond the classroom. "Do not write term papers for me," she told them. "Make sure they are useful for somebody else as well."[110] Rather than dictating the form their projects would take, she suggested options, such as an individual or collaborative annotated bibliography, performance art, a short story (for radio or TV), a magazine, puppet theater, or a street theater performance. These projects required students to think critically about the audience they wanted to impact, the message they hoped to convey, and the form that would be most effective. Though more difficult than simply writing an essay, this was more useful preparation for the various rhetorical situations they would encounter beyond the classroom. And instead of fifty book reports, this resulted in a more "unusual" array of submissions: "sceneries for films they one day hoped to make (inspired, I imagine, by 'Battle of Algiers')... dialogues, poems, notes for compositions, [and] blueprints for courses they'd one day like to take."[111]

Bambara believed so strongly in this kind of multimodal learning that she advocated for it beyond her own classrooms. While such methods were well funded in affluent, white school districts, she developed enriched arts curricula for high school students in predominantly Black schools in Newark, Trenton, and Atlanta so that their education would include photography, mass communication, drama, poetry, design, music, and creative writing.[112]

Often, the "multimodal turn" in English is understood as a response to the internet and developments in digital technologies. In the early 2000s, as multimedia came to saturate digital environments, scholars such as Kathleen Blake Yancey, Jody Shipka, and members of the National Council of Teachers of English (NCTE) urged educators to incorporate "multiple modes of communication and expression... [and] multiple ways of knowing," including "speech, images, sounds, movement, music, and animation."[113] Composing in different media, however, has a much longer history. In the late 1940s, for instance, Hugh M. Gloster, director of the Communications Center at Hampton College (and later president of Morehouse College), helped students improve their literacy by having them broadcast radio programs, produce plays, practice public speaking, publish their writing, and experiment with emerging media.[114] In addition, writing professors like Janet Emig, James Britton, and Peter Elbow have engaged students in multimodal composition at least since the 1960s when new and more affordable technologies such as slide projectors, photocopiers, televisions, tape recorders, and the Super 8 camera enabled broader access to new forms of recording, editing, copying, distributing, listening, and viewing.[115] During this period, Bambara also developed a multimodal pedagogy that guided students in telling their own stories in whatever media were most useful to them: from radio to journalism, fiction, and film.

In addition to reminding us of the longer histories of multimodal teaching, Bambara's work also highlights how such methods were shaped by Black feminism. Black feminist critics have historically valued the art, knowledge, and theory that exceeds white, patriarchal definitions. In Alice Walker's essay "In Search of Our Mothers' Gardens" (1972), written around the time that Bambara was teaching at City College, Walker argued that narrow notions of what constitutes art and literature obscure the long histories of Black women's creative production. For much of their lives, Black women like Walker's mother were forced to cook, clean, and work for wealthy white families. Not only did they not have expendable income or leisure time with which to write, but for much of US history, antiliteracy laws made it illegal for them to do so. For Walker, a narrow focus on the written word overlooks generations of Black women who "fed... [the] creative spirit" through "the only materials [they] could afford" and the "only medi[a] [their] position in society allowed [them] to use," such as singing, quilt making, and gardening.[116] Years later, Barbara Christian, herself a former SEEK instructor, would revisit this idea in her influential essay "The Race for Theory." Written in the 1980s, as French post-structuralist theory spread like wildfire through universities, Christian argued that Black women have historically theorized "but in forms quite different from the Western abstract logic": through poems, stories, and autobiographies.[117] Considering Bambara's teaching alongside Walker's and Christian's work, we can see how she developed a Black feminist pedagogy that honors the myriad means through which people produce and share knowledge.

Some of Bambara's most nuanced insights into multimodal pedagogy appear not in her archives but in the pages of her novel *The Salt Eaters* (1980). While scholars have read this novel about a wounded activist as a meditation on spiritual wholeness (Thabiti Lewis) and Black women's mental health (Belinda Waller-Patterson), and as a critique of nuclear power (Janelle Collins), it is also a cautionary tale about multimodality.[118] The novel dramatizes the healing of Velma Henry at the hands of Minnie Ransom and Ransom's spiritual guide, Old Wife. Velma is a community organizer, computer programmer, sister, wife, and mother who has been spread thin by these multiple modes of cultural work. We first meet her in the aftermath of a failed suicide attempt, "dry, stiff... frozen" and withdrawn from the world.[119] She has been torn apart not only by racism, sexism, capitalism, and environmental degradation but also by her own efforts to organize against these. Like Bambara, Velma saw possibilities to challenge injustice in every facet of her life. As a result, she, like her namesake John Henry, nearly worked herself to death. Velma's predicament thus warns readers that while possibilities for transformative cultural work are abundant, trying to do it all is a surefire recipe for burnout.[120]

Velma's healing offers a more viable way of moving through a world in which the opportunities to make change are abundant. Throughout the book, the healers guide Velma toward dancing, which becomes a way for her to reopen herself to the world—both its acute dangers and its wondrous possibilities. "Let her go," Old Wife advises Minnie, "dancing is her way to learn now."[121] Instead of trying to do everything, Velma embraces dance as her mode of cultural work: a way to bring joy to others and also to herself. As a healer and teacher, Minnie helped an artist find her art form and knew when to "let go," a pedagogy that closely approximates Bambara's own. In this way, *The Salt Eaters* suggests that the hands of patient healers and teachers are necessary to guide us toward our styles of flourishing: our path, our movement, our verbs, our dance.

There is another aspect of Velma's healing that is worth mentioning for its insights into Bambara's pedagogy. In addition to guiding Velma toward her particular mode of cultural work, the healers also ease her burden by restoring her place within a larger community. Though health is often understood in individual terms, Velma's healing is depicted as a collaborative effort. Her sickness, we are told, is so fierce that it "took twenty hard-praying folk to loosen... concentration was necessary to help a neighbor experience the best of herself and himself."[122] This is also conveyed through the polyvocal form of the novel, which takes a literary form associated with liberal individualism and explodes it into radical collectivity. Restoring Velma's position in the community gives her (and, by extension, readers) permission not to try and do it all but to pursue one's preferred modes of cultural work, bolstered by the knowledge that others are working alongside us, too, and in different ways. As we will see, this vision of strength in numbers can be understood in relation to Bambara's classrooms and the collectivist pedagogy she developed therein.

Anthologizing Alternatives

Today the success stories of SEEK students are well known. The program's graduates went on to become doctors, lawyers, teachers, professors, labor organizers, and some of the era's most exciting writers and artists. Among SEEK's notable alumni are Oscar Hijuelos, the first Latino recipient of the Pulitzer Prize for Fiction; Grammy-nominated writer, performer, and composer Sekou Sundiata; and Nellie Y. McKay, who helped establish the fields of African American literature and Black women's studies. As Shanna Benjamin has recently shown, McKay's experiences as a student in the Queens College SEEK program inspired a lifelong commitment to "opening doors for others" and expanding access to education.[123] While this list of notable alumni hints at the influence these classrooms had on the era's art, literature, and criticism, the anthologies edited by Bambara and other SEEK faculty bring that impact into even sharper relief.

During her time at City College (1964–69), Bambara compiled the entries for what would become her groundbreaking anthology *The Black Woman* (1970): a collection of essays, poems, stories, and interviews on subjects like motherhood, relations between Black men and women, educational racism, birth control, social work, poverty, and Black family dynamics. It is difficult to overstate the collection's impact. Perhaps more so than any other single text, *The Black Woman* helped establish Black feminist criticism.[124] In Robin D. G. Kelley's words, it is "a kind of manifesto for black feminism, a critique of both the women's movement and male-led black politics, and a complex analysis of how gender, race, and class worked together to oppress everyone."[125] As one of the first "multi-genre" anthologies, it paved the way for subsequent collections like *Third World Women* (1972), *This Bridge Called My Back* (1981), *All the Women Are White, All the Blacks Are Men, but Some of Us Are Brave* (1982), and *Home Girls* (1983).[126] Since its publication, *The Black*

Woman has inspired generations of students, activists, artists, and authors. It continues to appear on college syllabi across disciplines to this day.[127] Yet despite its profound impact both within and beyond universities, little has been said about its classroom context: the fact that it was written, in part, by Bambara's students. In fact, when filmmaker Louis Massiah asked Bambara "about the genesis of *The Black Woman*... How did that come about?" her initial response was only one sentence: "In 1968 I was teaching at City College in the SEEK program."[128]

In the SEEK program, students and faculty alike were galvanized by Bambara's classroom and campus lectures on Black literature and history, myths and propaganda, and the need for more relevant education. One student, Francee Covington, confronted her: "You've been saying this, that, and the other. Why don't you do a book, dammit?"[129] This was echoed by Gayle, who approached Bambara and said, "I heard you give eight talks. Why the hell don't you write them down and get them printed?"[130] According to Bambara, it was Gayle who "urged me to assemble a book on the black woman rather than run off at the mouth about it."[131]

While Covington and Gayle had suggested she publish her own writing, Bambara instead chose to edit an anthology. Initially, she envisioned *The Black Woman* as a collection of writings by women in the Student Nonviolent Coordinating Committee (SNCC), the Congress of Racial Equality (CORE), and the Black Panther Party. However, as time passed, she decided that rather than waiting for busy activists to slowly come around to the idea of publishing their work, she would collect writings from her friends, neighbors, colleagues, and students. Among the collection's twenty-seven authors, more than a third were affiliated with the SEEK program, either as students (five) or as instructors (five). Students' contributions include an essay titled "Black Romanticism" and a transcribed conversation among seven young women about appropriation, the politics of Black hair, and relationships among Black women. Some, such as Covington's "Are the Revolutionary Techniques Employed in the Battle of Algiers Applicable in Harlem?" were likely projects from Bambara's classes. If pundits were skeptical that these "new students" could withstand the rigors of a college education, little could they have imagined that their writing would be published in one of the most important anthologies of the twentieth century.

Among students' contributions, Joanna Clark's personal essay "Motherhood" is a particularly scathing indictment of society's abuse of Black mothers. Clark describes trying to support two children as a single mother while also attending college through the SEEK program. Her essay critiques the injustices she experiences as she is shuffled between inept institutions including the Department of Welfare, Support Court, and New York City hospitals. She encounters condescending doctors, flagrantly sexist lawyers, and an "investigator... extremely gung-ho about filling out forms" and equally eager to "throw [her] off welfare."[132] Her essay indicts a culture that frees fathers from responsibility, leaving all obligations to mothers, "as if... [she] went out behind a barn somewhere and knocked herself up with the nearest twig."[133] These observations are conveyed with wry, understated wit and humor, astounding given how cruelly she was treated. In a moment when Black mothers were being both blamed for destroying their families and praised for their extrahuman "resiliency," Clark describes the difficult realities she faced as a young, poor single mother, urging readers to develop a more nuanced understanding of the material conditions of Black women's lives.[134]

As Clark's essay demonstrates, *The Black Woman* circulated the knowledge and perspectives missing from mainstream journalism, publishing, and curricula, as well as the era's male-dominated anthologies of Black literature.[135] This is "knowledge" not in the capitalist sense of the term, as a commodity to profit from, but as insights that will enable others to navigate and challenge an unequal society. Echoing a common refrain throughout Bambara's work, Eleanor Traylor writes that the anthology picks up where educational institutions fall short: "In this collection, we gain the pedagogy of those who think better than they've been trained."[136] As such, it can be read as a kind of grassroots pedagogical formation and means of sharing knowledge beyond the guarded gates of university walls, what Lavan and Tomás Reed call a "feminist studies open curriculum."[137] And people wanted this wisdom. Bambara recalls that "within the second month the book came out, it went into a new edition. That book was everywhere. There were pyramids of *The Black Woman* in every bookstore."[138] According to Holmes, it was a "literary bombshell" that helped "black women across the age spectrum sense... a new age dawning," one in which "women exert[ed] their power."[139]

Considered alongside Bambara's teaching archives, *The Black Woman* highlights how classrooms have been central to the production of feminist criticism. In recent years, scholars like Rachel Sagner Buurma, Laura Heffernan, and Matt Brim have illustrated how classrooms do not merely introduce students to critical paradigms, they are where such discourses are actually produced.[140] More so than other fields, feminist criticism has been relatively forthcoming about its indebtedness to classrooms. While liberal individualism rewards those who claim ownership of ideas, feminist scholars tend to acknowledge the networks of knowers and collaborative labor of thinking: that no thought is ever singular. Key texts of this era like Patricia Meyer Spacks's *The Female Imagination* (1975) and Sandra Gilbert and Susan Gubar's *The Madwoman in the Attic* (1979) acknowledged that the ideas therein emerged from the college courses their authors taught at Wellesley and Indiana University, respectively. While these books emerged from women's literature classes, *The Black Woman* was born, five years earlier, in SEEK's basic writing classrooms. And, unlike Spacks and Gilbert and Gubar, who weave their students' stories into their own narrative, Bambara saw her students as authors in their own right, and she included their writing in her anthology.

But *The Black Woman* was not the only anthology to emerge from, or in close proximity to, the SEEK program. The 1960s and 1970s were, in a sense, the era of the anthology. This period saw both the publication of anthologies by marginalized authors—women, African Americans, Asian Americans, and Puerto Ricans—and the growing popularity of literary anthologies in college English courses. Amid the postwar expansions of higher education, Norton aggressively marketed its English literature anthology as a way to affordably aggregate work that was first published in different periods and by various authors and publishers.[141] However, in the SEEK program, such canonical collections merely consolidated a white-dominated curriculum. As educators scoured bookstores and fought with mimeograph machines to ensure that their students could read literature by authors of color, they also compiled anthologies of Black literature and criticism.[142] Gayle was teaching in SEEK when he edited his foundational collections of Black literary criticism, *Black Expression* (1969) and *The Black Aesthetic* (1971), as were James Emanuel and Theodore L. Gross when they published the anthology *Dark Symphony* (1968), Larry Neal when he and Amiri Baraka edited *Black Fire* (1968), and June Jordan when she published *The Voice of the Children* and *Soulscript* (she also had plans for a third anthology of writing by City College students). While the SEEK program is remembered today as a landmark educational opportunity program and the birthplace of basic writing, it also gave rise to some of the era's most important anthologies of Black literature and criticism.

In 1969 Bambara, Christian, and Gayle celebrated their students' victorious protests and the resulting open admissions policy, but by the time of its official implementation in 1970, they were all teaching elsewhere. Molloy suggests that an increasing emphasis on grammar instruction and testing—and the obvious harm this did to SEEK students—may have pushed them out.[143] Yet before we venture away from SEEK's early classrooms, it's worth noting their impact not only on Bambara but on Gayle and Christian, too. As Molloy has observed, Gayle's arguments with senior white English literature faculty shaped his famous theory of "the Black aesthetic."[144] In 1967 and 1968, he published two essays criticizing how they distorted Black literature through the lens of white liberalism, racism, and prejudice. He built on these ideas to develop his vision of a "black aesthetic" liberated from what white critics define as good art.[145] For Christian, it was with her SEEK students, not her Columbia professors, that she began seriously studying Black literature. At Columbia, literature meant classic British texts published by white men prior to 1900. But in SEEK she and her students debated *Native Son* and *Invisible Man*, catalyzing her career as a Black literary critic. It was also in preparation for these courses that Christian first laid eyes on a novel by a Black woman, leading, ten years later, to the first monograph on Black women novelists (1980).[146] These classrooms also shaped Christian's lifelong interest in questions of access: both to formal educational institutions—evident in her later advocacy for affirmative action at the University of California, Berkeley—and to such value-laden categories as "literature" and "theory."[147] Their presence can also be detected in her stylistic commitment "to being both rigorous and readable."[148]

In 1969 Bambara accepted a position as an assistant professor at Livingston College: a new, experimental college, part of the larger public Rutgers University system, located in Piscataway, New Jersey. Livingston was the product of the same Black campus movement Bambara had supported at City College. In fact, the same year that City College students had occupied their campus, Rutgers students barricaded themselves in buildings and staged cafeteria protests to demand more Black students and faculty and a more racially just curriculum. Livingston was thus established to quell this unrest, increase college access for Black and Puerto Rican students, and focus on "urban problems," the era's thinly veiled euphemistic language for racism and poverty.[149]

Livingston was, in those early years, a version of the Black university Bambara had dreamed of. One of its first catalogs proudly announced that the college "would have no ivory towers" and would prioritize access over exclusivity.[150] The college offered courses in new subjects like Afro-

American studies and computer science, had few required courses (thus allowing students to design their own curriculum), and supported activist student organizations. It also provided opportunities for students to participate in college governance and exercise the kind of community control that Bambara encouraged in her classrooms. Former student Marian Murray describes a "multi-racial, multi-generational, multi-religious, and multi-ethnic campus," where conga drums pulsed like a heartbeat and the chants of student protests served as a soundtrack to their learning.[151]

At Livingston, Bambara taught writing, especially for first-year students, and a range of courses that became legendary among Black students: Red Man/Black Man in American Literature: Racist Archetypes; Literature of the Colonial Experience; and Cross-Cultural Studies of Language as a Political Institution.[152] In these courses, Holmes writes, she "created equitable faculty-student relationships... sought to awaken students to an awareness of their own culture... and to their own political power," and generously shared contacts from her address book to help them "find jobs and resources."[153] Reflecting on her time at Livingston, Bambara refers to it as "one of the most stunningly profound periods of my life," during which she was "thoroughly enmeshed with students and their academic and otherwise lives."[154]

During her years at Livingston, Bambara also helped to establish the kind of creative community she had been a part of in the SEEK program. She recruited some of New York's and New Jersey's most influential writers, artists, and activists, many of whom were associated with the Black Arts Movement: figures like A. B. Spellman, Nikki Giovanni, Hattie Gossett, Jan Carew, Sonia Sanchez, and her former SEEK colleague Aijaz Ahmad, who, like Bambara, had left part-time work at City College for full-time employment at Livingston. Similar to the work of editing an anthology, these faculty recruitment efforts reflect what Traylor calls Bambara's pedagogy of "gathering": bringing people together to "think deeply and act decisively."[155] "A true New Yorker," Bambara could not drive, so poet Nikki Giovanni "picked her up two days a week to take [them] to Rutgers in [Giovanni's] 1960 VW Bug."[156] Through the Holland Tunnel and down the Jersey Turnpike, the two writers chatted for hours about their students, their writing, and ways "to change the world."[157] "We drove together," Giovanni recalls lovingly, "to Rutgers and through our careers."[158]

At Livingston, Bambara continued teaching working-class students of color from what she called "nonwriting backgrounds."[159] To interest them in writing, she developed assignments that honored their experiential knowledge and challenged them to write for audiences beyond their professor. One such assignment asked them to reflect on their experiences as Black students and extract a useful lesson to convey to a younger reader:

> Remember how you used to get all hot in the face, slide down in your seat, suddenly have to tie your shoe even though you were wearing loafers back then in fourth grade whenever Africa... or slavery was mentioned? Remember the first time the mention of Africa, of Black, made your neck long and your spine straight, made the muscles of your face go just so? Well, make a list of all the crucial, relevant things that happened to you that moved you from hot face to tall spine: then compose a short story, script, letter, essay, poem that makes that experience of change available to the young brothers and sisters on your block.[160]

As usual, Bambara did not dictate the forms their writing projects had to take. Instead, she offered suggestions such as "a short story, script, letter, essay, [or] poem."[161] While some students chose to write "position papers for organizations in their community," others "were working at the storytelling library hour, so they wrote stories."[162] Many of these were Black rewritings of classics, like "Little Black Riding Hood" and "The Three Little Panthers." Knowing that their words could make a difference in people's lives, students worked long hours revising and editing. The assignment resulted in midnight phone calls, "notes... outlines... rough drafts... cut-downs... editing... the search for form and metaphor."[163] Much to Bambara's delight, the students were teaching "themselves and each other in that process of sifting and sorting, dumping, streamlining, tracing their own process of becoming."[164]

Among their projects, the children's stories stood out as important alternatives to the uninspiring, genteel books that lined the shelves of mainstream bookstores. As a new mother, Bambara was all too aware of the ways children's stories reflected the values of a white supremacist society and offered few life lessons for Black children. She and her students traveled to local elementary schools, community centers, and children's hospitals to share their stories. After witnessing young people's enthusiastic reactions to her students' words (and with the success of *The Black Woman* in mind), she decided to compile them into an anthology that could reach even broader audiences. In 1971 Gayle helped her secure a contract with Doubleday for her second collection of student writing.

Similar to *The Black Woman*, *Tales and Stories for Black Folks* included student writing alongside the work of more "seasoned writers" and "well-honed analysts" like Langston Hughes and Alice Walker.[165] But unlike the multimodal assemblage of her first anthology, *Tales and Stories* is composed entirely of fables that use animals to explore human relationships and power dynamics. A collection of "kitchen table wisdom" that honored Black traditions of sharing insights through stories, the anthology aimed to equip young readers with relevant life lessons. And these pedagogical objectives were explicit: the introduction notes that the stories were designed to "instruct" and "teach" while also entertaining. Holmes writes that they helped "children develop tools... to evaluate what is often presented to them without criticism... [and] heighten children's awareness of the misguided beliefs and inequitable relationships... presented in mainstream literature."[166] For instance, "The Three Little Panthers," coauthored by Bambara and her student Geneva Powell, uses the story of an assignment to teach children to recognize the racism that may lurk behind a facade of benevolent integration. In their story, a cunning teacher sends three little panthers to live in the suburbs, where they are greeted with a specious welcome. Their story begins: "Once upon a time, there were Three Little Panthers. They attended Freedom School, not to learn how to make their fortune, but to learn how to survive."[167] Just as the Freedom Schools of the 1960s taught Black students the knowledge and skills that would help them "survive," so too did *Tales and Stories*.

While the book wasn't in print for very long, it was praised by critics as "a commanding and never ambiguous assemblage," with pedagogical potential to "[provoke] introspective reading and [encourage] creative writing."[168] And what Bambara valued most about the anthology was "that my students are in it."[169] Indeed, were it not for her students at City College and Rutgers-Livingston, we would not have such important collections today.

The Black Woman and *Tales and Stories* suggest that Bambara's teaching was not only multimodal but also anthological, a term, borrowed from Alexandra T. Vazquez, to describe how Bambara taught students to compose and think with others and collect and share that work.[170] If hierarchical models of the student-teacher relationship are "colonial" in nature, Bambara's work invites us to imagine teaching, instead, as editing an anthology: creating the conditions for students to collectively make something worth sharing beyond the classroom. In contrast to liberal philosophies of education that emphasize students as individual learners, this approach is grounded in collectivity: what students are capable of learning and making together in concert.

To Light New Fires

In 1974 Bambara did what for many was unthinkable. The professor who had given students permission to "walk out" of the classroom relinquished a coveted tenure-track job at Livingston to focus on her writing. To be fair, she never had both feet firmly planted in academia. Throughout her career, she maintained a critical ambivalence toward universities. While they, at times, created space for transformative learning, obstacles such as inadequate facilities, large classes, excessive workloads, racist and sexist policies, messy departmental politics, academic egos, frustrating bureaucracies, and the encroachment of standardized assessments often impeded learning and left little time for Bambara's own creative projects. "I like doing a lot of things," she writes, but "teaching is a jealous god... [who] takes everything."[171] That year she relocated to Atlanta, where her formal teaching became more sporadic. Throughout the late 1970s, she taught only the occasional course, including Introduction to Third World Literature (1974), at Duke University, and Images of Black Women in Literature and Film (1977), at Spelman College. With this lighter course load and reduced required service, she was able to continue developing the labor-intensive but "most worthwhile" community-controlled and multimodal pedagogies she had first explored in SEEK.

In Introduction to Third World Literature, at Duke University, students continued to take an active role in shaping the course's methods, objectives, and modes of evaluation. The syllabus announced that students would teach a portion of the course: "brief lecture[s]" would be delivered "by the instructor or students... the student can elect to report on one of the group reading assignments or provide background to class on the body of criticism in existence on a particular author or book."[172] The course also emphasized research: one assignment sent students to the library to create a bibliography on a topic of their choosing. Some options included "Anthologies of U.S. Black literature," "Anthologies of Caribbean Literature," "Books by and/or about a major Black, Puerto Rican, Chicano, etc. author," and "Periodicals carrying fiction and non-fiction." Once they had immersed themselves in the existing scholarship on their topic, students were instructed to "compose five questions worth raising about the field of literature," a literal example of what Freire called "problem-posing" education. Confronted with the ongoing legacies of colonialism, Bambara challenged students to articulate the value of literature in relation to these broader struggles.

In 1987, after nearly a decade away from formal classrooms, Bambara taught a course called The Text as a Rite of Recovery during her brief tenure as a visiting professor of English at the University of Delaware. The recent transplant to Philadelphia was anything but rusty. In fact, her passionate course descriptions and ambitious assignments suggest that she was sharper for her time away, able to approach teaching with renewed creative energy. The course (listed in the catalog as The Contemporary American Novel) focused on Maxine Hong Kingston's *The Woman Warrior* (1976), Leslie Marmon Silko's *Ceremony* (1977), and Bambara's own *The Salt Eaters* (1980). As was often the case, her syllabus identified what she called the "course's thesis," the primary idea about literature that they would test out that semester (and that students were welcome to disagree with or complicate). In this case, the thesis was that contemporary fiction by Black, Native American, and Asian American authors can be read as "diagnostic probes into the question of what constitutes health—for an individual, a downpressed community, a country not yet a nation."[173] Though the description foregrounds health, the course also thematized questions of learning, education, and access to information, reflecting her holistic understanding of the connections between the two.

That semester, they treated the novels as sources of "alternative education": as means by which communities critique dominant ideologies and share wisdom beyond formal institutions and as antidotes to the "monocultural bias" in mainstream curriculum.[174] Though this was a literature course, it began by surveying students' knowledge of racial and ethnic minorities:

 i Fill in the blank: Ellis Island is to European immigration as _____ island is to Asian immigration.
 ii Can Puerto Ricans on island of Puerto Rico vote in U.S. presidential elections?
    . . .
 v Name ethnic groups who make up the population of your home state. Did you include Anglos? If no, why not, so what?
 vi Name three famous American Indians.[175]

Rather than lecturing on the gaps in academic curricula, this activity asked students to draw their own conclusions about the extent to which their education had or had not taught them about immigration, Native American history, US imperialism, colonialism, race, and ethnicity. For some students, especially at a predominantly white institution like the University of Delaware, it likely revealed just how much had been absent from their education. For others, like Asian American, Puerto Rican, and Native American students, it signaled that their knowledge, culture, histories, and perspectives would be valued in this classroom. Though the specifics of this assignment remain unclear, we can imagine, given her penchant for research assignments, Bambara asking students to answer such questions for homework, then discussing in class the different sources they used to locate this information. Or she may have given this survey both at the beginning and at the end of the semester to illustrate what they had learned. Either way, this assignment allowed her to establish one of the motives for the course. That semester, the books they read would help them cultivate what she called a "multicultural literacy": ways of seeing that are informed by the histories, perspectives, and experiences of racial and ethnic minorities.

The Text as a Rite of Recovery was structured around assignments that prepared students for an open-ended project, like those she had assigned in SEEK. Throughout the semester, they were instructed to consider how each novel "offer[s] new categories of perception // encourage[s] and equip[s] the reader to change or otherwise alter her/his perspective // challenge[s] us with a new analysis of the past, present, or future?"[176] They then used these new ways of seeing to write a "perception paper" analyzing an outside text (something not on the syllabus). Though students were free to interpret this task in different ways, Bambara did provide some options. Students might review a "film...commercial movie...or tv drama that includes figures related to course readings," or explore "your own ethnic history and stereotypes of your people in vaudeville, books, artifacts," which "might prove...enlightening in a stunning way."[177] And the assignment sequence did not end there. Students then met with Bambara for conferences and revised their perception paper into a "term project" such as "a bibliography, a slide show, a picture book, a series of broadsides, etc." The one requirement was that their creation "can be shared with others."[178] As we will see, this insistence that students use their learning to benefit others would continue to shape the pedagogies not just of Bambara, but of all four teacher-poets, long after they left City College.

Over the years, Bambara grew increasingly frustrated with the racism, sexism, and elitism in academia.[179] Often, the courses she wanted to teach on Third World literature and Black women writers were met with skepticism from faculty and administrators who failed to see them as legitimate academic subjects. And at a structural level, changes in higher-education policy were shutting out the working-class students and students of color she wanted to teach. Beginning in the 1970s, conservative politicians, business leaders, and legislators enacted a series of policy reforms that elevated free market capitalism and transferred the cost of collective goods and social services—housing, health care, and education—from taxpayers to individuals. In terms of higher education, these neoliberal reforms involved decreased state funding for public universities; the end of open admissions initiatives and the implementation of tuition; cuts to affirmative action, opportunity programs, and remedial education; and a shift from grants to loans, all of which had disproportionately negative effects on poor and minority students.[180] Bambara often referred to universities as a kind of addictive drug, whose seductive promise of an income belied a greater danger to her health. "Stay[ing] off campus" was tantamount to "trying to stop smoking" or kicking "a lotto habit."[181] At one point, she pledged to avoid campus life altogether.[182] As the pitfalls of universities came to outweigh the possibilities, Bambara shifted her focus to local arts organizations like the Neighborhood Arts Center in Atlanta and the Scribe Video Center in Philadelphia, where her teaching could more directly serve working-class communities of color.

This turn toward community teaching coincided with Bambara's increasing fascination with film. Ever since the open admissions era, when her colleagues had dismissed popular visual forms as base pleasure and mind-numbing entertainment, she understood the power film had over audiences—a power that could be either politically manipulative or consciousness-raising. Inspired by the Third Cinema movement of the 1960s and 1970s, which rejected the neocolonialism and capitalism of big-budget Hollywood cinema, Bambara's writings from the 1980s critique how such films colonize our senses and imaginations by selling homophobic, misogynistic, racist, and imperialist desires, using pleasure to seduce audiences into accepting these ideologies "as inevitable . . . norm."[183] By contrast, she believed that independent Black films like Julie Dash's *Daughters of the Dust* (1991) and those produced by the Black British Sankofa film collective could teach viewers to recognize the conventions of the culture industry through which we are sold such dangerous desires.

In the documentaries she coproduced, Bambara also explored how film could help marginalized communities seize control over cultural narratives and tell their own stories. For example, *The Bombing of Osage Avenue* (1986), coproduced with filmmaker Louis Massiah, utilized participatory storytelling to counter the media's pathologizing, racist depictions of the 1985 bombing of a local Black liberation organization known as MOVE. On May 13, 1985, the Philadelphia police firebombed the MOVE residence, killing eleven people and destroying sixty-one homes in Philadelphia's historically Black Cobbs Creek neighborhood. As Karen Beckman has shown, mainstream media representations of this event blamed the activists themselves and Cobbs Creek residents for this horrific act of state-sanctioned violence.[184] Outraged at these inaccurate, distorted narratives, Bambara and Massiah interviewed members of the Cobbs Creek community in order to tell a more accurate story from the perspectives of those most affected. *The Bombing of Osage Avenue* thus illustrates the dual aims that would characterize Bambara's film pedagogy: to challenge dominant narratives and contribute to the healing of abused communities.

Bambara found a welcome home for her evolving cinematic interests at Philadelphia's Scribe Video Center, a nonprofit organization founded in 1982 by Massiah to "advance the use of electronic media, including video and audio, as artistic media and as tools for progressive social change."[185] According to their website, the initial workshop had "no equipment, no staff... [and] wasn't much of anything except a group of people who had come together to learn about documentaries."[186] In fact, it was Bambara who "pushed Scribe to look at video as a cultural form that would thrive in neighborhood settings and as a creative tool to explore community issues."[187] She would spend nine years there teaching courses on screenwriting and spearheading the Community Visions grassroots videography project.[188]

In workshops like Video for Social Change, Bambara taught local activists from organizations like Women against Abuse, the Philadelphia Unemployment Project, and the Black Women's Health Project to create documentaries. Twenty-five years after she had challenged her SEEK students to design their own course, she now asked these community organizers to decide "what... you want to do, and why, and in whose name, and so what?"[189] Of course, she made suggestions. They could "explore a community concern, demonstrate an innovative approach to social change, portray aspects of community life from a new point of view... reconstruct gender ID, recode representations, un-mask retrograde ideologies... demystify, decolonize, clarify (unmask) power configuration, promote the overthrow of internalized oppression."[190] Whatever they chose, the goal was to leave the "spectator... thinking or feeling differently." Describing her approach to these workshops, Holmes writes that Bambara "challenged students to use the video lens as a tool for transforming institutions rather than merely documenting them."[191] As in her college courses, these workshops were not entirely outward facing; there was also introspective work to be done. In addition to changing the hearts and minds of audiences, they aimed to nourish the spiritual growth of the activists involved in the filmmaking process.[192]

These film workshops were grounded in praxis: the testing of concepts through creative making, and, reciprocally, the generation of new insights from that process. As participants made their documentaries, they debated questions of aesthetics, representation, and "the politics of imaging"—how jump cuts or the mise-en-scène impacted a viewer. These conversations then informed their artistic choices. And the difficulties they encountered in using "the master's tools" led to discussions of power: how "the very conventions—the very tools, practices... were not designed to accommodate" their "stor[ies]... people... cultural heritage... [or] issues."[193]

As they created their documentaries, participants learned storyboarding, lighting, interviewing, camerawork, film and sound editing, and budgeting. These were concrete, transferable skills that they could use in their professional, creative, or activist work long after the workshop concluded. While neoliberal education paradigms often equate skills training with the production of more efficient capitalist subjects, Bambara's workshops remind us that such training is not inherently tethered to capitalist notions of productivity. Rather, learning a skill like video production can also be part of Black, Marxist, feminist pedagogies that aim to seize control of the means of storytelling and representation.

The resulting films address issues like affordable housing, unemployment, community-run schools, women's health, and sexual assault. "Women Housing Women" (1991), for instance, shares how activists in the Women's Community Revitalization Project successfully developed affordable housing for low-income and formerly unhoused women.[194] Others, like "Peace at Home: Getting a Restraining Order in P.A." (1991), are "educational, self-help video[s]."[195] Several, like "Montessori Genesis II: A Family Thing" (1991) and "To School or Not to School" (1993), focus on efforts to provide inspiring education to every student, not just those with racial and economic privilege. Since its inception in 1990, Community Visions has helped more than 150 activist organizations produce videos.[196] As the products of Bambara's program, these videos illustrate how the open admissions era continued to impact cultural production, including in unexpected places like the Scribe Center.

Bambara was, for the most part, able to kick the habit of academia. However, in 1988 she received an offer too good to refuse. That spring, Rudolph P. Byrd, a professor of African American literature, invited her to serve as a writer in residence and teach two courses at Carleton College, a small liberal arts college in Minnesota. By now, Bambara well knew the pitfalls of such majority-white institutions: the pervasive tokenism, inordinate demands on Black faculty, superficial celebrations of multiculturalism, and daily micro- and macroaggressions of campus life. She agreed to come only on the condition that she would not have to attend department meetings or assign the "blue book" exams she despised.[197] While other Black women of her generation like Nellie Y. McKay and Barbara Christian spent much of their careers creating institutional space for Black women's studies, Bambara, not unlike her protagonist Velma, recognized that teaching was her art form and that the classroom, not the department meeting, was where her battles were worth fighting.[198] There, she could advocate for social change without becoming too drained and depleted.

The final project in Bambara's Carleton course, Contemporary Black Women Writers, was both multimodal and anthological. It asked students to "revisit the major themes of the readings" by creating something that could be shared with a public audience: "painting, collage, music, recitation, and enactments."[199] Instead of an exam, they participated in an event. Reflecting on the unorthodox invitation he received to join Bambara and her students for their final, Byrd recalls, "As I entered the lobby of the performing arts center I was greeted by a blues, much loud but cheerful talk, and a throng of students."[200] The atrium had been transformed into a gallery displaying students' projects. Each student had selected a form that would best tell the story of what they had learned that semester, and Bambara, too, found a form that would fit. With this event, students shared what they learned with the college community in a kind of living anthological performance. Byrd recalls the "impressive ... creativity and beauty of the students' work," taking special note of a collage inspired by Toni Morrison's *Sula*.[201] Allowing students to speak first, it was only toward the end of the two-hour symposium that Bambara "delivered an abbreviated lecture" that connected the projects on display to "the core objectives of her course."[202] So inspired by the event, Byrd decided to apply this method in his own teaching.[203]

Unsurprisingly, Carleton students "love[d] her course." A group of Black women reported that they had "never felt so affirmed by a professor." Indeed, Bambara touched the lives of hundreds of students in classrooms both formal and informal. As former Livingston College student Linda Janet Holmes recalls, Bambara taught students to advocate for change while remaining grounded in their communities and taking care of themselves.[204] She also carved out spaces for them to "recreate ourselves and imagine," a gift they greatly appreciated.[205] Holmes used these "lessons in boldness" to become a writer and community health advocate. Another student, Marian Murray, dedicated a book to Bambara.[206] Additionally, Bambara's challenge to poet Nikkey Finney, to "do more than pearl and decorate the page," led Finney to lyrical explorations of poverty, sexuality, and the environment; a career as a poetry professor; and prestigious literary prizes, including the National Book Award. In the final weeks of her too-brief life, Bambara continued writing to Finney, requesting that she "send some paper and one of those fat juicy pens." "I would hunt down a tree for you," Finney responded, in a poem celebrating Bambara's life and the lengths to which she would go for her beloved mentor, teacher, and friend.[207]

Bambara's teaching archive contains a small, torn piece of paper with a short poem by Salvadoran writer Miguel Huezo Mixco:

> Because to write is not to run away
> nor to turn off the lights
> It is to love to pardon to redeem and condemn
> to search everywhere
> to break my heart against yours
> and when broken not to tranquilly await the future
> but to go out and light new fires[208]

As an instructor, Bambara challenged the hegemony of the written word and encouraged experiments with different media and art forms. She taught students to use whatever they had at their disposal—words, images, colors, light, sounds, and movements—"to love to pardon to redeem and condemn." Over the course of her thirty years as an educator, she helped countless individuals, from the SEEK program to the Scribe Center, find the right form for the story they wanted to tell. The only requirement was to go out and light new fires.

"This Class... Has Much to Teach America"

June Jordan's Public & Project-Based Pedagogy

2

JUNE JORDAN spent the tumultuous 1960s participating in sit-ins and freedom rides, reporting on the civil rights movement for the *New York Times* and the *Herald Tribune*, interviewing prominent Black activists like Malcolm X and members of the Congress of Racial Equality (CORE), and organizing against poverty with the Harlem-based community group Mobilization for Youth. Yet despite this extensive activism, in September 1967, she found herself feeling "powerless." She "had no job, nothing to do that I wanted."[1] She craved "real work: something unrelated to farce, and something poised against tragedy," a way to earn a living that would also be useful to broader political struggles.[2] That fall, Herbert R. Kohl asked her to take over his "Freshman comp" class at City College. "What's that?" she asked. A few days later, Jordan was hired. Upon arriving that first morning, she met "25 white, middle-class Americans. And they met me," initiating a semester-long exploration of "differing anger devolved from similar dreaming."[3] Soon thereafter, "teaching no longer seemed to me like an accident, a stunt, or primarily a distraction from my real work as a poet."[4] It helped her overcome her sense of powerlessness. And in the years to come, over the course of three decades as a professor, she would teach hundreds of students to do the same.

Jordan was a prolific author best known for her poetry and essays on racism, sexism, and imperialism. Her work addressed issues like the race riots of the 1960s, police brutality against African Americans, widespread poverty in New York City's immigrant communities, rape culture, racial profiling, apartheid, and US imperialism in Puerto Rico, Nicaragua, Guatemala, Lebanon, and Palestine. Through writing, Jordan implicated herself in violence against the vulnerable, challenging the ease with which we read about injustice without questioning our complicity, or asking what we owe to those we have harmed. Indeed, flipping through the pages of her collected poetry reveals a near-encyclopedic counterhistory of the United States, told from the perspectives of its victims rather than its victors.

While Jordan is most famous for her writing, she was also a creative teacher and educational activist. This chapter explores how, beginning at City College and for many years to come, Jordan developed teaching methods that emphasized the structural nature of inequality, while also helping students explore their own capacities for acting and intervening in such conditions. As we will see, what began, at City College, with assignments like "the problem paper" and early experiments with publishing student writing would eventually develop into a public and project-based pedagogy that taught students to use what they learned to advocate for social change. In addition, this chapter considers the products of that pedagogy, including nearly a dozen anthologies of student writing that she and Toni Cade Bambara edited throughout their careers. These anthologies remind us that classrooms have been sites where American literature is not only read but also written.

A Tale of Two Educations

In the late 1960s, as Jordan was raising her son in a public housing project in Queens, she became deeply invested in the critiques of educational racism emerging from the era's Black liberation movements. Though *Brown v. Board of Education* (1954) promised an end to America's long-standing legacy of "separate but equal" schools for Black and white students, educational resources remained unequally allocated along racialized lines.[5] Figures like Martin Luther King Jr. and Malcolm X argued that this refusal to invest in Black education maintained a white supremacist society. Scholars such as Kenneth Clark and Preston Wilcox described how the American school system committed "educational genocide" to keep minority children "undereducated" and "subservient."[6] As a former student of both New York City's public schools and an elite private boarding school, Jordan had firsthand knowledge of these conditions.

The daughter of Jamaican immigrants, Jordan was a scrawny but feisty young girl (with a pet raccoon) who grew up in Brooklyn's historically Black Bedford-Stuyvesant neighborhood. School, for her, was always about power. At her local public school, PS 26, she felt that teachers wielded an irrelevant curriculum against her and her peers, in an effort to discipline them into quiet and passive obedience:

> When I was going to school, too much of the time I found myself an alien body force-fed stories and facts about people entirely unrelated to me, or my family. And the regular demands upon me only required my acquiescence to a program of instruction pre-determined without regard for my particular history, or future. I was made to learn about "the powerful": Those who won wars or who conquered territory or whose odd ideas about poetry and love prevailed inside some distant country where neither my parents nor myself would find welcome.[7]

While school bored her to tears and there was the occasional fistfight with bullies, in the books she read at home, language came to life. Jordan was raised in a household shaped by West Indian beliefs in the importance of education.[8] Her father, Granville Ivanhoe, saw education as crucial for surviving their new city and country, and the largely self-taught Ivanhoe passed his reverence for art and literature on to his daughter. William Shakespeare, Edgar Allan Poe, and Paul Laurence Dunbar taught Jordan more about the beauty of language than any of her classes.[9] From this extracurricular education under her father's tutelage, she knew that literature could be thrilling, despite the "boring, inaccessible, irrelevant" books assigned in school.[10] She was later accepted to Northfield School for Girls, an elite preparatory institution in Massachusetts. While Northfield was largely "hostile to Jordan's racial and cultural identities," it further cultivated her love of words.[11]

After graduating from Northfield, Jordan dipped in and out of different colleges, including a few years at the University of Chicago and Barnard, where she was "completely immersed in a white universe."[12] As a student, she wanted knowledge that would help her better understand "the political and economic realities underlying our Black condition in white America" and address social problems like poverty and hunger.[13] But she was largely disappointed by the soporific "nonexperiment" pedagogies she encountered: classes in which the answer was known ahead of time and students were graded, for instance, on whether they correctly counted the number of white, red, and purple corn kernels on a given cob. There were, however, some important exceptions, including two assignments in a freshman English course at Barnard taught by writer and jazz critic Barry Ulanov. In one, Ulanov taught students the art of brevity by instructing them to write an essay "about anything you want, without using any forms of the verbs *to be* and *to have*."[14] This assignment invited them to experience how heavily we rely on these verb forms, when specific, active verbs can better bring writing to life—an assignment that clearly impacted Jordan's pithy poetry. The other assignment was an essay, daunting in its vagueness, to "somehow" connect British philosopher Alfred North Whitehead's *Aims of Education* and Edith Hamilton's classic collection *Mythology*. While Jordan's peers agonized over the task, she was excited by the creative challenge of synthesizing the disparate texts. Through the assignment, she began to connect classic works of philosophy and literature and her everyday experiences.

Having attended both elite, exclusive, and predominantly white institutions and underfunded schools in Black neighborhoods, Jordan was incensed by the ways our society withholds transformative learning opportunities from working-class students of color. In 1967 she published "You Can't See the Trees for the School," an interview with four students at an underresourced high school in Brooklyn about their "expectations, experience and ... [the] impact or irrelevancy of their education."[15] In this article, published a year before Paulo Freire's *Pedagogy of the Oppressed*, Jordan writes that schools turn students into "receptors" and perpetuate the myth that "students have nothing to offer (teach)."[16] Anticipating Freire's call for problem-posing methods, although from a different geopolitical context, Jordan writes, "Given conditions of black American life today, and yesterday, teaching should follow the form of a question, seriously raised."[17] That article would soon result in an opportunity to put her ideas into practice and ask students serious questions at City College.

How to Begin Is Also Where

In the fall of 1967, Jordan was hired as a part-time lecturer at City College, a temporary position that required teaching three composition courses per year. Her initial salary of $330 per month was promptly increased to $444, or, in 2023 dollars, roughly $8,000 per course.[18] Though excited to meet the students, she was also skeptical of universities: institutions that had long excluded people of color, disseminated the values of a racist society, and replicated existing power structures. "What is the university ... ?" she wrote in one essay. "It is where the powerful become more powerful."[19]

Toni Cade Bambara, who had been teaching at City College for the past two years, escorted Jordan to her first day of Freshman Composition, advising her new and nervous colleague to give students whatever she could and promising her they'd appreciate it. Though Jordan didn't have formal pedagogical training, she brought a wealth of knowledge and skills gleaned from her work as a poet and journalist. She could teach students to use language with precision, seek out missing perspectives, tell untold stories, reframe the era's political debates, and hold readers in rapt attention. Describing herself as "very young and very scared," Jordan later stated that she could not have done it without Bambara, who "psyched me and prepared me."[20]

On the first day of English 1K2, Jordan shared her view of writing with the twenty-five students seated in front of her. "Writing," she told them, "is the conquest of language ... [and] the control of tyranny."[21] That semester, they would practice writing as a means of "truth-telling" and precise communication—a way to pierce through the lies we are sold by media and textbooks. Their method would be to "work hard with ideas and toward ideas: We would write sentences (ideas) in two or three papers a week."[22]

It was clear to Jordan—a writer documenting the on-the-ground struggles of local communities—that the question of "how" their class should begin was also "where." Recalling how alienating her own education had been, she asked students not to write about "those who won wars or who conquered territory" but about where they were and what they knew, especially their classrooms, schools, and neighborhoods. The first book she assigned was from Professor Ulanov's course at Barnard: Whitehead's *Aims of Education*, which argues that education should teach students not rote memorization of facts but "the art of the utilization of knowledge."[23] Students were then asked to write an evaluation of their own education, either by using Whitehead's criteria or by developing their own (a version of the creative mimicry assignment we saw in Bambara's classroom). In response, one student reflected on the shortcomings of his education: "I was given no concept of life, much less an appreciation of it, with which I could go out into the world on my own and become somebody important and useful to the community."[24] Through such assignments Jordan taught students to see schools as something they have an active stake in and are capable of improving.

As a professor, Jordan honored students' unique writing styles and guided them in pursuing their own art. While some students wrote essays like "Hell Is Other People and Other Thoughts in the Singular ... ," steeped in literary language and philosophical reflections grounded in concrete observations, others explored "Should the American Sterilization Laws Be Abolished?"

with footnotes to sociological and economic studies at the end of nearly every sentence. "Good, trenchant, clear & thorough," Jordan wrote in the margins of one essay. On another she commented, "I admire your determination to master your own inclinations of style." And because they were allowed to choose their own topics and develop idiosyncratic writing styles, the students spent hours researching, drafting, and revising their writing. Together they "worked hard" and "worked well," as their words became "more and more their own words."[25]

Before long, Jordan realized just how much young writers are capable of, should adults stop underestimating them. In fact, she came to believe that "the thoughts and the thoughtfulness of seventeen-year-olds are worth thinking about," even beyond their classroom.[26] That semester, in the first course she ever taught, Jordan decided that students would publish their final essays in an anthology titled "Tomorrow in English."[27] She compiled nine papers and drafted a two-page proposal, a four-page introduction, and a table of contents. The collection, however, was never published. Instead, it sits in Jordan's archives at the Schlesinger Library, raising just as many questions as it does answers about her teaching. Though the class had twenty-five students, "Tomorrow in English" includes only nine essays, written by seven students. What happened to the others? Why, despite so much editorial labor, was the collection never published? While the fate of "Tomorrow in English" remains unclear, its aims were unequivocal:

> To celebrate some Americans
> To compile an enjoyable, astonishing anthology of good and even extraordinary writing
> To challenge the orthodox of English instruction... [and] document the black-of white learning process that never ends, but seldom enters public knowledge.[28]

"Tomorrow in English" is, like Bambara's *The Black Woman* and *Tales and Stories for Black Folks*, an anthology of student writing, one of the genres of open admissions. Similar to its published counterparts, this dormant anthology indexes Jordan's understanding that her students were writing things worth reading beyond the classroom. The introduction reverses conventional educational relationships (in which students learn about society) by depicting her students as teachers and the nation as their pupils, stating, "This class, in English, has much to teach America."[29] Soon, publishing her students' writing would become far more than an aspiration: it would become a hallmark of Jordan's pedagogy.

In addition to teaching traditional City College students, who "were mainly young, white men interested in engineering or medicine," Jordan taught older Black and Puerto Rican students in the SEEK program.[30] She notes that these students were "most articulate and genuinely wise" but had been abused by the schools of a racist society: "forced to spend themselves in compulsory attention to people convinced that children are ignorant, and that Black children are stupid... they have been taught to believe they will fail."[31] Her goal, as their instructor, was to counter "the butchery performed by city high schools" and instead support their self-determination. In her words, this meant helping them develop their "own naming of the world."[32]

In 1969 Jordan adapted an assignment she borrowed from Mina Shaughnessy (who was, by then, directing the writing program), known as the "problem paper." For this assignment, students read *The Will to Survive: A Study of a Mississippi Plantation Community, Based on the Words of Its Citizens*, a report by civil rights activist and community organizer Anthony Dunbar, who spent seven weeks interviewing poor Black families in the Mississippi Delta to figure out how hundreds of thousands of people still go hungry in one of the world's wealthiest nations. Following Dunbar's example, students then wrote a paper analyzing a social issue in their local neighborhoods. The resulting essays bear titles like "Inferior Education in the Williamsburg Community," "Drug Addiction in the South Bronx," and "Inadequacy of Acceptable Food and Inadequate Systems of Food Supply in Harlem."[33]

Through this assignment, students learned to formulate questions "seriously raised," locate reputable information, evaluate possible solutions, and organize their findings into a report. In addition to strengthening their reading, writing, and research skills, the problem paper also helped students cultivate a structural imaginary: a way of seeing social problems like racialized poverty as the product of long, ongoing histories and policy decisions made manifest in physical spaces, structures, and environments. This structural imaginary was present throughout Jordan's writing from this era. To take just one example, in the wake of the Harlem Riots of 1964, she embarked on an urban redesign project with architect and planner R. Buckminster Fuller titled "Skyrise for Harlem": "a proposal to rescue a quarter million lives by completely transforming their environment... which may actually determine the pace, pattern and quality of living experience."[34] Whereas mainstream media pathologized Harlem as a crime-ridden and depraved slum, "Skyrise" blamed the state for neglecting this historically Black community. It proposed structural solutions to these long-standing histories of disinvestment: replacing the neighborhood's inadequate housing, dangerous roads, and underfunded schools with safe and clean streets, desirable apartments (complete with hanging gardens, skyline views, and ample outdoor space), and cultural centers that would allow residents to thrive—a veritable blueprint for reparations.

The problem paper similarly taught students to see issues like drug addiction, low test scores, and poor health not as individual problems but as the products of a society that invests more resources in certain communities than others.[35] With their essays, students brainstormed ways to address these conditions and bring about equitable access to health care, housing, food, and education. Through such assignments, Jordan began developing an activist pedagogy that guided students in advocating for more just institutions and policies.

In an enthusiastic letter to Shaughnessy, Jordan describes how much she, too, learned about persuasive political writing from the problem paper:

> Dunbar's model guided us into valuable, tactical conclusions concerning the presentation of a social problem we want to move people (who have money) into solving. Examples: If you delimit the community of your concern, the problem will seem correspondingly limited and, therefore, amenable to solution. If you literally present the people who suffer a particular, social problem, then the problem correspondingly seems real.[36]

As these remarks suggest, the assignment prompted Jordan and her students to think more deeply about audience: how an awareness of the reader who will be receiving any piece of writing can help us to write more effectively. And according to Scott MacPhail, this ability to carefully tailor arguments for different audiences would become a defining feature of Jordan's writing, as she shifted the contours of her claims for the primarily women readers of *Ms.* or the progressive audience of the *New Republic*.[37] In addition, in later essays like "Nicaragua: Why I Had to Go There," Jordan analyzed "particular social problem[s]" using the strategies she developed with students. Published in *Essence* in 1984, the essay presents readers with "the people who suffer," in this case the voices and stories of Nicaraguans struggling under the weight of US imperialism. While acknowledging the massive scale of the necessary changes—"an absolute reversal of northamerican habits ... the end of northamerican power imposed by force"—the article concludes with a section titled "What You Can Do about Nicaragua," a list of immediate, concrete actions that readers could take, including educational resources to consult, phone numbers and addresses of elected officials to contact, and a list of organizations to join and support.[38]

As is often the case with teaching archives, it's difficult to determine where, or with whom, the problem paper originated. Unlike the individualism often associated with pedagogical innovation, such archival assignments foreground the networks and collaborations that support transgressive teaching. Certainly, neither Jordan nor Shaughnessy was the first to ask students to analyze social problems. As Jarvis R. Givens has shown, throughout the Jim Crow era, Black schoolteachers asked students to analyze local issues like unequal housing "in order to help address these matters as future leaders."[39] In addition, James A. Berlin has demonstrated how the Great Depression led to a rise in college writing courses that addressed problems in local neighborhoods.[40] In the SEEK program, assignments like the problem paper were successful, in part, because they honored students' desires to improve their underresourced communities. Though she never took a course with Jordan, former SEEK student Francee Covington appreciated assignments that allowed her to write about the communities that were important to her. Decades later, she still remembered one of her essay's argument about toxic lead paint in Spanish Harlem: "Instead of putting a man on the moon can we put some men in these apartments to clean up all this mess so that kids don't suffer as a result."[41] "It couldn't just be ranting," Covington recalls; each point had to be supported with persuasive evidence and analysis.[42] And because students were writing not solely to fulfill a requirement and pass a course but to improve the quality of life for their families, friends, and neighbors, they actually enjoyed working on these assignments. As Jordan notes in a letter to Shaughnessy, "Most of my students immersed themselves in this project according to the most ambitious criteria; they were spontaneously striving for usefulness, accuracy, power, and the kind of authoritative tone that can only be earned by defensible research."[43]

As they worked on assignments like the problem paper, Jordan's skepticism toward universities began to wane. Such assignments highlighted how higher education could make a positive impact on individual students as well as their families and communities, to whom they could return "with newly formed questions, and newly devised answers."[44] Gradually, she began to sense what Roderick Ferguson refers to as the university's "fragile possibilities": that perhaps, at times, through initiatives that invested in working-class students, universities could create space to challenge the status quo, however temporarily and imperfectly.[45]

Jordan described these early years at City College as a "time of extreme excitement and revolution."[46] In the SEEK program, she met activist "poets and writers and thinkers" who became "much more than colleagues."[47] While English literature faculty saw SEEK courses as dull skills instruction, these writers saw an opportunity to interrogate with students the underlying conditions that had left them in need of remedial education. Allied against their elitist colleagues and in support of their students, SEEK educators, Jordan writes, "got to know... and also respect each other."[48]

While Jordan's significance as a feminist poet and critic today is undisputed, it was her City College colleagues who first introduced her to women's poetry. Intrigued by the petite, fire-eyed poet Adrienne Rich, Jordan first began to read her work "as a result of our shared commitment at City College."[49] And what began with Jordan reading the women poets who were her colleagues eventually led her to writers like Emily Dickinson, Alice Walker, and Sonia Sanchez. For Jordan, whose political consciousness had been forged through the civil rights and Black Power movements, these authors awakened her "to another dimension of love, and of struggle."[50] They helped her connect Black liberation to the ideas emerging from the women's movement, and she soon began writing for feminist publications like *Chrysalis* and *Ms*. This feminist awakening is also reflected in her teaching. Many of her early courses, including a class titled Literature and Social Change, included not a single woman author. But by the end of the 1970s, she was teaching courses like Contemporary Women's Poetry and Contemporary Global Issues for Women, thanks, in part, to her City College colleagues.

While Jordan, Rich, and Audre Lorde would go on to move through similar poetic circles, City College also introduced Jordan to Bambara, who primarily wrote fiction. After walking her new colleague to that first day of teaching, Bambara became Jordan's mentor. Without many records detailing their relationship, we can only speculate about what this might have entailed. Perhaps Bambara showed Jordan the ins and outs of City College, suggesting whom she might trust and whom to avoid. Maybe she demonstrated how to use the department's temperamental mimeograph machine. As two of the few Black women faculty in a predominantly white, male institution, this would not be surprising. We do know, for certain, that the bonds the two forged had an enduring impact on both writers, the nature of which is explored later in this chapter.

In the spring of 1969, as Jordan was teaching students to evaluate their educations and advocate for greater resources in their classrooms, schools, and neighborhoods, City College erupted in protests for more relevant education and more equitable admissions policies. The college was divided between faculty and students who wanted open admissions and those who saw it as an "atrocity" that "would catapult the University into a trough of mediocrity" and tarnish the college's prestigious reputation.[51] Reflecting on this moment, Jordan recalls that they were at the epicenter of "a revolution": "from faculty petitions to student manifestos, to the atmosphere in the cafeteria and the bathrooms . . . [n]obody was eating, sleeping, thinking, or moving around anything except the issues at stake."[52] She, Bambara, and Lorde demonstrated their support by moving their regularly scheduled classes to a local middle school, IS 201, which students had taken over and renamed Harlem University. As Ferguson writes, Jordan also criticized the racism that underwrote open admissions opponents' cries for "excellence" and "standards."[53] And though these battles were waged on the South Campus of City College, she saw that the stakes of their struggle extended far beyond Harlem. She writes, "It was quite amazing. . . . [W]e thought that if we could make democracy come to City College that probably we could have an impact on the concept and perhaps even the practice of public education through the country."[54]

Like Bambara, Jordan wrote a campus essay, "Black Studies: Bringing Back the Person" (1969), in support of students' demands. But while Bambara's essay had helped galvanize the historic protests, Jordan's was written in the afterglow of victory, in the months following the strike. It appeared not in the student newspaper but in *Evergreen Review*, a left-wing literary magazine with a national readership. There, it shared the news of their local triumph to motivate similar efforts on other campuses across the nation.

"Black Studies" illustrates another key characteristic of campus essays: the ways this literary genre ties issues of curricula—what is taught—to the admissions policies and tuition costs that determine who has access to higher education. Jordan's essay was, observes Conor Tomás Reed, the "first major published document on Black Studies by a Black woman educator at the time."[55] While the majority of the essay makes the case for Black studies as an antidote to dehumanizing white society, it concludes with a discussion of City College students' controversial fourth demand: "that City College's admission policy be changed to reflect the ethnic and racial composition of the city's high schools," which eventually led to open admissions. Jordan urges "students everywhere" to build on their example and suture their demands for curricular change to an insistence on more racially just "admission policies that will guide and accelerate necessary, radical change, at all levels of education."[56] This connection between educational content and material conditions of access also appeared in Bambara's reminder to her colleagues that the movement for mass education had long resulted in new academic subjects.

While the campus essay speaks directly to the educational politics of the open admissions era, predecessors to the genre can also be found in earlier essays like Anna Julia Cooper's "The Higher Education of Women" (1890), which, in Cooper's own, distinctly nineteenth-century way, ties questions of knowledge to women's access to education.[57] In our current moment, when universities are eager to publish antiracist statements, and academic departments are (to varying extents) willing to address questions of "diversity" and "inclusion" in terms of course content, these essays remind us that the struggle for curricular change needs to be tethered to changes in admissions policies, education funding, and the fight for free, high-quality public college for all.

In the fall of 1970, the first semester open admissions took effect, Jordan entered a classroom that was both more crowded and more diverse, with far more women, students of color, and ethnic-minority white students. That year, CUNY's incoming freshman class nearly doubled, from 20,000 students to 35,000. Inadequate funding for the initiative also led to predictable problems: long registration lines, increased class sizes, a scarcity of textbooks, and trailers, ice-skating rinks, hotels, and Jewish community centers haphazardly transformed into makeshift classrooms. While some professors saw this, in Geoffrey Wagner's words, as "the end of education," Jordan and her coconspirators viewed it as a tremendous opportunity to reinvent college and make it more useful to the "new students" now seated in their classrooms.[58]

In her open admissions courses, Jordan increased opportunities for student decision-making. Like Bambara, she believed that students should participate "fully and equally" in decisions both in the classroom and on campus; "otherwise, once again, the people most affected by a decision will have been excluded from the decision making process."[59] In her courses, "tactical decisions" were "not imposed upon them, but arrived at by vote."[60] Initially, many students were "dumbfounded" when she, the educator in charge, told them, "This is not my class, this is our class, I do not want to hear what I think, I need to know what you think."[61] From preschool through high school, they had been trained to see classrooms as the domain of ruling teachers: rewarded when they conformed to the instructor's rules and expectations and punished when they disobeyed. But the benefits of this collective, less hierarchical approach quickly became clear.

In Jordan's course on children's literature, the fact that students helped select the readings and discussion topics meant that they were eager to participate. While it's common, in many classes, for only a handful of outspoken individuals to contribute to the conversation, the astonished author of a classroom observation report notes that "the entire class was totally involved in the discussion for the entire hour."[62] To ensure a fruitful dialogue, Jordan asked "deceptively simple question(s)" about relationships between parents and children, violence, sexism, and didacticism that connected their analyses of *Winnie the Pooh, Alice in Wonderland,* and *Grimms' Fairy Tales* "to our actual existence in contemporary society."[63] The result was "an informed, serious, solidly intelligent discussion under the firmly gentle but skillful direction of the instructor."[64] Jordan would eventually formalize this expectation that students help design the course by incorporating it into her syllabi. As one later course description notes, "Political realities and individual concerns of class members will determine the emphasis of our progress."[65]

Jordan's advocacy for students' self-determination extended beyond her classrooms. In 1970 she delivered a graduation speech to middle school students in Brooklyn's Ocean Hill–Brownsville school district (made famous when parents wrenched decision-making power from the New York City Board of Education and implemented community control). In the speech Jordan celebrates the soon-to-be-high schoolers' accomplishments and encourages them to continually evaluate the relevance of their education:

> Let me urge you to examine every subject given to you for study, and every assignment demanded of you. Ask this question, again and again, and again:
> How does this study,
> how does this subject, relate to the
> truth of my life?[66]

If students found that their education was not adequately preparing them for the life they wanted to live, she advised them not to "turn off" but instead to "take it over: Don't drop out. Change it ... compel that school to serve your life.... For, what is the purpose of a school if it will not prepare you to live your own life of your own choosing in the community of your choice?"[67] Whereas Bambara had invited young people dissatisfied with their education to "walk out," Jordan challenged them to hold their schools accountable and demand the learning they desired.

✱ ✱ ✱

It's difficult to overstate the enduring impact the open admissions era had on Jordan's work. Prior to teaching at City College, she had understood universities as bastions of privilege, where the already powerful go "to become more powerful." However, SEEK and open admissions demonstrated how higher education can change people's lives and benefit disenfranchised communities. There, she witnessed hundreds of working-class students, including many students of color, shed internalized ideas about their unintelligence and use their voices to advocate for change. She watched them access the "power" one needs to "spring free from dependency upon those who exploit, isolate, and... destroy" and achieve the kind of "self-respecting self-sufficiency" enjoyed by many adults.[68] For the rest of her career, she would continue to advocate for "just and democratic access to first rate, higher education."[69]

In addition to inspiring Jordan's educational activism, these classrooms also influenced some of her most impactful writing. During the decade she spent at City College, her oeuvre expanded to include two poetry collections, two edited poetry anthologies, four works of children's literature, a biography of Fannie Lou Hamer, and essays in some of the nation's most prestigious newspapers. A significant portion of this writing responded to the era's debates over Black English, which divided their college campus as well as schools nationwide. In the late 1960s and 1970s, educators debated how to teach English to increasingly diverse students, many of whom had grown up speaking variations of English. The famous resolution "Students' Right to Their Own Language," (1974) written by the Conference on College Composition and Communication, succinctly captures the spirit of these debates: "Should the schools try to uphold language variety, or to modify it, or to eradicate it?"[70] At City College, some faculty viewed the linguistic diversity of these students as a deficit and obstacle to overcome. Theodore L. Gross, for example, wrote that the Black, Hispanic, and Asian American students who entered City College through open admissions brought "with them language and dialect problems that prevented them from understanding the most elementary texts."[71] According to Gross, "The greatest difficulty for blacks ... seemed to be to put an 's' on the third person singular."[72] Jordan, by contrast, saw Black English as vital.[73] She wrote poems and essays in and about Black English, challenging her colleagues' discriminatory beliefs and practices. In essays like "White English/Black English: The Politics of Translation," she argued that "white/standard" English should be taught as a second language, different from, though no less valuable than, Black English, each useful in different contexts. She also advocated for methods of writing instruction that honored the dialects students grew up speaking in their communities.

Among her many works from this period, Jordan's young adult novel *His Own Where* (1971) highlights the reciprocal relations between her teaching and writing. One of the most acclaimed children's books of 1971, *His Own Where* is written in breathtakingly lyrical Black English without "the 's' on the third person singular." The novel is remarkable not only for its dazzling prose, or as a clapback to colleagues who wanted to eradicate Black English, but also for its pedagogy: how it introduced young readers to the ways of seeing that Jordan was teaching students in her classrooms.

The novel follows the blossoming romance of two New York City teenagers, sixteen-year-old Buddy Rivers and fourteen-year-old Angela Figeroa, amid conditions that make love the unlikeliest of responses. Their relationship unfolds in a world of structural ironies.[74] The institutions that ostensibly exist to usher them into adulthood do more harm than good: Angela's family is abusive, Buddy's school is oppressive, and child services imprison Angela in a Catholic charity house. Though legally children, both are the primary sources of care in their families: Buddy raises himself while his father lies permanently comatose in the hospital; Angela raises her siblings while enduring the verbal and physical abuse of her tyrannical father.

Buddy, who speaks the language of young people's lives and whose very name invites readers to see him as a trusted companion, encourages them to adopt the kind of structural imaginary that Jordan was teaching to her students. He is a vivid dreamer, an agile carpenter, and a charismatic student organizer who sees people's lives as products of environments deliberately designed to facilitate the flourishing of the few at the expense of the many. While the doctors refer to the "accident" that landed his father in the hospital, Buddy understands this as a failure of urban planning to protect pedestrians: "The street set up . . . so cars can clip the people easy kill them even. Easy."[75] When the doctors finally identify Angela's injuries as "child abuse," Buddy asks readers to consider the structural conditions that contribute to these violences: "They call it child abuse. . . . But why Angela parents have to work so hard and long and why they have to live so crowded up they say nothing. Point no finger. Take no action. Still the consequences standing pretty terrible and clear."[76] Buddy thus repeatedly draws our attention to how material conditions, including low wages and poverty, as well as physical spaces like roads, sidewalks, and crowded apartments, impact people's emotions, sense of self, and relationships and the paths and possibilities available to them.

Similar to "Skyrise for Harlem," *His Own Where* insists that there are better ways of sharing social spaces. In one of the novel's most fantastic scenes, Buddy drifts off into a dream about the skyscrapers in Manhattan: those offices occupied during the day by white-collar workers but left vacant during the evenings, when the Brooklynites he knows are stuffed into "the crowded, cold, the peeling painted rickety and rusted the unlit shamble Brooklyn housing."[77] Buddy wonders what would happen if instead they shared the skyscrapers as a workspace by day and living room by night. He imagines the Hudson River swallowing the housing projects while "all the Brooklyn people reach the evening empty towers and fill them up with cribs and toys and parties on the intercom and blankets on the leather couch and turnip greens cook steaming in the cafeteria."[78] In this exhilarating example of structural imagination, Buddy shows young readers a way of thinking that starts with material conditions—actually existing structures and people's needs for shelter—and figures out a way of rearranging space to promote mutual flourishing.

But Buddy does not merely imagine alternatives; he also brings these visions to life. Depressed by the clutter and lack of "peoplespace" in Angela's home, Buddy renovates his brownstone into a whimsical, kaleidoscopic oasis full of pure "living room," where the two can enjoy each other's company.[79] He also convinces his neighbors to tear down the fences that separate their yards, creating a giant "openspace." And changing the space changes the neighborhood: now "people on the block say hello and talk awhile," and come together for barbecues.[80] It's worth noting that, at the time when CUNY opened its doors to the city, Jordan wrote a novel depicting how tearing down barriers allows for new modes of being together and more joyful encounters. As "peoplespace" and "openspace" illustrate, she invents new language to show young readers that these places are not simply there and given but are socially constructed, and therefore alterable. Rather than accepting the urban landscape he inherited as inevitable, Buddy insists that structures should shift to accommodate the desires of those they serve. In the novel's final scene, Buddy and Angela steal away to a cemetery sanctuary and build their own world. Thus, the novel concludes by celebrating the collaborative placemaking of two working-class Black adolescents, those who are least often consulted in decisions about resource distribution and the social construction of place.

His Own Where extended Jordan's lessons about a structural imaginary to young adult readers beyond the limited confines of her individual classrooms. She herself described the novel in explicitly pedagogical terms: as a "means of familiarizing kids with activist principles of urban redesign... [and] activist habits of response to environment."[81] As such, the novel highlights the aesthetic dimensions of open admissions: the ways this era's emphasis on educational access also shaped literature. Indeed, at the same time that creative writing MFA programs were giving rise to what Mark McGurl identifies as "self-involved" fiction obsessed with individualism, these authors were writing works of literature shaped by the open admissions ethos: the idea that transformative learning should be available to anyone who wants it.[82]

The Practice of Publishing Student Writing

During the same period in which Jordan was teaching at City College, she also cotaught a weekend writing workshop for Black and Puerto Rican youth. The workshop was part of the Teachers and Writers Collaborative (TWC): an organization that sent writers into public schools to collaborate with teachers in empowering students through writing. The TWC aimed to equip these young people with the skills possessed by writers: problem-solving, comfort in open-endedness, and creativity, among others.[83] In contrast to the reading comprehension quizzes and rote memorization of grammar rules that dominated classrooms in poor school districts, they advocated for eliminating grades on written work and nurturing children's creative use of language. And it was in these weekend workshops, cotaught with Brooklyn teacher Terri Bush, that Jordan began to experiment with publishing student writing.

On October 7, 1967, Jordan arrived at the Harlem Community Resource Center eager to meet the peculiar students—ranging in age from twelve to fourteen—who had elected to take an extracurricular Saturday writing class. After a few shy exchanges, the students began their first warm-up writing activity (a predictable prompt: introduce yourself to the class). As the children tentatively shared their writings with the group, Jordan swallowed deeply, fighting not to let the supportive smile stray from her face. Despite her awareness of educational inequity, she was still shocked to encounter students who spelled *him* with an *n* and could not distinguish a fragment from a sentence, producing "a sense of desperation" that threatened to derail the entire undertaking.[84] These young people, she writes, arrived with a "history of no education," battered by years of "shit treatment" and "despisal pedagogy" at the hands of underfunded schools.[85] The question then became, "How can you correct completely illiterate work without entering that hideous history they have had to survive as still another person who says: You can't do it. You don't know. You are unable. You are ignorant."[86] Determined not to be part of this stifling history, she and Bush explored other ways of being together and doing things with language with the goal of "enablement": "the encouragement of Black children to trust and then to express their own response to things."[87]

In their weekend workshops, no classroom convention was held sacred; nearly every aspect of the learning process was available for questioning. Jordan's teaching diaries depict the slow, careful, and deliberate process of asking the students about their relationships to school, to reading, and to writing. She and Bush also inquired about what they wanted from these workshops and from their lives, never assuming that they already knew the answers, and adjusted the workshop based on their responses. "How would you like this place to look?" they asked, inviting the participants to imagine a learning environment that they would actually enjoy.[88] Eventually, a pattern emerged. Jordan would share readings (her own poetry, poems by Victor Hernández Cruz, Langston Hughes, and Gwendolyn Brooks); they would review their writings from the previous week; Jordan would offer a writing prompt ("Write about 'white power' or 'black power'" or "What would you do if you were president?"), and together they would write, eating snacks and listening to music.[89] According to Richard Flynn, Jordan gave them "good poetic models in order to enable them to write 'real poetry,'" exemplifying her broader "refusal to underestimate children."[90] Over time, such practices of creative mimicry would become central to her pedagogy with college students as well.

This approach led to poems like "Hands," "No Way Out," and "The Last Riot," in which the young authors issue trenchant critiques of stereotypes, racist schools, and anti-Black violence, made all the more powerful when we consider that their average age was thirteen. Poems like Arlene Blackwell's "Sands Junior High School" criticized the unfairly "harsh" and disinterested teachers who "pin a reputation on you back ten times quicker than you earn it."[91] Similarly, Isabel Velez objected to the treatment of children as if they "are slaves to teachers."[92] Michael Goode's poem "April 4, 1968," elegizes Martin Luther King Jr. and urges readers to honor his legacy by continuing to ask, "What kind of world is this?"[93] Amid a stratified society that sought to silence these young people, poetry allowed them to express their opposition to unjust policies, beliefs, and practices and to imagine the world anew.

And yet, just beyond the walls of these thrilling classrooms brimming with young people's poetry, journalists were describing these same students as "silent creatures ... [who] didn't know the names of things, didn't know that things had names, didn't even know their own names."[94] The TWC instructors were outraged at the ways news media naturalized and even exacerbated conditions of educational apartheid. During this moment of heightened national attention to educational inequality, they began to experiment with publishing their students' writing. This was seen as a way to both address racist stereotypes of illiterate urban youth and give students an actual audience for their words. As one TWC instructor observed, "A student will only be concerned with his own use of language... [and] be able to improve its effectiveness... when he is talking to an audience, not just one that allows him to say what he wants as he wants, but one that takes him and his ideas seriously."[95] And what was true in the 1960s remains so today: students value writing that makes an impact on the world.

Jordan and Bush's first publishing experiments took the form of "folios." The two spent hours typing students' poems into collections that they could take home, "making something they have done seem more permanent and... valuable via a kind of simple-minded, physical change of appearance."[96] Jordan describes this potentially tedious labor as "effectively pedagogic."[97] By March 1968 the folios had transformed into a student-written and -edited newspaper, *The Voice of the Children*, and, soon thereafter, a published anthology.

Around the same time that Bambara was gathering her SEEK students' submissions for *The Black Woman*, Jordan and Bush published *The Voice of the Children*: a poetry anthology authored entirely by students in their workshop. The original cover photograph depicts a group of children, their bodies entangled and hands clenched tight into confident fists, radiating a sense of intimacy, pride, and power. They stand together, a visible incarnation of the collective strength in numbers facilitated by the anthology format. This collaborative spirit is underscored by Jordan and Bush's organization of the poems not by individual authors but into sections ("Politics," "Observations," "Blackness," "Love and Nature," "Very Personal") that highlight the conversations among them, especially, as Rachel Conrad observes, the "themes of racial politics and black identity."[98]

While anthologies are typically introduced by an editorial foreword, Jordan's view of the collection appears as an afterword, letting the children speak first and on their own terms. The first words we encounter belong to fourteen-year-old Vanessa Howard, whose foreword, titled "Ghetto," explores how stereotypes reduce the complexity of individuals:

> Nine out of ten times when a person hears the word "ghetto" they think of Black people first of all.... Ghetto has become a definition meaning Black, garbage, slum areas.... I think they put all Black people in a box marked "ghetto" which leaves them having no identity. They should let Black people be seen for themselves, not as one reflection on all.[99]

In Conrad's words, Howard's poem critiques "white supremacist hegemony... [and] claims for plural 'Black people' an authority over their own identities."[100]

For students who had been taught that their voices did not matter, publishing gave their weekend workshops "a sense of clearer purpose," a sense that their work with words could make a difference.[101] Once they knew that people would be reading their poems, they started asking questions "about punctuation, stanzas, paragraphs, and form."[102] Jordan writes, "They want to avoid adult errors of understanding; they want people to receive the message, and no mistake about it."[103] In a moment when educational debates focused on student illiteracy and error, through publishing, students learned both how narrow notions of correctness can maintain dominant power relations and also how they could use those very conventions to gain adults' attention. In short, they learned to write for different audiences.

That same year, Jordan included her students' writing in another edited collection: *Soulscript* (1970). Unlike *The Voice of the Children*, which was written entirely by students, *Soulscript* included their poems alongside the work of literary luminaries such as Paul Laurence Dunbar, Langston Hughes, and Jean Toomer. As noted in Jordan's introduction, *Soulscript* was intended as a corrective to the classroom's "typical textbook," with its omissions and distorted visions of Black Americans. The original cover prominently announces that the collection was "edited by June Jordan," using her hard-earned name recognition to attract readers. While the cover does not indicate that a significant number of the poems contained therein were authored by students, archival records reveal that circulating their poetry was a crucial motivating force in its publication. In a letter to her editor, Milton Meltzer (an acclaimed author of history books for children), Jordan wrote that inclusion in the anthology would "testify to the ordinary, earnest talent of all youngsters."[104] When Meltzer wanted to cut several of their poems, she fought back, insisting that eleven student-poets "are necessary to support my contention that children flow among the wellsprings of poetry as much as any adult."[105]

Soulscript was an instant success. It was lauded as "an exemplary, tasteful anthology" and "an enjoyable volume of thought-provoking reading."[106] Reviewers praised these poems as "the best, represent[ing] a striking convergence of the vocabulary of individual recognitions and historical immediacy."[107] Today it is understood as a foundational anthology of African American poetry. Yet scholars rarely consider that it includes student writing. This erasure of the collection's classroom context shortchanges the role that education has played in literary history and silences the student voices Jordan fought to include. It also limits our imagination of what might emerge from our own classrooms and teaching.

Both anthologies sold well, primarily to libraries and schools, allowing students' words to travel to classrooms as far away as Houston and Albuquerque. Their poems were published in the *Village Voice* and the *New York Times*, and they were invited to read their work on local television and radio stations and at universities. Of course, not everyone thought their poetry was worth reading. One review in the *Courier Post* claimed, "The editors are the heroes of this anthology of ghetto kids' poems and paragraphs," which the reviewer deemed unworthy of being "listened to" (and clearly he didn't listen to Vanessa Howard's "Ghetto").[108] But the students themselves proved this curmudgeonly critic to be in the minority. Howard, for example, went on to publish her own collection of poems and mentor younger writers.[109] While Jordan initially believed that audiences would be interested in her students' writing, the popularity of these anthologies confirmed it: their poems were filling important gaps in mainstream literature and curricula.

In the late 1960s, the publication of young people's writing increased exponentially, due in no small part to the TWC. Workshop instructors published participants' work in a wide range of genres: from memoirs like Herbert R. Kohl's *36 Children* (1967) and *Teaching the "Unteachable"* (1967) to anthologies like Kenneth Koch's *Wishes, Lies, and Dreams* (1970) and Steven Joseph's *The Me Nobody Knows* (1969), which was made into an award-winning rock musical. However, some of these texts, like Kohl's and Koch's, convey an implicit savior narrative and aesthetic. For example, while *36 Children* incorporates student writing, the children become characters who helped Kohl, the white male teacher and narrator, on his journey to overcome "an impossible teaching situation" and his fear of the "thirty-six black faces before me."[110] By contrast, the very few words we hear from Jordan in *Soulscript* and *The Voice of the Children* position her students as authors and help readers appreciate their literary achievements.

What sets Jordan's anthologies apart from these other collections is their definitively student-centered ethos. This was facilitated by Jordan's decision to publish their writing in a "textbook" intended for classroom use. In doing so, she created the conditions for TWC participants to speak to other young people across the partitioning walls of classrooms and schools. The textbook format allowed them to write to and for other students, those who might be trapped in classrooms with irrelevant curricula, oppressive policies, and racist instructors, and who might benefit from the ways these young authors had learned to see the world. The result was collections of student writing primarily for student readers, not the adult gaze. And some reviews acknowledged this. Whereas many of the era's collections of adolescent writing were little more than "coffee-table literature for adults," Marvin Hoffman praised *The Voice of the Children* as "one of the finest, most balanced representations of student thought and creativity to date.... One senses in reading their work a group of young people writing for their own and each other's pleasure; the adult reader just has the privilege of listening in."[111]

During the open admissions era, both Jordan and Bambara began experimenting with publishing pedagogies that they would continue developing for many years. Often, this involved countless uncompensated hours corresponding with publishers, negotiating contracts, and organizing publicity events. Their editorial labor ranged from convincing publishers that these writers had something important to say to convincing the authors themselves. They did this because of the multifaceted impact that publishing could make in the lives both of their students and of readers beyond the classroom. Publishing allowed students to insert their voices into dominant narratives; to address gaps in the literary, educational, and cultural record; to call out to collectives of readers who had been ignored by publishers; and to share survival strategies across classrooms and institutions. Among the many metaphors that feminist pedagogy has generated for thinking about teachers—as maestros, gardeners, or midwives—their work suggests that we might also think of them as "editors": people who guide students in realizing their writerly vision and sharing their work with broader audiences.[112]

While the publication of student writing in college classrooms dates back at least to the 1930s, Bambara's and Jordan's approaches responded to the distinct conditions of the open admissions era. Publishing, in this context, was both a way of empowering students who had been abused by underfunded and oppressive schools and a means of getting more useful and relevant books into the hands of readers who needed them. Their publishing pedagogies can also be understood in relation to longer histories of Black editorial labor. Amid a sea of white editors serving as gatekeepers to coveted contracts, Black writers have not been afforded the luxury of focusing solely on their craft. Rather, they have taken on work as editors in order to counter the racism within the publishing industry.[113] At least since the 1920s, some of the most influential authors of African American literature—Alain Locke, Claude McKay, W. E. B. Du Bois, Jessie Fauset—have also worked as editors in order to publish, in Zora Neale Hurston's words, "what white publishers won't print."[114] In the late 1960s, Jordan, Bambara, and other Black women writers, most famously Toni

Morrison, took on work as editors to circulate the writing of their friends, colleagues, neighbors, and, crucially for this book, students.[115] Looking back, we can understand their practice of publishing student writing as a form of both pedagogical and editorial activism.

The products of this pedagogy were anthologies of student writing, another one of the genres of open admissions. Among the many anthologies that emerged from, or in close proximity to, the SEEK program, Bambara's and Jordan's stand out for their inclusion of student writing. While anthologies are often produced for classroom use, with students as their intended audience, their construction occurs, in Kenneth Warren's terms, away from the "site" and "sight" of the classroom, reflecting a hierarchical model of knowledge transmission from expert scholar to presumably novice student.[116] By contrast, these writers engaged students in the production of grassroots anthologies that modeled alternative configurations of power and knowledge. In a moment when journalists and tenured faculty were obsessing over the reading skills their students lacked, Jordan and Bambara saw them as capable not merely of reading complex literature but of writing it. Reflecting on a course that concluded not with a traditional final paper but with an anthology, Jordan notes that "the class was producing its own literature: A literature reflecting the ideas and dreams and memories of the actual young Americans at work."[117]

Inventing Routes to Power

Because Jordan's position at City College was only part-time, she also took on teaching positions at Connecticut College, Sarah Lawrence College, and Yale University. Unlike at City College, where insufficient funding led to crowded classes, and students scrambled to access books, courses, advising appointments, and precious time with their overworked professors, on the lush, quiet campuses of these elite colleges, classes were small, resources were abundant, and professors were expected to spend extensive time nurturing students' intellectual development in office hours. We can picture Jordan during this period, speeding down the Henry Hudson Parkway, checking her watch and praying for traffic to ease while mentally sorting her Sarah Lawrence lesson plans from her City College syllabus. Commuting between these schools sharpened her sense of educational inequality: how much time, money, and attention are devoted to wealthy, predominantly white students as compared to working-class students of color. In her words: "The best universities have continued the worst kind of class privilege."[118]

However, the students she met at these elite institutions challenged her assumptions. Unlike City College or TWC students, the majority of them had grown up with wealth and an excellent K–12 education, often at expensive private schools. While she perhaps expected to encounter confident and self-assured individuals bolstered by affluence and exceptional academic training, what she found, even at these elite schools, were "innocence," "vulnerability," and a sense of powerlessness. At Sarah Lawrence, for instance, students were incensed at the US invasion of Cambodia and came to her with "hysterical tears running every which way down their cheeks and into their own mouths."[119] "We have to do something to stop this," she told them, to which they responded, "No . . . They won't listen to us. Who are we?"[120] Jordan was shocked that students at Sarah Lawrence, Connecticut College, and Yale did not realize the skills they possessed, or the fact that they were poised to graduate and join the ranks of power. There, she resolved "to dent the extremely low self-esteem, and the commonplace sense of impotence that seriously disfigured the formulating worldview of my students, regardless of race."[121]

Though one might expect Jordan to use different teaching methods at these private schools, there's a surprising degree of continuity in her approach. In fact, her Sarah Lawrence course Literature and Social Change (1969) originated in a course she initially developed for "Black teenagers from economically impoverished backgrounds" in an Upward Bound program.[122] While the earlier Upward Bound version of the course was organized around "the human experience of poverty," and the Sarah Lawrence version focused on "the creative experience of revolution," many of the readings and assignments were identical. In both courses, students read classic works of literature like Percy Bysshe Shelley's *The Masque of Anarchy*, Jonathan Swift's *A Modest Proposal*, and John Steinbeck's *Grapes of Wrath* alongside works by Richard Wright (and, in the college version, Frantz Fanon) and discussed their relevance to current events: the plight of migrant workers, starving children in Biafra, and the Poor People's Campaign.[123]

In addition to analyzing these books, Jordan challenged students to use each text's insights into language and power to move audiences to action through their own writing. In both courses, this took the form of collaborative, public projects. Students in the Upward Bound program organized a "Wrath Rally" "to focus public concern on the appalling status of migrant workers in America" and a letter-writing campaign in which they wrote to the governor, Congress, and newspapers "asking for action" against poverty in Biafra.[124] In the Sarah Lawrence version of the course, the undergraduates "hypothesize[d] appropriate written forms, and polemical strategies, to further serve The Poor People's Campaign."[125] Reflecting on what happened when students were asked to move beyond mere analysis of the assigned literature and use what they had learned from the books to advocate for change, Jordan notes that their "writing leaped into an eloquent fluency that had never even been hinted in their earlier work."[126] Though these campaigns generally did not produce legislation, reform, or revolution, she writes that "this very failure instructed us all" about the nature of what they were up against. She viewed both versions of the class as successful because "everything we read and everything we wrote, quite literally, translated into action."[127]

Jordan's letter of resignation from Sarah Lawrence describes just how deeply the students she met there changed her understanding of politics. She writes:

> [They] affected my thinking about possibilities for social coalition in America that will produce ... spectacular change. I used to envision interracial coalition as primarily a chance existing among the poor.... I no longer regard ... poverty as a necessary condition of alliance. Indeed, the opposite of poverty ... power, seems to me an essential ally of the powerless. I realize this sounds fatuously sophomoric ... but it's true, and I am already acting on ... my changed understanding.[128]

These students thus sharpened her sense that change should not be the sole responsibility of the poor but that those with power should become "allies to the powerless." And this realization, that everyone has something to contribute to the production of a better world, expanded her "conception of the community I wanted my lifework to encompass."[129]

Back at City College, things were not looking good. In 1975, during the worst economic downturn since the Great Depression, New York City was on the brink of bankruptcy, and neither the big banks nor the federal government responded to the requests made by city and state officials for a bailout (President Gerald Ford infamously told the city that it could "drop dead," according to one newspaper headline).[130] The only way city officials were able to secure modest financial assistance was by surrendering their decision-making power to the Emergency Financial Control Board, which was managed in part by the banking industry.[131] This board slashed CUNY's budget and demanded that the Board of Higher Education dismantle open admissions and terminate the college's 130-year history of tuition-free education.[132] Jordan, now a full-time assistant professor, and others rushed to defend the policy. She and twelve other Black faculty members went on a three-day hunger strike to protest the decision, which they rightly believed would "resegregate" the college.[133] At the board's hearing on the implementation of tuition, she delivered an impassioned speech emphasizing that the decision would "result in a 65% decline in Black enrollment."[134] Speaking on behalf of Black faculty, she declared "that the impending end of Open Admissions, the impending establishment of tuition requirements are, one and all, racist events that we cannot countenance, nor in any way accept. . . . We will fast. We will take a cut in salary. We will fight."[135] Without such policies, the university would revert to a place "where the powerful become more powerful."[136] But the decision had already been made. Two months later, the petition passed, open admissions ended, and Jordan, along with five thousand other faculty and staff members, received notice that their appointments would be terminated. As predicted, Black and Latinx student enrollment plummeted by 50 percent.[137]

Following their time at City College, Jordan and Bambara maintained a lifelong correspondence, the sporadic nature of which did not lessen its intensity. As their archival letters indicate, the two dreamed of collaborating on a film about Zora Neale Hurston and corresponded about a document mysteriously referred to as "the cat piece." Their care for one another is evident in Jordan's review of Bambara's short-story collection *Gorilla, My Love* for *Black World*, celebrating it "as teaching beautiful plus make you laugh out loud."[138] It is present, too, in Bambara's review of Jordan's essay collection *Civil Wars*, in which she admires Jordan's "deep-rooted belief in the sanctity of life."[139] In a letter to Jordan, Bambara describes how *Civil Wars* "got me to start keeping a journal. I thank you so very much for your example, June."[140] Though seemingly a small decision, for an author like Bambara this new practice of daily recording her thoughts and actions had a dramatic impact on her writing. Formally, her posthumous novel *These Bones Are Not My Child* (1999) consists of daily journal entries that correspond precisely to the year Bambara reviewed *Civil Wars* and began keeping her own diary. In addition, following the success of their early anthologies, both authors continued developing the publishing pedagogies they had first explored at City College. But whereas Bambara largely withdrew from formal academic institutions and shifted her focus to community arts organizations, Jordan took a different path.

In 1978 Jordan accepted a tenured position at SUNY Stony Brook, where she would teach for nearly a decade. As a professor in the English Department, she directed the Poetry Center and Creative Writing Program and taught courses like Contemporary Women's Poetry, In Search of the Invisible Black Woman, and the nation's first-ever course on Black English. What Jordan valued about public universities like City College and Stony Brook was the diverse students they attracted, and the wide range of experiences and perspectives they brought with them to the classroom. She "cherish[ed]" the opportunity teaching "represents: to be in serious contact with many different kinds of people," and the more "random" and "heterogenous," the better.[141] While she, like many professors, sometimes struggled to find time for both writing and teaching, she also "depend[ed] upon the teaching experience for the testing... and the provocation of new ideas."[142]

In her Stony Brook course The Art of Black English (1984), Jordan's classroom projects took on new urgency. Midway through the semester, one of her students, Willie Jordan, experienced something no one ever should. His brother, Reggie Jordan, was killed by the Brooklyn police. Having sought legal counsel for their family, Jordan was advised that "unless the execution of Reggie Jordan became a major community cause for organizing, and protest, his murder would simply become a statistical item."[143] With Willie's permission, she brought this problem to the class: "We had talked about the politics of language. We had talked about love and sex and child abuse and men and women. But the murder of Reggie Jordan broke like a hurricane across the room."[144] As their professor, she helped them channel this grief and rage into action. They decided to write personal statements of condolence to Willie's family and letters of condemnation to the police, which would also be sent to *Newsday*, a Long Island newspaper, to raise awareness about Reggie's murder. In working on their letters, the students faced a major decision: whether to write in Black English, the language of Reggie's life, or adhere to the conventions of Standard (read: white) English, "the language of the killers." Jordan helped them consider the implications of their decision, but she insisted that only they could make it. She writes, "At the end of one of the longest, most difficult hours of my own life, the students voted, unanimously, to preface their individual messages with a paragraph composed in the language of Reggie Jordan."[145] This decision honored Reggie's life but "doomed... [their] writings," guaranteeing that they would not be published in major newspapers.[146] As Alexis Pauline Gumbs has shown, this exemplifies how Jordan taught students to become accountable to those whom society deems "nobody," an experience that ultimately shaped Jordan's own vision of solidarity.[147]

It's hard to imagine a more meaningful course than The Art of Black English. Students cared so deeply about their work that semester that "more than 40 percent... were graded A or A–." We know this because the director of undergraduate studies was not pleased. In October 1985 Jordan received a letter requesting an explanation as to how she was planning to fix this excessive number of high marks (she wasn't). One can only imagine the ire she must have felt receiving a memo that reduced such a painful, complex experience to a letter grade, and that treated a course in which many students succeeded as if it were a problem to be solved. Though she received pushback, rather than praise, from the administration, the job security of tenure allowed her to continue this transgressive teaching.

In 1989 Jordan made a cross-country move to the University of California, Berkeley, where she was hired as a professor of African American studies and women's studies. Because of affirmative action, nearly half of Berkeley's students were people of color and many were progressive activists.[148] During Jordan's tenure at Berkeley, she joined students' political rallies and supported their demands for more diverse faculty, an ethnic studies program, and the establishment of a gay and lesbian studies center. A cheerleader and champion of all students, she was particularly enamored with those at Berkeley, whose "competing opinions and conflicted/commingling identities enflamed my imagination."[149] She wanted to teach in ways that would honor "that enormous complexity, and pride—I wondered if I could try to preserve, and even embolden, that fabulous, natural energy of assertive, polemical young hearts and minds, inside the classroom."[150] Drawing on early assignments like the problem paper and her experience publishing students' writing, here she would develop the fullest expression of her public and project-based pedagogy.

From her earliest years at City College, Jordan taught students to consider not only the interpersonal but also the structural nature of inequality: how deeply entrenched racism, sexism, and homophobia are in our institutions and society. She continued this in Berkeley courses like Contemporary Global Issues for Women, which explored how access to material resources and opportunities such as education, health care, and employment differ globally and in relation to race, gender, sexuality, and class. In that course, they read Margaret Atwood's novel *The Handmaid's Tale* and Jordan's "Poem about My Rights," alongside United Nations reports on teenage fertility, *New York Times* articles on family planning in Kenya, and essays on forced sterilization and reproductive rights in Native American, Black, and Mexican American communities. Students' reactions to this knowledge varied. Some were ready to take action; it was just a question of how and where to begin. Others felt guilty for all the privileges they had that many people did not. Many felt despair, given the magnitude of injustice and the scale of what we're up against. One semester, in The Politics of Childhood, students' understanding of structural inequality "became perilously keen and threatened to immobilize/demoralize all participants."[151] To salvage the course, Jordan assigned a project: to create something that could improve the lives of children. She writes, "At this point, I tried to invent a route to power: I asked students to conduct research into the status of children in California, and the U.S.A. I asked them to organize their findings and then integrate their individual lives, as children, with the big picture of children's needs unmet, in America."[152] Together they produced a radio broadcast that shared these findings with a larger audience. Jordan contacted local radio station KPFA and arranged to air their program, which was picked up and broadcast nationwide by Pacifica National Radio. This assignment helped students rise from felt positions of powerlessness to positions of advocacy. It also resulted in "a new organization advocating [for] children's rights... [with] Berkeley students... at its helm."[153]

During Jordan's time at Berkeley (1989–2001), these kinds of public projects became a more robust, central assignment, around which the rest of each course was organized. Her course Martin and Malcolm: Flipsides of the Same Black Revolutionary Coin, for instance, concluded with the production of a dramatic radio program called "The Trial of the American Conscience," "written by African, Asian, Chicano, Chicana, and White Americans who want to change the destiny of South Central [Los Angeles] from despair and violence to justice, empowerment and reason."[154] Like Bambara's assignments, Jordan's were often multimodal, with forms suited to the task at hand. Another semester, in her women's studies course Coming into the World Female, a reporter from *Mother Jones* published an editorial denigrating women's studies, and Berkeley's renowned department in particular, as mere "therapy" that does not "belong in a university classroom."[155] Jordan's students voted to take action. They prepared a press conference, a mock women's studies class, and a demonstration outside the newspaper's office. While their peers laughed and drank in local bars, they voluntarily "spent hours and hours in solemn, wearisome research" for these projects.[156] They assigned themselves extra "homework into the facts," to make sure their points were accurate and persuasive, and gave everything down to "the design and the wording of their flyers maximal painstaking and meticulous execution."[157] They did all this not to get a good grade and pass the course but to counter the lies of dominant discourse and instead spread the truth about women's studies.

These kinds of public project assignments, which were developed by both Jordan and Bambara, asked students to use what they learned not just for personal gain but to contribute to the public good. Their public nature offers an interesting counterpoint to the covert traditions of Black transgressive teaching that Jarvis R. Givens calls "fugitive pedagogy."[158] While Givens highlights the clandestine means by which Black schoolteachers have historically subverted white supremacist curricula, Jordan and Bambara remind us that activist educators have also taught students to write out loud and intervene in public discourse. Their work can thus be understood as part of a longer history of what Roopika Risam calls "academic insurgency," an effort, led by scholars of color, to reimagine research and teaching in the service of public and community engagement.[159]

What emerges from these courses is a public and project-based pedagogy that helped students realize their capacity for action, even amid widespread, deeply rooted structures of injustice. With Jordan's guidance, students identified what was obscured by dominant narratives, gathered missing information and perspectives, and crafted projects that could move audiences to action. We might think of this, in her terms, as inventing routes to power: helping students identify how they could use their knowledge, skills, and resources to advocate for change. Contemporary poet and National Book Award finalist Solmaz Sharif distilled what she learned as Jordan's student into the following principle: "When you see work that's not being done, you go and you do it. You don't wait for someone else to."[160] Writing with the special exuberance teaching seemed to elicit, Jordan describes how this pedagogy transformed "the fixed, predetermined, graveyard nature of... formal education."[161] Instead, school became "a place where students learned about the world and then resolved, collectively, and creatively, to change it!"[162]

Nowhere is this public and project-based pedagogy more evident than in Jordan's famous Poetry for the People program.[163] The program began in 1991 as a Berkeley course in which students read, wrote, published, and performed poetry. There, as she recalls, "the ethnic, racial, intellectual, and sexual diversity" of her students allowed her "to devise a syllabus that is, for me, unprecedented, and even unwieldy in its range."[164] One semester the course covered units on "African American Oral Traditions," "Caribbean Poetry," "White Male Poetry," "Native American Poetry," "Gay and Lesbian Poetry," "Asian American Poetry," "Chicana/o Poetry," "Women's Poetry," "Canonical Poetry," and "Irish Poetry."[165] Because Jordan was not an expert in all of these poetic traditions, she frequently invited guest lecturers, practicing poets, and advanced students to help them "handle the course materials responsibly."[166] One semester, a student pointed out that the course neglected a rich tradition of Deaf poetry and invited Deaf poets to campus. Together, they explored how poems could be "more than a private catharsis."[167] Student Kelly Elaine Navies describes "a classroom filled with stories: stories of political oppression, sexual rape, the psychological rape of miseducation, domestic violence and loss of language, stories of love stomped on and love celebrated."[168] Through poetry, they explored the effects of uneven power structures on daily life and the ways people navigate and resist these conditions.

Part of what made the program so revolutionary was that students were not only reading poetry but also writing it. Each week, around seventy students in the popular course would engage in creative mimicry and write poems inspired by a particular poetic style. The week they discussed oral traditions in African American poetry, for instance, students wrote "How Do I Love Thee?" poems inspired by Queen Latifah, Toni Braxton, and the Company. In class, they met in small groups to read, share, and revise their poems, treating each other's work with the same care and scrutiny given to assigned authors.

In the resulting poems, the student authors examine individual lives—their own and those of loved ones—in relation to broader histories, current events, and geopolitical conditions. In "Tio Juancho," Ruben Antonio Villalobos locates his experiences "coming of age as a Panamanian American" within the broader history of US-Panama relations.[169] The poem, which takes the form of a letter to his uncle, explores the "connections between the songs mi tio sang and current political events in Panama."[170] Elizabeth Riva Meyer wrote a poem depicting her grandmother's suicide as an act of resistance to the exploitation of women.[171] Another student, Shanti Bright, wanted to write about "issues of tribal enrollment, mixed-blood identity, the history of patriarchal domination and Native women," and she realized, "A term paper could not express my own connections to these issues as powerfully as a poem."[172] She penned the lyric, "Crouching in the Shadow of Columbus's Tomb," which explores "the Columbus in me," including Bright's own imperial attitude of "discovery" on a high school trip to Costa Rica.[173] Reflecting on the pedagogical approach that led to the production of these poems, Kirsten Bartholomew Ortega writes that "the teacher provides the students with access to context, history, and literary structure and examples, but the students are an essential factor in the construction of knowledge because they provide new insights and new forms of expression."[174] By connecting the assigned readings and their own experiences, they generated insurgent knowledge: the ideas and perspectives obscured by mainstream media and curricula.

With Poetry for the People, Jordan continued developing the kinds of "democratic...instruction modes" that had proven so effective at other institutions.[175] Among these was a set of ground rules that were used to create a classroom where students would feel "safe enough" to explore difficult subjects, feelings, and ideas. As she well knew, and as extensive research confirms, classrooms are not inherently welcoming and supportive to all students in equal measure. Rather, they tend to reproduce the structural inequalities of society writ large.[176] Everything from who gets called on to who is disciplined and whose experiences are reflected in the curriculum vary based on race, class, and gender. Always attentive to structure, she designed three ground rules to create a different learning environment. Enrolling in the class meant students agreed not to exclude "anyone on the basis of race, ethnicity, language, sexual preference, class, or age."[177] Each participant also pledged to "respect and to encourage each other" as they crafted "messages...for the world to contemplate."[178] Finally, their work was informed by the notion that "the art of telling the truth" is a "healthy way" to forge "powerful connections" among people who would otherwise remain strangers.[179] By taking the course, students agreed "not to kill connections" but to deepen them. We can read these ground rules as an experiment in alternative worldmaking, where Jordan sought to enact, in the classroom, the social relations she (and many others) desired for society. As one student notes, these rules—and the different classroom dynamic they created—convinced her to stop cowering in the corner: "Take down those barriers it's safe to come out of hiding."[180]

In the intervening years, educators have built on these kinds of ground rules to involve students in coauthoring the principles that will govern their classroom, often in the form of contracts or constitutions. Inspired by Jordan's example, my students, every semester, coauthor a set of community guidelines that we agree to adhere to in our classroom. Involving students in this kind of collective placemaking generates a learning environment that everyone has a stake in.[181] And because students write these guidelines, they tend to respect them. Though one could criticize the ways such practices fail to prepare students for a harsh, violent, and cutthroat reality, the opposite seems more true. Asking students to create a more just, equitable, and pleasurable classroom alters what they're willing to settle for in the world beyond its walls. It prepares them to build better ones.

Jordan also democratized their classroom by employing students as instructors. After completing the course, participants applied to be student-teacher poets (STPS) who took a course called The Teaching and Writing of Poetry and led discussion and writing groups for Poetry for the People's next cohort.

Similar to the community knowledge-sharing practices we saw in Bambara's classrooms, STPs worked with Jordan to create handouts—"Technical Checklists," "Helpful Reading Tips," and how-to guides—that imparted the lessons they had learned to the program's incoming students. The first rule on the "Technical Checklist" was the same lesson Professor Ulanov had taught Jordan decades prior at Barnard: Use "strong, descriptive words.... Eliminate all forms of the verb 'to be.'"[182] "Helpful Reading Tips" reminded student poets to "read slowly & loud ... remember not to 'swallow' the last words of a line ... no disclaimers before you read!"[183] These handouts demystified the process of writing and performing poetry so that any student, not just those with confidence or advanced language skills, could participate. And serving as an STP also benefited the student leaders: recent research has shown how teaching course material to someone else helps students effectively learn difficult concepts.[184] In 2016 Jordan's successor Aya de Leon noted that this "peer-to-peer, each-one-teach-one model continues as the foundation of the program to this day."[185]

Each of Poetry for the People's semester-long adventures concluded not with an exam but with poetry performances and the publication of student work. Jordan believed that "public performance, publication, and media appearances ... are natural and necessary steps to the acquirement of power through language."[186] At the end of each term, students (with her guidance) organized a public reading, where they read their work alongside invited poets such as Ntozake Shange and Sherley Anne Williams in front of a packed auditorium. One poet whom they often invited was Jordan's former SEEK colleague, Adrienne Rich, who by then had also moved to California, where she became a frequent collaborator and ardent advocate of Poetry for the People. Crucial to these events was the democratic notion that student poetry should receive the same fanfare as that authored by established poets. In addition, rather than outsourcing the labor to administrators and custodial staff, students were responsible for every aspect of the readings: teaching each other the art of reading poetry aloud, inviting poets, reserving rooms, publicizing the event, coordinating refreshments, setting up sound and lighting, archiving the readings, and cleaning up afterward.

Their semesters also culminated in the publication of students' poetry in an anthology. In fact, what began in the late 1960s with *The Voice of the Children* and *Soulscript* would evolve into nearly a dozen anthologies of student writing that Jordan (and Bambara) compiled throughout their careers. In collections like *Whose Country Is This, Anyway* (1995) and *Poetry in a Time of Genocide* (1993) (the proceeds of which went to "Bosnian women and children, victims of ethnic cleansing"), students responded to social and political issues of their era.[187] *Profiles in Conflict* (2002), for instance, addressed racial profiling in the wake of the September 11 terrorist attacks on the World Trade Center. It speaks back to a world in which "58% of those surveyed would require special security checks for Arabs and Arab Americans, 49% would mandate special IDs, and nearly a third would support the internment of American citizens of Arab descent."[188] And whereas at City College, Jordan had only dreamed of publishing student writing, now, after twenty-five years as an educator and editor, and with access to the resources of Berkeley's campus, she was able to involve students to a far greater extent in the publication process. Just as students were responsible for the unglamorous logistics of organizing their performances, so too were they involved in editing, proofing, binding, budgeting, distributing, and marketing their anthologies.

On the one hand, these performances and publications equipped students with a range of skills that they could use beyond the classroom: from copyediting and public speaking to archiving, marketing, and event planning. But equally important was the way these collaborative undertakings—group projects at a massive scale—invited students, on a more philosophical level, to think beyond the liberal individualism promoted by much of formal education. From grade school through graduate school, students are taught to compete rather than collaborate with those sitting next to them. Grades, exams, and prohibitions against cheating all enforce the notion that one must accomplish things by one's own merit, a pernicious fantasy that obscures the systems, structures, and interconnections on which we all depend. Most university courses teach students, in Stefano Harney and Fred Moten's terms, to "deny . . . what one produces with others" and thus contribute to "the impoverishment . . . [and] immiseration, of society's cooperative prospects."[189] Jordan's assignments, by contrast, highlight the labor at the heart of collaboration: how many different hands are involved in making things happen. Her students combined their knowledge and skills to create performances and publications that were more robust than what any one could have produced individually. In this way, we can see how these teacher-poets extended the 1960s-era ideals like collective power into classrooms across the country, and for many years to come.

In their later teaching, Jordan and Bambara built on their early experiments with the publication of student writing to develop teaching methods that introduced students to the material practices of the publishing industry. In fact, around the same time that Jordan was teaching Berkeley students to bind and publicize their anthologies, Bambara was teaching undergraduates at the University of Delaware to "deglamorize publishing and study marketing, distributing, printing—the entire process including bookbinding."[190] While creative writing workshops often emphasize craft—discussions of language, structure, and form—she wanted them to "realize that the packaging/designing and distribution ... are an integral part of your work."[191] For their midterm, they created visually appealing publicity posters (known as broadsides) for their short stories. This emphasis on publishing highlighted how language and literature are part of a larger ecosystem that involves editors, copyeditors, publishers, booksellers, readers, teachers, and students. It also equipped students with a range of transferable skills that they could use outside the classroom.

In addition to drawing on their earlier teaching, these publishing pedagogies were also shaped by developments in Black and women-of-color feminism. One by-product of the Black women's literary renaissance of the 1970s was a heightened focus, in the 1980s, on addressing the racism and sexism many had experienced throughout the publishing process. While the early 1970s saw Black women like Jordan, Bambara, and Lorde take up work as editors, in the late 1970s and 1980s many resigned from their positions in white-dominated presses and publications and instead formed their own publishing networks. Around the time that Jordan and Lorde resigned as editors of the women's magazine *Chrysalis*, owing to its racist policies, Jordan and Alice Walker convened the Sisterhood: a group of Black women writers who focused on securing publication and publicity opportunities.[192] And in 1980 Lorde and Barbara Smith established Kitchen Table: Women of Color Press in order to "make visible the writing, culture, and history of women of color."[193] As Smith writes, the press was born from

> our need for autonomy, our need to determine independently both the content and the conditions of our work and to control the words and images that were produced about us. As feminist and lesbian of color writers, we ... had no options for getting published except at the mercy or whim of others—in either commercial or alternative publishing, since both are white dominated.[194]

In the introduction to the anthology *This Bridge Called My Back*, editors Cherríe Moraga and Gloria Anzaldúa describe the additional labor they undertook to circulate the work of women of color. As editors, they "bore the burden of the book... not only doing the proofreading and making editorial decisions, but also acting as a telephone answering and courier service, PR persons and advertisers, interviewers and transcribers, and even, occasionally, muses for... contributors [experiencing] 'writing blocks.'"[195] In the 1990s, writes Kinohi Nishikawa, Black women writers would increasingly take up self-publishing to circumvent the racism in mainstream presses.[196] Considered in this context, we can see how Jordan's and Bambara's efforts to involve students in the publishing process were part of broader efforts to seize control over the means of literary production. As we look back, their work illustrates how feminist publishing impacted the era's teaching practices and, reciprocally, how classrooms were sites of what Courtney Thorsson calls "Black feminist literary organizing."[197]

In the 1960s and 1970s Jordan had advocated for Black English and open admissions; in the 1990s she engaged in a parallel struggle for bilingual education and affirmative action, both of which came under threat during her time at Berkeley.[198] She also continued to critique injustices in education funding. Her essay "Finding the Haystack in the Needle, or, the Whole World of America and the Challenge of Higher Education" (1992) criticized how California's tiered public university system—of community colleges, state universities, and elite University of California schools—distributed the majority of taxpayer dollars to campuses with the greatest number of white students, while working-class students of color were often relegated to community colleges bereft of counseling, job placement, and health centers; African American or ethnic studies programs; and sometimes even bathroom stall doors. She writes, "Per student, per year, the state spends $2,899 on the community college level, $6,617 on the California state university level, and $13,260... at the University of California" schools. "What's the operating principle here?... 'To them that have it will be given'? 'From those that have not it will be taken away'?"[199]

Jordan challenged this upward consolidation of resources by working to expand access to transformative learning. Throughout her career, she had success with what Moten and Harney call "steal[ing] from the university": diverting funds away from the accumulation of wealth and power to instead provide relevant and empowering education for marginalized communities.[200] At Stony Brook, for instance, she utilized university funds to support broader public education efforts, including an extensive public teach-in on apartheid. At Berkeley she again "stole from" the university (and external funding agencies) to secure a series of grants that allowed her and her students to bring Poetry for the People to local schools, community organizations, and prisons—like Yerba Buena Center for the Arts, Dublin Women's Prison, and Glide Memorial Church—where they could reach working-class communities. At each site, the STPs would introduce the week's writing exercise, read some of their own poems, and then guide participants in writing, sharing, and revising their poems.[201] They might bring in a blues record, a Georgia O'Keeffe painting, or fruits and veggies from the local farmer's market to teach participants how to write vivid sensory descriptions. In one exercise titled "Today they vote in South Africa," the college students explained to Highland Elementary School students the importance of South Africans having their first free elections and then asked them to write about "something they have always wanted, but have known will be very hard to get, just as Black South Africans must have felt about voting."[202] As an instructor at Oakland's Computer Academy notes, for students who had been subjected to standardized, disciplining, and disempowering schools, the program's "self-esteem building" and "accessible and fun kind of literacy" had "visible, real, and truly life changing" effects. He writes, "The workshops were so powerful and uplifting" that they later replicated them in their high school, so that "those same students—now seniors—have just spent eight weeks teaching poetry to my sophomores, using many of the same techniques they learned in Ms. Jordan's program."[203]

Not only was Jordan the charismatic visionary driving these extensions of Poetry for the People into broader communities, but she also did the administrative labor that made them possible, including writing budgets, grant proposals, schedules, and progress reports. The amount of paperwork it took to coordinate the course The Teaching and Writing of Poetry for advanced students, who would then lead smaller sections of undergraduate poetry workshops; to secure funding for their performances, anthologies, and visits by famous poets; and to extend this work beyond the university would send many of us running for the hills. In addition to everything else she was—a brilliant teacher, writer, editor, and activist—Jordan was also a fierce administrator who understood pedagogical labor, not unlike poetry, as an effort to make things happen within formal constraints: to redistribute power, move people to action, and expand our sense of what is possible. And she taught students to perform this kind of administrative activism as well: they reserved auditoriums for poetry readings, hired American Sign Language interpreters for public events, designed and printed programs, and negotiated with their institutions for funding to bring their favorite "hot shot poets" to campus.[204]

Jordan also continued to share teaching materials, understanding this as key to social justice pedagogies. In 1995, she, her coteacher Lauren Muller, and students published *June Jordan's Poetry for the People: A Revolutionary Blueprint* (1995), a how-to guide that includes the methods, decision-making processes, poems, stories, syllabi, and reading lists that went into producing the program. And readers were eager for such models. In 1999, Yolanda Wisher came across *A Revolutionary Blueprint* at a bookstore in Philadelphia and used it to create Poetry for the People Philadelphia. Their group hosted public poetry readings and writing workshops, engaged in "guerilla poetry tactics" in supermarkets, and organized open-mic nights in women's and children's shelters.[205] More recently, in 2021 Felicia Rose Chavez used *A Revolutionary Blueprint* to develop her model for an "antiracist writing workshop": one that replaces orthodox methods of creative writing instruction that silence students of color with approaches that decenter whiteness and redistribute power equitably among participants.[206] Indeed, through this published collection of teaching materials, Jordan's pedagogy continues to transform classrooms to this day.

Thirty years before Jordan dreamed up her now-famous poetry initiative, teaching had helped her overcome her sense of powerlessness. And the public and project-based pedagogy she developed throughout her career passed that gift of enablement on to students. It taught them not to dutifully recite the professor's ideas but to understand themselves as active knowledge producers and creative cultural workers with the power to make a difference. In a "Merit Review Statement" submitted to the Berkeley administration, Jordan wrote, "My students have understood—sometimes reluctantly, that the point, at bottom, is for them to assume power—over the English language, over the classroom, over all campus policies, over their own lives."[207] And students attest to the empowering nature of learning in the service of social change. "Most English classes," one wrote, are "disempowering," teaching deference to a literary tradition that they will never ascend to.[208] By contrast, Jordan's classrooms helped students like Kelly Elaine Navies discover "the political significance of my own voice."[209] Another student recalls that learning to write poetry gave him "a godlike feeling... you begin to make up your own rules, define your own world."[210] Poetry for the People helped him feel, not like a tyrannical, omnipotent god, but one among a poetic pantheon, part of "a poetic community—joining Joyce, Baraka, Hughes, but on one's own terms."[211]

And join the pantheon they did. Poetry for the People graduates went on to author works of literature (like Michael Datcher's memoir *Raising Fences: A Black Man's Love Story* and Ruth Forman's poetry collection *Renaissance*) and were named poet laureate of the University of California system (Samiya Bashir, 1994) and National Book Award finalists (Solmaz Sharif, 2016).[212] Equally important are the many students who did not go on to become famous poets but brought the program's lessons to bear on other fields like museums, teaching, counseling, and law. Today, Kelly Elaine Navies works as an oral historian of African American culture at the Smithsonian.[213] Elizabeth Riva Meyer is a school counselor who provides mental health services to children. Ruben Antonio Villalobos and Shanti Bright (now Shanti Bright Brien) both became lawyers: Villalobos advocates for Latinx communities, and Brien recently published *Almost Innocent: From Searching to Saved in America's Criminal Justice System*, which draws on her experiences as a lawyer to advocate for a more just legal system. As we saw in Bambara's work with the Scribe Video Center, Poetry for the People illustrates how the pedagogies of open admissions far outlived its brief existence as formal educational policy and continued to impact cultural production for many decades to come.

Of Parallels & Intersections
Adrienne Rich's Pedagogy of Location

3

IN 1968 ADRIENNE RICH was widely recognized as one of America's most promising young poets. A graduate of Radcliffe, she had published four venerated poetry collections and earned such accolades as the Yale Younger Poets Award, a Guggenheim Fellowship, and the National Institute of Arts and Letters Award. Having skillfully ascended the ranks of literary and educational institutions, she was teaching students in Columbia University's MFA program to do the same. That year, however, Rich made a surprising professional move. Amid protests against the Vietnam War, the assassination of Martin Luther King Jr., and critiques of educational racism, she felt, "In order to live in the city, I needed to ally myself, in some concrete, practical, if limited way, with the possibilities."[1] That spring, she traded in her advanced creative writing seminar to teach remedial writing at City College. Though she didn't know it at the time, that decision would fundamentally alter her writing and, with it, the course of feminist literature and criticism.

Today Rich is remembered as one of the twentieth century's most influential feminist authors and public intellectuals. Her twenty-five poetry collections and eight works of prose addressed subjects such as marriage, lesbian love, war, Judaism, and motherhood. In poetry collections like *Diving into the Wreck* (1973), she explored how women have been erased from history and distorted in literature—their lives curtailed by patriarchy. Her essays on authors like

Anne Bradstreet, Emily Dickinson, and Lorraine Hansberry helped establish feminist literary criticism, and her formulations like "compulsory heterosexuality" and "the lesbian continuum" remain central to queer theory. She is also regarded as one of the few white second-wave feminists who confronted issues of race and class. This work has earned her a reputation as a "pioneer, witness and prophet" of the women's movement.[2] Yet before Rich ever identified as a feminist, she thought of herself as "a teacher of language... someone for whom language has implied freedom, who is trying to aid others to free themselves through the written word."[3]

Though Rich spent more than twenty years teaching writing, literature, and women's studies to hundreds of students at universities across the country, relatively little has been said about her work as a professor.[4] This chapter focuses on her experiences teaching basic writing in the City College SEEK program. While her journey as an educator began at elite institutions, SEEK introduced her to an "activist style of teaching": student-centered and access-oriented methods that she would continue developing throughout her career.[5] This chapter also demonstrates how Rich was radicalized by her experiences at City College. More specifically, it illustrates how teaching basic writing to working-class students of color, advocating for open admissions, and collaborating with Black women teacher-poets helped her see beyond second-wave feminism's celebrations of sisterhood to develop an intersectional politics. And by tracing Rich's trajectory from 1960s Harlem through her time at Douglass College and her later courses in California, we will see how these early experiences would eventually lead to pedagogy of location: ways of teaching students to analyze the material conditions and power structures that undergird their lives.

Poetry and Protest

Born in 1929, Rich was raised in the affluent suburbs of Baltimore and homeschooled until the age of nine. Convinced that his daughter was a prodigy, Rich's father transcribed her stories before she could write, gave her poems by William Blake and John Keats to copy, and arranged for the publication of her first poetry collection when she was only six.[6] Under her father's strict tutelage, she learned "to feel, at a very young age, the power of language and that I could share in it."[7] In the 1940s, she attended Roland Park Country School, a private all-girls school. There, students like her "who showed special intellectual interest or ability" were given additional time, energy, and attention: "We were taken to libraries, art museums, lectures at neighboring colleges, set to work on extra research projects, given extra French or Latin reading."[8] At Radcliffe, the women educators of her high school disappeared, but this did not bother Rich, who, at the time, dismissed "damned sterile feminism."[9] It seemed like the natural progression into the serious intellectual world of elite universities where "now I would have great men as my teachers."[10] While most courses focused on intrinsic "textual criticism," (an emphasis on literary devices rather than culture and context) Rich was drawn to professors like F. O. Matthiessen who discussed literature in relation to history, politics, and social issues—lessons that "would inform her thinking and writing for the rest of her life."[11] And she relished the professorial praise that Harvard bestowed on her. In 1952 she wrote to her father, "This place has been my life—remove Harvard and you'd have no Adrienne Rich."[12]

In her final semester, at the age of twenty-two, Rich published her first major poetry collection, *A Change of World* (1951). Formally precise and exquisitely crafted, these early poems assume a cool, detached, observational tone. Unlike in her later, more famous poems, Rich didn't yet use *she* or *I* for the speaker's voice. She "had been taught that poetry should be 'universal,' which meant, of course, non-female."[13] But while gender may have been missing from the poems, it was all too conspicuous in their reviews. As is often the case with women writers, these early poems were lauded by male critics for their humility and deference to tradition. W. H. Auden described them as "neatly and modestly dressed" and commended Rich's "respect for elders"—an admirable trait for a young female author.[14]

In the 1960s, Rich experienced what critics have called a "feminist awakening" as she joined the civil rights, feminist, and antiwar movements.[15] Though Alexandra J. Gold has identified a nascent feminist dissatisfaction in some of her early poems, it was in Rich's poetry of the 1960s that her feminism became explicit.[16] Beginning with *Snapshots of a Daughter in Law* (1963), Rich broke with the edict that good literature should be universal and began to explore the particular experiences of women in a patriarchal society. As part of this transition, she also moved away from traditional poetic forms like sonnets and rigid rhyme schemes and started to experiment with free verse. While Rich's awakening has been understood as a response to the era's social movements and her experiences of motherhood, it was also shaped by her work as a professor.

Rich's teaching career began in the same kind of elite institutions where she had studied. In 1966, having recently relocated to New York City with her husband and three sons, she was hired as a lecturer to teach a poetry workshop at Swarthmore, a small liberal arts college near Philadelphia, and as an adjunct in Columbia's creative writing MFA program. Her early workshops were, like Rich's own education, an intense immersion in what Matthew Arnold famously called "the best which has been thought and said."[17] Her reading lists were extensive: one semester, students were told to read three poetry textbooks; essays by D. H. Lawrence, A. E. Housman, and Paul Valéry (among others); and, independently, the work of eight other poets (all white men) as well as essays by Martin Heidegger and Ludwig Wittgenstein, two of the era's densest and most difficult philosophers.[18] Her early syllabi include few women despite the fact that she personally knew Anne Sexton, Denise Levertov, and Sylvia Plath. Nor do they include writers of color, though she occasionally mimeographed poems by Amiri Baraka. Her assignments often asked students to emulate the poetry they were reading by W. B. Yeats, Wallace Stevens, and Robert Frost. One asked them to compose poems in the three styles identified by Ezra Pound: melopoeia, phanopoeia, and logopoeia.[19] This was hardly the spontaneous overflow of excess emotion often associated with poetry; it was a rigorous study of poetic structure and form, meter, rhythm, and diction, what Rich calls in her syllabus "prosody."[20]

At Swarthmore and Columbia, Rich and her students bonded over their shared opposition to the Vietnam War. Gradually, amid the countercultural zeitgeist of the 1960s, her courses became more casual, sometimes meeting on her living-room floor, with students referring to her as Adrienne.[21] As an educator, Rich occasionally relied on her star power; sometimes her feedback on students' poems was as lackluster as stating, "I dig it" or "I don't dig it."[22] While she sensed that these courses might "bring new focus to her own study of poetry—an unexpected boon," little could she imagine the changes soon to come.[23]

In 1968 Columbia erupted in political demonstrations. Hundreds of students occupied the campus to protest the university's research on military weapons and their plan to construct a segregated gym in nearby Harlem. The New York City Police Department retaliated with violence: students were beaten, tear-gassed, and detained in one of the largest mass arrests in US history. Yet many faculty, even those self-proclaimed humanists, ignored these events. They wanted to get "back to business," continue on "in the name of scholarship, neutrality, [and] objectivity," and "pretend that nothing has happened."[24] But for Rich, these events were a turning point. In a letter to fellow poet Jean Stafford, she describes how they connected seemingly freestanding courses to the larger universities in which they are taught:

> It was not until the occupation of the buildings that I became concerned with what Columbia was, how it functioned, who had power and how it was used. It ... [took] that occupation to make me aware that I was associated with a university which was actively threatening, as part of its policy, the minimal social values which ... were essential for me as a woman, a writer, a human animal.[25]

Newly conscious of her complicity in a racist and imperial institution, Rich soon abandoned her post to teach in an educational opportunity program committed to racial justice.

Asbestos Gloves and Scaffolded Assignments

In 1968, when Rich applied to teach in the City College SEEK program, she was offered a more prestigious and less demanding position as poet in residence, but she declined, insisting that she wanted to teach in SEEK.[26] At the time, she held what she later called a "romantic notion of teaching." She imagined herself as the schoolteacher heroine in Emlyn Williams's play *The Corn Is Green* (1938), who takes a job in a remote countryside village and discovers "a nascent poet" buried among his otherwise "undistinguished" and unremarkable peers.[27] While "birth and family background had destined him for a life in the coal mines," through the special tutoring she gives him, "another path opens up," and he is whisked away to Oxford.[28] In retrospect, Rich called this "the secret fantasy of many teachers: the illscrawled essay, turned up among so many others, which has the mark of genius."[29] Today we might call it, more simply, a savior narrative.

At City College, Rich met educators who thought differently about teaching. In preparation for her first semester, she wrote to Mina Shaughnessy, who had recently taken over the writing program, asking for advice, especially about how much reading to assign. The Columbia professor who had bombarded her students with Heidegger and Wittgenstein knew things would look different at City College, though she wasn't sure to what extent. Likely through Shaughnessy, Rich obtained a document titled "Report on the Summer Seminar, Pre-baccalaureate Program, City College" (1968), a collection of writings by the SEEK educators who were soon to become her colleagues. In the pages of that collection, Rich read Fred Byron's proclamation that "teaching is partially an attempt to show students that all knowledge, no matter how formidable it might first appear, is approachable."[30] She also encountered Barbara Christian's "hypothesis": "that most of the students suffer from a lack of awareness of the importance and relevance of their own lives."[31] Here were educators who aimed not to cultivate the talent of an exceptional few but to undo the damages of a racist society that systematically denied their students opportunities. They understood teaching not as charity but as part of broader movements for collective liberation.

In that document, Rich first encountered, in her words, an "activist style of teaching": practices that centered students' ideas and experiences, challenged them to make decisions about their learning, engaged them in research, and asked them to produce reports, filmscripts, and syllabi for their own courses.[32] The most creative proponent of such methods was Toni Cade Bambara, whom Rich met for the first time in the pages of that report (she made quite an impression). Bambara argued that conventional teaching methods can reinforce social hierarchies and described what happened that summer when students, instead, were given control over the "content, direction, and goals of the course."[33] As someone who was gradually unlearning her own fidelity to patriarchal authority, this radically student-centered classroom lit a fire in Rich's imagination.

In the fall of 1968, Rich began her position as a part-time lecturer in SEEK. She taught three or four sections of basic writing per year, with around fifteen students in each. Though her exact compensation is unknown, given the racial disparities in academic salaries combined with the fact that the college had tried to recruit her for a more prestigious position, it's likely that she would have been compensated at a higher rate than June Jordan, Toni Cade Bambara, or Audre Lorde.

In these classrooms, Rich met "black and Puerto Rican freshmen entering from substandard ghetto high schools, where the prevailing assumption had been that they were of inferior intelligence."[34] Many had been subjected to a racist school system, inexperienced and apathetic instructors, and a curriculum that largely ignored their cultures. As someone who found freedom in language, Rich now faced students who had had "language and literature used against them to keep them in their place, to mystify, to bully, to make them feel powerless."[35] Over the next five years, she would help them cultivate a different relationship to the written word.

Despite their uninspiring, bureaucratic titles like "English 1.8" and "English 1-T," Rich's SEEK courses were organized around the enticing idea that writing is a form of empowerment. One of her earliest syllabi states, "This class will start from the idea that language—the way we put words together—is a way of acting on reality and eventually gaining more control of one's life."[36] These early courses combined discussions of assigned readings with in-class writing exercises and brief lectures, often on writing skills or historical context for a reading. Students wrote one short in-class essay and one take-home essay per week, which were "read aloud in class frequently and discussed."[37]

Initially, Rich borrowed the "activist teaching methods" of SEEK's earliest educators. Following the examples in the report, students' lives and experiences took center stage. Her syllabus for English 1-H states, "The people in the class and their experiences will be the basic material of the course, about which we will be talking and writing."[38] She assigned readings that she hoped would help them "define the actual experiences we ourselves are having, and to make others more aware of our reality as we perceive it."[39] This included a wide range of texts, from existentialist plays like Jean-Paul Sartre's *No Exit* and Albert Camus's *The Plague* to poems by Native American, African, and Chinese authors. Often, Rich assigned classic works of philosophy like Plato's *Republic*, alongside works of African American literature like Eldridge Cleaver's prison memoir *Soul on Ice*, "maintain[ing] where possible a dialogue between the works of those writers. (E.g. between Eldridge Cleaver and Plato)."[40] As this pairing suggests, they analyzed both the liberal philosophies that have influenced society and the violence and injustice that such philosophies have permitted. Rich was candid about her selection principles; her 1969 syllabus notes that "the only unifying device for the course is that each book studied is one which has strongly affected the instructor."[41] And students were equally frank with Rich; they did not always accept her decisions. In one instance, they challenged her inclusion of D. H. Lawrence's *Sons and Lovers* on the grounds that it "had nothing to do with them."[42] Unlike Bambara, who had adjusted her syllabus based on students' interests, Rich did not change course. Instead, she explained her belief that Lawrence's depiction of "certain aspects of family life, sexuality, work, anger and jealousy ... carried over to many cultures" but noted that if they didn't find it meaningful, "we could talk and write about why not and how not."[43]

Rich also adapted her colleagues' creative mimicry assignments. While she had previously instructed Columbia students to "write a Wordsworth poem," at City College her focus switched to Black writers. She borrowed, for example, Bambara's writing prompt, which used Amiri Baraka's (then LeRoi Jones's) essay "Cuba Libre," a critique of the lies in mainstream journalism, as inspiration for their own compositions. Rich's version reads, "Write an essay on lies, or a lie, that you encountered while growing up ... lies told by teachers; by parents; lying by other children; lies you told yourself; lies in newspapers and magazines; in advertising, political speeches, sermons, movies, tv etc. How did these lies affect your thinking, and how and when did you begin to identify them as lies?"[44] Another creative mimicry exercise (also obtained from Bambara) asked them to read Eldridge Cleaver's vignette "Eyes" and then write about an insight gleaned through a particular body part, such as their hands or hair.[45] Pleased by the writing these assignments produced, Rich developed similar ones using Ann Petry's novella *Darkness and Confusion* and Richard Wright's short story "The Man Who Lived Underground."[46] These assignments—which used Black literature to guide students in drawing lessons from their lives—laid the grounds for what would ultimately become her pedagogy of location.

A reasonable reader might question the ethics of a white woman using assignments developed by a Black woman in her classroom. Rich herself seemed aware of how closely it resembled theft. She described how SEEK educators adapted each other's teaching materials as a kind of "poach[ing]."[47] (To avoid receiving credit for an assignment borrowed from Bambara, she added "acknowledgments to Toni Cade" in at least one memo to SEEK administrators.[48]) However, this exchange can also be understood as part of their collective efforts to empower students. As Jarvis R. Givens writes, such sharing of materials has historically been important among Black educators looking to subvert a white supremacist curriculum.[49] In the SEEK program, it was also a time-saving measure for overworked professors. Though better compensated than today's instructors, SEEK professors still performed extensive labor to support their students. In addition to their classroom teaching, they provided detailed feedback on students' writing; coordinated with counselors; wrote midsemester reports on each student; met them outside of the classroom (and reviewed their work beforehand); answered "phone calls at home" from absent students; constructed and evaluated makeup assignments, all trickling in at different intervals; and continued to mentor those who ran "into writing problems" in advanced courses.[50] They also spent hours searching for relevant readings and revising their syllabi, lesson plans, and assignments. Exchanging materials meant they didn't have to reinvent the wheel but could build on each other's research into what worked and what didn't.

Among the successful assignments they traded were writing prompts that tapped into the era's critiques of education and asked students to analyze their schools. Rich, for instance, asked them to read George Orwell's essay "Such, Such Were theJoys," a satirical critique of his boyhood boarding school, and compare Orwell's depiction of Crossgates with City College. Suggested grounds for comparison included the "purpose of each institution... the physical environment... meaningfulness of education given... how institution reflects the society outside."⁵¹ They were also instructed to draw on their observations, experiences, and "what you feel" in formulating their analysis. Rich's archives contain questions about educational power and authority that they likely took up while working on such assignments. Strung through a document titled "Student Passes—Education Fails," they read, "Who decides what you are allowed to learn?... What determines the courses you take each semester?... Where is the power that controls your life here?... What does quality education mean? What is a university?... What are your expectations here and what do you have a right to expect?... And who makes the decisions that are even now shaping your future life?"⁵² Through these questions and writing prompts, students analyzed the institutions in which their lives were unfolding.

Rich also challenged students to imagine how a better education might look. Like Bambara's assignment to design a syllabus for their dream course, one of Rich's writing prompts states:

> Write a description of a course you would like to take some day—on any subject, or covering any kind of material. Talk about how you feel this material could best be taught, and what you would hope to be doing in the course... how you'd like [it]... to be run, under what conditions you would most enjoy and profit from it... why this particular course would seem valuable to you, and what you hope to gain from it for your life.⁵³

For students who had come through stultifying and repressive schools, this prompt instead centered their intellectual interests and curiosity. It carved out time and space for them to give texture, language, and form to the education they desire. Such acts of poiesis can help sharpen our critique of the present, allowing us to measure the distance between what we want and what we have and to challenge the forces that stand between the two. And who knows what concrete changes might emerge from such imaginative assignments? Students might be inspired to continue their studies or demand changes to City College. Though SEEK instructors may have been hired to fulfill the assimilationist aims of basic writing, these assignments illustrate how they instead encouraged students to think, feel, imagine, and desire beyond the status quo.

❋ ❋ ❋

One day, as Rich perused the City College bookstore, she was drawn to a slim book with a marigold cover and an alluring black design, full of angles and arches, evoking both a hookah pipe and the sensuous curves of a female figure. The title, in Gothic lettering, was *The First Cities*, its author an unfamiliar poet named Audre Lorde. Rich was captivated by Lorde's quietly devastating poems—poems that mourn murdered children, convey the mysteries of motherhood, and dwell in the long shadows fathers cast over daughters. Like many of Rich's poems, Lorde's were intimate, deceptively simple, and steeped in an awareness that women know the world differently. And Rich was thrilled to learn that their author was teaching a mere stone's throw away. "On the South Campus of CCNY [City College of New York]," she recalls, the two "began a conversation that was to go on for twenty years."[54] Their friendship would evolve to include joint readings and panel appearances at conferences such as the Modern Language Association (MLA) and National Women's Studies Association (NWSA), providing feedback on each other's writing, and extensive correspondence and published interviews.[55] "We were hard on each other, we listened to each other, but we didn't always take each other's advice," Rich recounts in the documentary *A Litany for Survival* as a loving, conspiratorial smile spreads across her face.[56]

City College also introduced Rich to June Jordan, with whom she formed an equally intense, though less frequently discussed, friendship. The two "bonded fast, and regularly frequented their favorite Indian restaurant on the Upper West Side to talk poetry, teaching, politics, [and] motherhood."[57] While Rich and Lorde's relationship left a more robust public record, archival documents reveal a joyful, symbiotic, and occasionally romantic friendship between Rich and Jordan. Among other things, they were regularly asked to review each other's work. Jordan praised Rich's poems of "severe force, beauty, and confrontation," writing that they capture "the grief driving all of us crazy" and hold up a mirror to society's devaluation of sexuality.[58] Rich, in turn, praised how Jordan's poems in *New Days* "bite like the teeth of a saw" and register the moving journey of "woman, black, totally vulnerable—into the historic force-field of violence."[59] And their interactions extended beyond the sound bites of book jackets to include phone calls, letters, and later faxes. As Hilary Holladay writes, the two shared a fascination with "power in all its dimensions, twinned with the pursuit of meaningful relationships."[60]

Like Lorde and Jordan, Rich became involved in educational activism at City College, including advocating for greater resources for SEEK students. To take one example, when administrators wanted to increase the number of classes SEEK instructors taught, she wrote a fervent memo explaining how that decision would harm students by reducing the amount of personal attention each received. She was also an outspoken advocate of open admissions. In fact, her husband, Alfred Conrad, a distinguished professor of economics, helped generate the data that the students used to formulate their demand for "a student body that was 43 percent Black," and he regularly appeared on television news to drum up support for open admissions.[61] The two also attended rallies, though Rich's arthritis sometimes kept her home, eagerly awaiting detailed reports from Conrad and their students.

Rich's educational activism also involved using what poet David Henderson describes as her "enormous influence with the white faculty" to challenge their racist and elitist attitudes towards students.[62] In 1970, when CUNY opened its doors to the city, the students who arrived were working class, women, and people of color with a wide range of skills, backgrounds, and levels of academic preparedness. But not all faculty were excited about these "new students." In the sensationalist editorial "Surviving the Apocalypse: Teaching at City College" (1972), professor Leonard Kriegel describes them in dehumanizing terms as "untrained monkeys" and "lions caged in a zoo," and the campus as a "circus ring" and "human beehive." In a statement delivered at a CCNY faculty meeting, Rich chastised her colleagues, as Jordan also had, for viewing the "admission of a larger non-white population" as "a serious threat to the educational standards, the academic excellence, of the College."[63] She writes:

> In admitting ghetto students we are not admitting simply a collection of social and educational problems.... We are admitting a wealth of intelligence, toughmindedness, and motivation ... [students who] have a concern for justice, truth and freedom which many of our better prepared students unfortunately do not.... Let's not sell our ghetto students short by imagining that they have everything to gain from the College, and little to give.[64]

Rather than obsessing over the skills these new students ostensibly lacked, she and the other teacher-poets valued the different knowledges and skills that they brought with them to the classroom.

With the advent of open admissions, writes historian James Traub, "history professors were tearing one another to shreds, and English professors were seeing the end of the world around every corner."[65] However, the basic writing program, where Rich and the other teacher-poets taught, was the "one corner of City College... alive with a sense of possibility."[66] While other faculty whined that these new students were not the ones they wanted, these writers and their coconspirators developed teaching methods that would be effective and inspiring for the particular individuals sitting in front of them.[67]

One of the major ways they supported these diverse learners was by making writing less intimidating. They developed, for instance, structured assignment sequences that broke large writing tasks into smaller, more manageable components. In Rich's ENG 1-G 11 (1971) course, the task "write a story" was divided into a series of five exercises that students completed over the span of several weeks. Though writing a story might seem like a simple, straightforward task, it could prove daunting for students who had been taught that they weren't good at writing, whose papers had been handed back with their words buried beneath an instructor's corrections. The sequence began with "Assignment One: Description of Place," then proceeded to "Assignment Two: Description of a Person" and "Assignment Three: Narrative Dialogue."[68] These culminated in "Assignment Five: Writing a Story," which incorporated the different skills they had practiced. Each of the five assignments also included explicit step-by-step instructions. "Assignment One: Description of Place" states:

STEP ONE: Choose a place that you remember well or one that you can observe directly—a room, a street, a subway stop, a store, a place on the campus, etc.

STEP TWO: Try to set down in a few words the major impression or mood the place creates in you. It might be cozy and familiar, or depressing, or sinister and creepy, or suggestive of things—good or bad—that have happened there. . . .

STEP THREE: Write down all the details you have observed about the place—colors, sounds, smells, etc.[69]

In class, they discussed students' progress, difficulties they encountered, and questions that arose. They also received feedback from Rich, which they used to revise their drafts.

These assignments foreground the "structure" at the heart of "instruction." For Rich, as a novice poet, the constraints imposed by structural forms like the sonnet had functioned as "asbestos gloves," allowing her to work through difficult experiences, emotions, and ideas that felt too dangerous to touch directly.[70] Her sequences and instructions provided similar support, which today we would call *scaffolding*.[71] Five years before the term was officially introduced into education science, Rich was, in her words, developing "well thought out lessons which have some logical sequence."[72] Like the "how to write poetry" handouts that Jordan used at Berkeley, these clear steps leveled the playing field, ensuring that all students, regardless of prior training or talent, could successfully complete each assignment. While educators informed by critical pedagogy might view such approaches as heavy-handed or overly prescriptive, the work of these teacher-poets highlights how structure is not inherently antithetical to creativity. If liberatory pedagogy conjures anarchic images of a leaderless classroom, they remind us that structure, too, can be empowering. In fact, we might think of these instructions, sequences, and pathways as a form of radical scaffolding.

Rich and her colleagues also made writing more accessible by teaching it as a process composed of multiple, discrete activities that get collapsed under the umbrella term *writing*. As practitioners of what would, in the next two decades, come to be known as "process" pedagogy, they guided students through each stage of the writing process: brainstorming, outlining, drafting, revising, and proofreading.[73] For example, Rich, Christian, Bambara, Henderson, Shaughnessy, and Lorde all assigned what Peter Elbow calls "low-stakes," or informal, ungraded assignments like journals in which students could brainstorm ideas they might later build on in their essays.[74] Rich's version instructed them to "write at least half a page daily" in their journals about the "ways in which the reading and discussion intersect with your own life and thinking."[75] The journals were "handed in every few weeks," read by Rich, "and returned ungraded but with comments."[76] This alleviated anxieties about grammatical correctness, allowing students to express ideas without fear of red ink encircling their mistakes.[77] And what Rich found was that "many students first show the writing they are actually capable of in an uncorrected journal rather than in a 'theme' written 'for class.'"[78]

What emerges from these classrooms are teaching methods designed to engage and inspire a wide range of students, not just those with exceptional academic training or a preexisting interest in the subject. Together, these scaffolded, process-based approaches along with Jordan's and Bambara's collaborative, multimodal, public, and project-based methods illustrate the access-oriented pedagogies of the open admissions era. Though such practices are likely well known to K–12 educators, community college professors, and those at teaching-focused institutions, they may be less visible from atop an ivory tower, where many students have had access to advanced academic preparation.

During her time at City College (1968–74), Rich began to think more deeply about the political implications of different teaching methods: the implicit ideas about power, obedience, and agency that students learn in the classroom. As was common among SEEK instructors, she sat in on courses in different disciplines to observe students' reactions to different instruction methods. From this, she realized that even "the most thoughtfully prepared, witty, or provocative lecture" precluded "active participation... critical thinking... dissent or even the asking of questions." Instead, lectures induced "boredom" and "detachment" among students, many of whom had long been tracked, through the educational institutions of a racist society, away from lives of inquiry.[79] She writes:

> Although the lecture as art form and social event may still have a place in the university, the first needs of our freshmen are for something else—for a kind of classroom in which students find themselves having to learn for themselves, and to teach each other more than they have ever been asked to do. The value of this is not merely to "increase participation" but to break, once and for all, the modes and patterns which 12 years of public or parochial education have left as their legacy.[80]

Though Rich may not have gone as far as Bambara in turning her courses over to students, she did experiment with giving them greater control, such as voting on how their writing would be evaluated (they chose to receive "critical comments" instead of grades).[81] She also reimagined remedial English as a "long-term project," ideally extending over three semesters, in which students would help define, design, and evaluate the work of the course, with an emphasis on group work and peer learning.[82] The goal would be to produce the kind of collaborative public projects we witnessed in Jordan's and Bambara's classrooms: "a proposal, a study, a set of interviews or a newspaper."[83] Yet some dreams, like this one, never came to fruition. It's not always clear what institutional obstacles—or maybe just life—got in the way. In the years to come, as her involvement in the women's movement intensified, Rich would become increasingly committed to the kinds of student-centered teaching that she envisioned at City College.

As Rich was guiding students in gaining greater control of their learning, she was also helping her sons to do the same. In 1970, having witnessed how school left them feeling "disenchanted" and "disaffected," she allowed them to withdraw and enroll, instead, in a school that did not yet exist, where the first lesson was how to squat in an abandoned laundromat and the second how to fix a toilet. At the Elizabeth Cleaners Street School, located on the Upper West Side, attendance was optional, decisions were collectively made by students and parents, and courses ranged from surrealism, "Marx and Lenin," and community law to photography, comparative religion, and Cuba.[84] The tensions of that school speak to the broader issues that plagued the alternative school movement. As the parents learned through their failed efforts to recruit students of color, absconding from official institutions can sometimes be too risky for families without the economic security net afforded by white privilege. Such experiences showed Rich that while "we need alternate education... we also need to reach those students for whom unorthodox education simply means too much risk."[85] For years to come, she would continue teaching in colleges that did just that.

✳ ✳ ✳

While Rich was hired to teach remedial writing, she came to think of her experiences at City College as "the remediation of our own education."[86] There, she and her colleagues engaged in "a constant, active effort... to educate ourselves to meet the needs of the new college population."[87] In preparation to teach her SEEK courses, Rich read widely: from the educational philosophies of Paulo Freire and books like Ellen Lurie's *How to Change the Schools* to linguistics and the works of Black and Latinx literature and history that had been absent from her education. For example, in order to help students understand the historical context of *Narrative of the Life of Frederick Douglass*, she read extensively about slavery. Cautious not to assign too much homework, she instead created a lecture containing definitions of key terms like *plantation* and a brief history of the Atlantic slave trade focusing on such topics as "indenture... difference between this type of servitude and chattel slavery of later centuries... first legal distinction between white & Black servants made in 1660's in Maryland & Virginia... laws defining slave as property," and details regarding Douglass's own conditions of enslavement.[88]

This simple fact, that Rich began studying Black literature and history in order to teach it, had a dramatic impact on her writing and politics. Though she had been active in civil rights efforts prior to her arrival at City College, this immersion in Black literature deepened her understanding of "the bitter reality of Western racism" and established the basis for her antiracist feminism.[89] Sometimes the lessons of these classrooms appear in poetic lines like "Frederick Douglass wrote an English purer than Milton's."[90] Other times, they influenced the formal aspects of her work. Rich cites Amiri Baraka's break with "anglicized formalism" in *The Dead Lecturer* (which she read for teaching) as the inspiration for her own departure from conventional poetic forms in collections like *The Will to Change* (1971).[91] In addition, writes Holladay, Rich's engagement with the autobiographical works of Douglass, Malcolm X, and James Baldwin inspired her to incorporate autobiographical excerpts in her own writing.[92] While she has since been recognized for such feminist writing methods, it was these Black male authors, whom she read in preparation for teaching, who showed her how to make the personal political.

Though Rich's professorial career began at elite institutions, it was at City College that she started writing about education. Initially, this took the form of poems about teaching, though they haven't always been recognized as such.[93] "The Burning of Paper Instead of Children" (1968), for instance, has been praised for weaving together dissent against the Vietnam War and questions of female desire and sexuality.[94] While scholars occasionally mention that it was written while Rich was teaching in SEEK, it can actually be read as a commentary on that program, as well as the era's debates over Black English.

The five-section poem opens with two burnings: the Catonsville Nine igniting their draft notices and a phone call from the speaker's neighbor, angry that their sons have burned a math textbook in the backyard. Its five numbered sections then proceed from the speaker's home through a library, a lovers' bedroom, a sylvan temple, and back to the speaker's office, where they're composing the poem late at night on their typewriter.

"Burning" is one of Rich's first poems to include prose, the form of writing she taught at City College. In the third section, halfway through the poem, we are taken into one such classroom:

> 3. "People suffer highly in poverty and it takes dignity and intelligence to overcome this suffering. Some of the suffering are: a child did not had dinner last night: a child steal because he did not have money to buy it: to hear a mother say she do not have money to buy food for her children and to see a child without cloth it will make tears in your eyes."
>
> (the fracture of order
> the repair of speech
> to overcome this suffering)[95]

Archival materials reveal that the quoted text was written by a City College student. But even without that information, readers like David Montenegro recognized that the poem "includes a passage in so-called poor grammar, Black English," a topic of fierce debate during this era.[96] The parenthetical reflection that follows the quoted material asks us to focus not on the images of a hungry child but on how the writer deviates from Standard English. Yet there are other mechanical idiosyncrasies throughout the poem beyond the quoted material: *It* is capitalized following a comma, colons are used to curious effect, and periods are absent. Why, the poem invites us to ask, are these interpreted as interesting poetic choices, worthy of debate and interpretation, and not mistakes in need of repair? Why do we praise in the lines of Adrienne Rich what we jump to correct in these anonymously quoted lines? Years later, Rich wrote that the poem explored the distance between students who were "expected to fail" and instructors with the privilege "to speak so people will listen."[97]

Written just a few weeks into her first semester at City College, "Burning" explores some of the questions that would come to define that experience. On the one hand, the poem speaks to the era's debates over Black English. As writing instructors, Rich and her colleagues were tasked with teaching students from different racial and ethnic backgrounds to write in Standard English, though many recognized that such standards for acceptable language and grammar use reflected the ways English was spoken among upper-middle-class white people. By incorporating this student's words into her poem, Rich foregrounds her own potential complicity in the eradication of students' home languages. By teaching students from linguistically diverse backgrounds to compose in Standard English, was she equipping them with language that would help them achieve socioeconomic mobility or denying the validity of the words they grew up with? Was she challenging the status quo or reinforcing it? Four years later, she would revisit these questions in her essay "Teaching Language in Open Admissions" (1972). There, she recalls that at the same time that they were trying to figure out, "How do you make standard English verb endings available to a dialect speaker?" they were also questioning the ethics of such practices: "Is standard English simply a weapon of colonization?"[98] Considering "Burning" alongside her later essay illustrates how poetry created space to meditate on her uncertainty, doubt, and misgivings, eventually leading to a nuanced, lyrical, and decidedly unromanticized narrative that foregrounds the ethical murkiness of "teaching language in open admissions."

"Burning" is a classroom lyric, one of the genres of open admissions explored by Rich and Lorde. Though both authors worked tirelessly to produce transformative courses and advocated for SEEK students, poetry created space to ask deeper questions about their work. In contrast to some of Rich's more impassioned rhetoric describing the urgency of remedial education, the poem is ambiguous about the efficacy of teaching to address entrenched conditions of injustice. Can "the repair of speech" help "to overcome" the "suffering" of poverty? Or is this simply a naive liberal fantasy? Lyric poetry, and the exploration of individual, subjective experience it affords, thus allowed Rich and Lorde to examine ideas and feelings that didn't fit neatly into—and were sometimes at odds with—the public narratives they embraced. While campus essays demanded greater resources for minoritized knowledge and students, and anthologies publicly affirmed students' voices and visions, classroom lyrics convey greater skepticism about the politics of learning in a society structured by pervasive injustice and inequality.

This ambivalence is also evident in a poetic fragment in Rich's archive:

Classroom as cell—unit—enclosed & enclosing space in which teacher & students are alone together

> Can be prison cell   commune
> trap   junction—place of coming-together
> torture chamber[99]

This small poem imagines the classroom as a microcosm of society. In the left-hand column, images of a "prison cell" and "torture chamber" emphasize how such spaces can reproduce the privatized, individualized, carceral logic of society. Similar images appear in Lorde's poem "Teacher" (1973). There, in the ring of the recess bell, signaling for students to come inside, they instead hear

> freedom's bell deaden
> in the clang of the gates of the prisons.[100]

Though these poems were written before the rise of the prison-industrial complex and the school-to-prison pipeline, Rich and Lorde saw in their students (and Lorde, through firsthand experience) the ways that schools were already effectively functioning as prisons: institutions designed and governed by white people that confine, "trap," and "torture" students, especially working-class students of color. Yet the images along the right in Rich's poem suggest that the classroom can also become a site of prefigurative politics, where we can enact the better world we desire. More specifically, they depict the classroom as a "commune...junction—place of coming-together" where decisions are made collectively, labor and resources are distributed equitably, and participants work toward common goals. There, these images suggest, we can explore foundational questions about how, as a society, we can best be "alone together" and organize social life. These dual and dueling images thus capture the seemingly contradictory realities of classrooms: how they are sites of social reproduction that can be transformed into sites of alternative worldmaking. And the poem refuses to state, definitively, which of these the classroom is. Instead, it oscillates between these two poles, back and forth like an electron, suggesting how neither state is permanent—how, with every decision, we can choose to make our classrooms one or the other.

Rich was the first to admit that City College catalyzed "a profound change in [her] conception of teaching and learning."[101] On first arriving, she had hoped to discover an unlikely Shakespeare buried among mediocre students, whose gifts she could help cultivate. But immersed in the SEEK community, she came to see "compensatory" (or "remedial") education as part of a broader "movement for social change," the goal of which was to "break down false barriers of class & color to make all education truly open to all people who want it."[102] There, she realized that the "veins of possibility" run through all students and that the political potential of teaching lies not necessarily in mentoring a select handful of highly skilled individuals but in developing teaching strategies that would benefit all, regardless of their previous academic training, ability, or interest.

I want to suggest, however, that these classrooms played an even greater role in Rich's shifting political vision than she recognized. In addition to altering her understanding of the politics of teaching, they helped her unlearn the liberal individualism that had shaped her early thinking about feminism. One place we see this is her poetry. Rich's earliest feminist poems were what Marianne Whelchel calls "individual portraits" of female achievement: they celebrated "strong women" like Emily Dickinson, Russian poet Natalya Gorbanevskaya, and astronomer Caroline Herschel who "achieved, but often in isolation and at the cost of misinterpretation and actual physical threat."[103] But as she learned to see the "veins of possibility" that course through all students, her poetry also shifted focus to the experiences of unnamed women "who have simply carried on the ordinary, day-to-day activities necessary to sustain life."[104]

In fact, throughout her time at City College, Rich's feminism came to focus less on individualism and more on the material conditions and institutional structures obscured by liberal ideologies. Her essay "Teaching Language in Open Admissions" demonstrates the role that the college played in this transformation. The essay reflects on her move from Columbia to City College, two geographically proximate but disparately funded schools. She describes how, though physically separated by only fifteen blocks, the two felt like different worlds. But what distinguished them was not so much students' abilities or intelligence but the physical conditions of each campus. At Columbia, every last detail—"gray stone dormitories, marbled steps, flowered borders"– was designed to give students "wide spaces of time and architecture in which to talk and think."[105] At City College, by contrast, students had to navigate an "overcrowded campus... [with] no place to sit between classes... two inadequate bookstores... two cafeterias and a snack bar that are overpriced, dreary, and unconducive to lingering... the incessant pressure of time and money driving at them to rush, to get through, to amass the needed credits somehow, to drop out, to stay on with gritted teeth."[106] For the many open admissions students who were neither wealthy nor white, City College was just one underfunded, inadequate school in a long line of many. Unlike that of their Columbia counterparts, their education had long been characterized by schools that "reward conformity, passivity, and correct answers... obsolete texts"; ugly, decaying "buildings"; and "the demoralization even of good teachers working under such conditions."[107] In the years to come, these analyses of physical educational institutions would develop into critiques of the institutional forces underlying more abstract concepts. In books like *Of Woman Born: Motherhood as Experience and Institution* and essays like "Compulsory Heterosexuality and Lesbian Existence," Rich illustrated how seemingly natural phenomena like motherhood and heterosexuality are, in fact, patriarchal institutions that incentivize and reward certain behaviors while punishing others. And from these materialist critiques would emerge her politics—and pedagogy—of location.

The Women's Movement and the Classroom

In the early 1970s, the women's movement began to change how Rich, and many other women, thought about education. Growing up, she had seen universities as "the dwelling place of permanent values... of beauty, of righteousness, of freedom" and "enduring, universal" education, "civilizing to the mind and sensitizing to the spirit."[108] However, the women's movement highlighted how universities were not "a breeding ground of humanism, but of masculine privilege"—privilege that she and her students began interrogating in the classroom.[109]

In 1973 Rich returned to City College after a yearlong position at Brandeis University. The recently promoted full professor brought with her a new course she had designed titled Images of Women in Poetry by Men.[110] Likely inspired by Susan Koppelman Cornillon's anthology *Images of Women in Fiction* (1972), the course explored many of the principles now associated with images-of-women criticism. Students read canonical white, male writers like John Keats, Walt Whitman, and W. B. Yeats alongside critiques of patriarchy by Simone de Beauvoir, Mary Daly, and excerpts from Bambara's *The Black Woman* to analyze how male poets depicted women as "myth, persona, image, muse, and metaphor."[111] The syllabus demonstrates how Rich tested out her shifting politics in the classroom. On the one hand, it announces a focus on not only language and literature but the material conditions in which they circulate. A section titled "Assumptions behind course" states, "In a patriarchal society—all institutions, economic, social, religious, educational, are dominated by men . . . I see no excuse for studying literature in a way which does not come to grips with this fact."[112] In addition, in a moment when she was immersed in debates over lesbian separatism and the role of men in dismantling patriarchy, she added a note on the "bias I come with": "I identify with women, but I am interested in teaching men who want to explore thru poetry what the patriarchal system in which they collaborate is doing to them. I can communicate with men who want to think, struggle and change, but my primary loyalty is to women."[113] Reading these words today, it's difficult not to wonder if someone with less cultural capital—like one of her Black female colleagues—could have similarly expressed a preference for some students over others without facing repercussions. Such examples suggest how white privilege may have afforded Rich greater liberty to experiment in the classroom.

That same year, Florence Howe solicited an essay from Rich for an edited collection on academia and the women's movement. Though Rich could have chosen any format for her contribution, what came to mind was Bambara's essay "Realizing the Dream of a Black University" (1969), "which appeared in the student newspaper" four years earlier and "was a complete proposal for a truly community-grounded college."[114] In that essay Bambara both critiqued the white supremacy of universities and outlined changes that could support the flourishing of Black communities. Four years later, Rich adapted Bambara's essay into her own feminist treatise: "Towards a Woman-Centered University" (1973).

While one might object that women-centered universities already existed in women's colleges, Rich, a Radcliffe graduate, knew the two were not synonymous. At worst, a women's college could be little more than a finishing school to make women more eligible for marriage. At best, it introduced them to a traditional curriculum dominated by men. In fact, by 1973 Rich saw Radcliffe's promise of "equal chances [and] equal opportunities" comparable to Harvard as "an illusion and a lie. . . . Harvard is an intensely patriarchal institution, in every way."[115] This is a radically different view of universities for someone who once proclaimed, "Remove Harvard, and you'd have no Adrienne Rich."[116]

Following Bambara's example, Rich's essay offers a blueprint for a better university. Instead of supporting research in the service of "Sputnik, [the] Cold War ... [and] the Air Force," a woman-centered university would "organize its resources around problems specific to its community: ... adult literacy, public health; safer, cheaper, and simpler birth control; drug addiction; community action; geriatrics and the sociology and psychology of aging and death; the history and problems of women and those of people in non-white, non-middle-class cultures."[117] Its curriculum would help women "know our foremothers, evaluate our present historical, political, and personal situation, and take ourselves seriously as agents in the creation of a more balanced culture."[118] Echoing Bambara's call for courses taught by local Harlem activists and community members, Rich's university would center "nonacademic women ... the grandmothers, the high-school dropouts, the professionals, the artists, the political women, the housewives. And it would involve them at an organic level, not as interesting exhibits of specimens."[119] Considered together, Rich's and Bambara's essays illustrate how, at the same time that these writers were asking students to imagine their dream courses, they were also envisioning their own ideal universities. Their essays also remind us that, as V. P. Franklin and Marilyn Jacoby Boxer have written, Black liberation movements helped lay the foundations for women's studies and feminist pedagogy.[120]

"Towards a Woman-Centered University" is, like the text it was modeled on, a campus essay. Like the campus essays written by Bambara and Jordan, Rich's ties questions of academic content to the material conditions of educational access. In contrast to elite women's colleges like Radcliffe and Barnard—"the familiar city-on-a-hill frowning down on its neighbors"— Rich posits that any truly "woman-centered university" would need to be "non-elitist" and access oriented.[121] It would thus more closely resemble an open admissions university, committed to "serv[ing] the needs of the human, visible community in which it sits."[122] In addition, just as the SEEK program addressed the material externalities associated with education, through things like book and travel stipends, Rich's university would include a health center and free child care so that working-class women and mothers could pursue their studies.

Following the publication of their essays (and perhaps even emboldened by them), both Bambara and Rich made potentially risky but politically significant career moves. In 1969 Bambara left City College to participate in the formation of Rutgers University's new experimental Livingston College. Six years later, in 1975, Rich made a parallel move. That year, she left City College, where she had taught on and off for the past five years, to teach at Douglass College for women, also part of Rutgers. In her letter of resignation, Rich admits to having "far more than institutional feelings about City College."[123] She described it as "an extraordinary and intense teaching and learning environment" and would later call it "the most exciting teaching I've ever done."[124] Through SEEK and open admissions, she watched students gain the "kind of critical perspective on their lives and the skill to bear witness that they have never before had in our country's history."[125] But over time, she saw "the original concept of SEEK diluted, then violently attacked and betrayed."[126] Class sizes grew, teaching loads increased, and many of the most dedicated faculty were fired.[127] Rich explained her decision to leave as "a statement of my desire to commit myself... to teaching women."[128] She believed her writing would be "nourished by the Douglass environment... just as... the early years of SEEK teaching were enormously important to me as a writer."[129]

Though a women's college like Barnard would have been closer to her uptown apartment, Rich was drawn to the fact that Rutgers was a public university that served less affluent students. In 1975, when she began her job as a professor of English, Douglass was experiencing a feminist overhaul catalyzed by the women's movement. Several years prior to her arrival, Elaine Showalter and Mary Howard had produced a report on how Douglass could become "a feminist model of higher education," which closely paralleled Rich's vision of a "woman-centered university."[130] The college had recently created one of the nation's first women's studies programs, a women's studies institute, and a women's center that served both Douglass students and women in the local community. Immersed in this women-centered environment, the critiques of the patriarchal canon evident in Rich's earlier courses gave way to courses on women's literature and feminist approaches to writing.

On Douglass's suburban campus, in classes filled almost entirely with women, Rich encountered "stunning parallels" to what she had experienced "in teaching the so-called disadvantaged students at City [College]."[131] One such parallel was the fear and uncertainty that seemed as present in her Douglass course American Women Poets (1976) as it had been in her basic writing classes. Whereas another instructor might have interpreted students' quietude as a sign of apathy or inability, SEEK had taught Rich that silence is not synonymous with absence—that, more likely, it is indicative of students' past educational experiences or their relationship to the institution. "Freshmen," she writes, "really aren't sure of college expectations" and "are likely to be scared and therefore withdrawn."[132] This was doubly true when poetry was the subject of their studies. Many students believe that poetry is difficult, inscrutable, layered with hidden meanings that only the brightest can detect (this, despite the song lyrics that they can recite verbatim and that constitute the soundtrack to their lives). To help them overcome this fear, Rich adapted the step-by-step instructions that she had used to make writing more accessible at City College. Rather than simply telling them to go home and read the assigned poems, she provided explicit directions that they could follow. She writes:

> Read the poems in several sittings; read both silently and aloud a number of times. Read to a friend, lover, member of your family, and talk about the poems. Look up in a dictionary every word of whose meaning you are not absolutely sure. Pay attention to punctuation and typography.... Listen for sounds—not just rhymes, but echoes within a line or stanza, repeated consonants, rhythms. Use a pencil and mark lines that especially move or disturb you; mark lines or phrases or images which you find puzzling... or obscure. But, at the beginning, don't anxiously search for "meaning"; let the images enter your imagination, the sounds resonate in you, allow yourself to react to them at a sensuous, emotional level. Then begin to ask yourself, *why* do these combinations of words affect me as they do?[133]

Such instructions ensured that all students could analyze poetry, not just those who excelled in prior English classes or had effective teachers. They are less a dictatorial statement that "this is the only way to read a poem" and more of an invitation to try one particular method.

Rich's teaching also drew on the critiques of power emerging from the women's movement. In the early 1970s, as women took to the streets to protest oppressive policies that kept men in positions of power, feminist educators were concerned with the ways that classrooms reproduced these conditions by placing teachers in authority positions over students. Just as SEEK educators had earlier questioned whether lectures and exams were stultifying students, scholars in the new field of women's studies interrogated whether, or to what extent, such methods were the products of patriarchal education, and the ways conventional classrooms encouraged obedience and conformity rather than nurturing student decision-making.[134] For Rich, these discussions reaffirmed the importance of the student-centered teaching she had been introduced to at City College. She wrote that "the underlying mode of the feminist teaching style is ... by nature antihierarchical."[135]

Rich's experiments with "antihierarchical teaching" are evident in the final project for American Women Poets. Instead of a paper, this large, lower-level course (where Rich was aided by a teaching assistant named Lynn Hanley) concluded with a research project that challenged students to edit an anthology of women's poetry "around a specific theme ... relevant to your own life."[136] Their anthologies were to include "15 poems by various women" on a theme such as "political protest, heterosexual relationships, work, anger, death, childhood, the mother and daughter relationship, lesbian poetry, the female body, war, food and eating" and a "critical introduction of at least 8 pages which connect[ed] the poems to the overall theme" and analyzed the similarities and differences among them.[137] According to composition scholar Christopher Leary, anthology assignments like this encourage students to identify patterns among texts, analyze how writing can function differently in distinct contexts, and consider audience reception.[138] And while Rich may not have gone so far as the other teacher-poets in publishing anthologies of student writing, editing a collection centered their ideas in other ways. By writing a critical introduction, students identified how poems offer unique insights into philosophical questions, current events, relationships, and politics—whatever topics they were interested in. This also reinforced the notion that students didn't need a syllabus compiled by an award-winning poet to determine which poems were valuable; they were capable of deciding literary merit on their own terms. As the deadline approached, students brought in one poem from their anthology to share with the class and discussed their work on the assignment, thus allowing them to learn from one another. In recent years, such assignments have become more common and evolved into new forms, such as the curation of online exhibits of artifacts. Rich's work illustrates how such archiving, editing, and curation assignments have a longer history, shaped by the social movements of the 1960s and 1970s.

A similar centering of students' ideas is evident in Rich's advanced creative writing seminar Writing out of Female Experience. On the first day of class, it was snowing, and Rich's arthritis was likely throbbing. She arrived dressed in black, "brushing her gamin-like hair out of her eyes with one hand, carrying a briefcase in the other."[139] Rich was unfazed by the student who brought her toddler to class amid a snowstorm that had shuttered her daycare. With a clear concern for students' minds and bodies, she "brought nutritious snacks for students who might not have had time to eat before the lengthy seminar."[140]

Each week, the course began with students either discussing their reactions to the assigned readings or sharing something they had written. In either case, Rich was never the first to speak. Aware that her fame could dissuade the class from expressing ideas that might contrast with her own, she stayed silent. Only at the end would she deliver a brief lecture to "tie up the strands" and connect their conversation to course concepts.[141]

That semester, Rich and her students practiced listening to, and reading for, what patriarchy suppresses. She describes this as "listening and watching in art and literature, in the social sciences, in all the descriptions we are given of the world, for the silences, the absences, the nameless, the unspoken, the encoded—for there we will find the true knowledge of women."[142] She also developed writing prompts that would allow students to address these gaps by drawing lessons from their experiences. For example, she adapted an earlier assignment (borrowed from Bambara) to convey an insight obtained through a body part. Whereas at City College she had asked students to write about their hair, eyes, or hands, she asked Douglass students to write about their breasts. The prompt reads:

> Study your breasts. (Either in the mirror or as you see them when you undress.) Think how you have felt about and perceived them during your life, how they are related to your sense of yourself, to the rest of your body... try to perceive the relationships between your hands/breast/body and the "you" that has been and will be writing, acting, thinking in the world. (1 typewritten page)[143]

In order to complete this assignment, thirty-eight-year-old student Joyce Greenberg wrote that she "studied my now-wrinkled breasts in my bedroom mirror and thought about how I had perceived them as inadequate all my life except during the blissful times I was pregnant or nursing."[144] That night, Greenberg wrote a poem based on her literal and figurative reflection. But after completing what felt like a decent draft, something gave her pause. Throughout the semester, Rich kept insisting that "there are places you have yet to reach into and sources you aren't yet touching." She wanted Greenberg "to include all the complexities, the imperfections, the confusions," not sweep them away to sustain an illusion of tidiness.[145] With this feedback in mind, Greenberg "wrote on a piece of scrap paper in ink, 'What is it I'm not writing about?' And in pencil underneath, I replied, 'My grandmother's bathing suit, my mother's yellow toes... [their] varicose veins.'"[146] In doing so, she confronted what patriarchy dismisses: the fear, fascination, and mystery surrounding aging women's bodies. And by asking students to write about their schools, or their breasts, or what they knew as mothers, Rich taught them that their experiences could be sources of wisdom, however "unofficial, unpaid for, [and] unvalued by society."[147]

Archival documents indicate just how much students learned from Rich, though what they learned wasn't always what she intended to teach. In one thank-you note, a student describes how Rich's course "helped us learn to heal the separations in our own lives," including "between ourselves and writings."[148] She recalls that "no matter how hard & tough she might be on us," Rich "always conveyed tenderness, sincerity, and strength." This particular student went on to establish a magazine for women's writing and start a women's writing group that focused on integrating writing and life. Another student admits that Rich sometimes made her "want to forget poetry and crawl into [her] lap to be mothered," a response that must have elicited mixed emotions from a writer who critiqued motherhood as a patriarchal institution.[149] Yet another described how Rich's courses catalyzed her "awakening into consciousness of being a woman."[150] Prior to these classes, she had felt "restless in an atmosphere where I was forced to take what is written in books for granted." She felt like she existed "within this closed realm of self-defeat...hopelessness...[and] loneliness." Rich's teaching, however, "awakened me out of the intensity of my introspection into a realization that my own struggles were insignificant compared to the vast suffering around me." She left the course determined to write "an archaeology of living women, the realities of whose lives go unnoticed, the intensity of whose experiences are continually hidden."[151]

At Douglass, Rich continued advocating for the downward redistribution of educational resources. In 1977, when asked if she wanted to help establish a creative writing MFA program at Rutgers, she instead offered a counterproposal, suggesting that an MA in *creative teaching* would be a more worthwhile investment. In a memo to her colleague, she describes how such a program could prepare educators to teach basic writing to students from different socioeconomic backgrounds. Rather than investing the school's limited resources in an exclusive MFA program that would provide advanced training to a handful of students, she advocated for a program that would draw out the "talent and expressiveness" that go "undeveloped" in the majority of the nation's students. In contrast to the ease with which one can teach those who are already strong writers, teaching "remedial writing makes constant demands on the imagination, requires rigorous training, and is finally a far more productive pursuit societally."[152] As such remarks suggest, teaching in open admissions catalyzed a lifelong concern with transformative learning for those disenfranchised by society.

※ ※ ※

As predicted, these classrooms inspired Rich's writing. During her four years at Douglass (1975–79), she wrote essays like "Claiming an Education" (1977) and "Taking Women Students Seriously" (1978), interrogating the patriarchal biases at every level of academia, from campus life to curriculum and teaching methods. And even in these essays about women's education, Rich's experiences at City College loom large. For it was there that she first witnessed the damage that schools can inflict on individuals. Seeing how their K–12 schools had discouraged, disempowered, and failed SEEK students helped her apprehend how they also "reward female passivity, indoctrinate girls and boys in stereotypic sex roles, and do not take the female mind seriously."[153] She wrote that as educators, "we can either teach passively, accepting these conditions, or actively, helping our students identify and resist them."[154]

In "Taking Women Students Seriously," first delivered as a talk for the New Jersey College and University Coalition on Women's Education, Rich identifies a series of questions that she first learned to ask at City College and then adapted for students at Douglass: questions about how past experiences affect one's attitude toward learning, how canonical literature comes across to the people whose experiences it has "excluded" and "depreciated," and how to help students understand education, not in terms of mere correctness, but as a search for truth.[155] On the one hand, these questions, and the "stunning parallels" she identified between City College and Douglass College students, allowed Rich to develop a range of empowering teaching methods. But the language of "parallels" also belies how a singular focus, on either gender or race, constrained her thinking about pedagogy at this moment. In the speech, Rich views City College students through the lens of race and class, and Douglass students through gender, thus overlooking the gendered experiences of SEEK students and the racial and class dimensions of Douglass students. Years later, and largely through her engagement with the work of Black women writers like her former colleagues, Rich would revise this vision in ways that accounted for the multiple, overlapping axes of difference.

In addition to inspiring essays on women's education, Rich's Douglass courses shaped some of her most influential writing on other topics like sexuality. In 1977, after publicly coming out as a lesbian, she began teaching a course called Woman to Woman Relationships in Literature. Such relationships, the description states, have tended to be treated "as rivalrous, destructive, or as secondary to romantic attachments to men." By contrast, the course would focus on "a spectrum of female relationships ... mothers and daughters; sister-siblings; female co-creators and fellow artists; fellow-victims; lesbianism as passionate love and as a primary loyalty to women; women in political comradeships."[156] The course included assignments such as a research project that asked students to analyze "a woman-to-woman relationship in your own family or one you know well."[157] In the months after she first taught this course, Rich wrote one of her most famous essays: "Compulsory Heterosexuality and Lesbian Existence" (1980).[158] Their course exploration of "lesbianism" as both "passionate love" and "a primary loyalty to women" anticipates what she would call, in that essay, the "lesbian continuum": a range of experiences among women "from the infant suckling her mother's breast, to the grown woman experiencing orgasmic sensations while suckling her own child ... to two women ... who share a laboratory."[159] The classroom thus allowed Rich to test hypotheses about relationships among women before formalizing them into her theory of the lesbian continuum. While it is almost certain that her conversations with Douglass students influenced the production of that groundbreaking text in other ways as well, archival absences leave us to wonder about the precise nature of those collaborations.

At Douglass, Rich remained close with the teacher-poets she first met at City College. As Black and "Third World" feminists critiqued the ways the mainstream women's movement centered the voices and concerns of upper- and middle-class white women over those of working-class women of color, Rich and Lorde maintained a public friendship that dramatized these tensions at an interpersonal scale. As Marion Rust writes, their friendship "honed their ability to recognize and articulate particular failures in second-wave feminism."[160] Through their conversations, Rich learned to identify what "is mine and not mine," what experiences of patriarchal oppression they shared and what was distinct, related to their class, race, and religion. Similarly, Lorde, who often wrote in her journal imagining herself in dialogue with Rich, asked her to "teach me what you know that I do not."[161]

But such learning across differences wasn't easy; it often involved misunderstandings, disagreements, and bruised feelings. In 1974 Rich pressured a reluctant Lorde into joining her and Alice Walker in jointly refusing the National Book Award. Without considering what such a prize might mean, personally and financially, to Lorde, or the repercussions a Black woman might face for such a flagrant rebuke of a literary institution, Rich coerced Lorde, who publicly smiled but privately fumed.[162] While this was seen as a heroic act of solidarity against the tokenism of the patriarchal literary establishment, it also signaled a potential rift in their still-blossoming friendship. Another notable incident occurred in Rich's 1981 interview with Lorde for the feminist publication *Signs*. Lorde was upset by Rich's request for explanations for her more abstract sentiments. "I felt a total wipeout of my modus, my way of perceiving and formulating," Lorde recalls.[163] But in Rich's eyes, "if I ask for documentation, it's because I take seriously the spaces between us that difference has created, that racism has created. . . . [H]elp me to perceive what you perceive."[164] The public nature of their friendship also made both writers uneasy. The fact that it unfolded in a space "beyond Audre/Adrienne" left them feeling "recklessly exposed," like theirs was an "intimacy rigged with terrors."[165]

But it was through this fear-laced friendship that Rich developed one of her signature rhetorical techniques, what Rust calls "additive emendation": a method of revising her writing "through prefaces, afterwords, footnotes, parenthetical remarks, and other forms of supplementation" that preserve rather than erase the shortcomings in her earlier thinking.[166] And it was this willingness to learn in public that Jordan most admired about Rich. In her unpublished "Sonnet for Adrienne Rich," Jordan depicts Rich as a poet who acted on her "will to change" and whose public accounts of this "changing helped us grow."[167] This esteem was mutual. Rich counted Jordan among her closest companions and literary interlocutors. As Kate Partridge writes, it was Jordan who inspired Rich's documentary-style poems, in which questions extend from the self rather than from historical documentation.[168]

By the 1970s, Jordan was convinced that she, Rich, and Lorde were "working on the same poem of a life of perpetual, difficult birth": generating language to describe their continual journeys of self-discovery as well as the shifting political conditions they inhabited.[169] During this period, all three joined in efforts to challenge the racism and sexism within literary publishing. In 1977, following Rich and Jordan's brief but painful affair, the two put their trysts aside to coauthor a petition demanding that the *American Poetry Review* change its racist, sexist, and antiyouth review policies, which Lorde also signed.[170] And when Jordan and Lorde resigned as editors of the feminist magazine *Chrysalis* because of its racist practices, Rich showed solidarity by following suit.[171]

Jordan and Lorde also both gave feedback on Rich's writing, including an early draft of her famous essay "Disloyal to Civilization: Feminism, Racism, Gynephobia" (1978). In her feedback, Lorde urged Rich to be less sentimental and more nuanced about the history of Black and white women's relationships. Rich took this advice and incorporated analysis of historical touchstones like white women married to slave owners and the origins of women's suffrage in abolition. The result is a complex analysis of the "special history of polarization, as well as of shared oppression and shared activism" among Black and white women.[172] In a moment when white feminists ignored racial difference or felt paralyzed by ignorance and guilt, Rich instead urged them to become "disloyal" to racist patriarchy. In Jordan's words, Rich took "on a lot of things that nobody else would touch.... [H]er engagement with racism as well as with the rift between the sexes... was just startling in its honesty."[173] While she is remembered as one of the few white feminists who refused to sing the praises of sisterhood and insisted on an antiracist feminism, we can see how such insights were sharpened both by her classroom experiences and by the women she met at City College.

Bambara also remained a key interlocutor, though their relationship unfolded primarily on the page. It also seems a bit lopsided, perhaps meaning more to Rich than it did to Bambara. In addition to adapting Bambara's assignments, assigning her work to students, and using "Realizing the Dream" as a model for her woman-centered university, between 1980 and 1981, Rich wrote a two-part review essay on Bambara's novel *The Salt Eaters* for *New Women's Times*. At a time when discussions of women's literature focused on white authors, Rich's essay, "Wholeness Is No Trifling Matter: Some Fiction by Black Women," argued that Black women's literature should be central to anyone trying to "comprehend female struggle and woman-to-woman bonding."[174] It also addressed how differences of race, class, and sexuality may impact readers' reactions to such fiction. For instance, she advised white women readers that they may experience "resistance" when reading the work of Black women writers because it "sweeps away illusions of any sisterhood which depends solely on either shared female or economic oppression" and addresses white women's complicity in racial violence.[175] Though she explored the implications of Black feminist literature for others differently positioned amid intersecting axes of power, this was not without complication. Then, and still today, the problem identified by bell hooks and Gloria Joseph remained: Black feminist ideas and works of literature were seen as more legitimate, and taken more seriously, when echoed by white critics like Rich.[176]

A Pedagogy of Location on the California Coast

As we have seen, the students and professors Rich met at City College were central to her development of a lesbian feminist criticism that was also antiracist. And as the 1970s gave way to the 1980s, she continued exploring how gender and sexuality intersect not only with race and class but also with other vectors of difference such as religion, ability, and nationality. During this period, writes Megan Behrent, Black feminist socialists, including her former colleagues and members of the Combahee River Collective, introduced Rich to versions of Marxism "not mire[d] in the sexism and homophobia of the male New Left" and expanded her thinking about the simultaneity of oppressions.[177] In addition, as her arthritis worsened, requiring her to hobble to classes and speaking engagements with the assistance of a cane, she wrote more explicitly about her experiences of chronic pain in a world designed for those who are "temporarily able-bodied."[178] Rich also renounced her earlier belief, in Virginia Woolf's words, that "as a woman I have no country."[179] As she traveled to Nicaragua to learn about the Sandinistas and studied global feminist movements in India, the Caribbean, Latin America, Africa, and the Middle East, she became more conscious of the privileges and power afforded by her US citizenship.[180] She came to see US foreign policy as an important site for feminist interventions, through which US women could take actions like trying to get "the foot of the United States off Central America."[181]

Throughout this later work, Rich developed a way of seeing that she called "a politics of location."[182] Drawing explicitly on Black feminist notions of identity politics and intersectionality, Rich's politics of location reject abstract, universal, and disembodied approaches to thinking and theorizing. Instead, they begin with one's concrete, lived experiences as they unfold in bodies marked by differences, and within particular geographic locations, and connect these to broader material conditions and questions of power. As Caren Kaplan has shown, Rich's politics of location have impacted scholars in a range of fields.[183] bell hooks used this concept to expand on her own theories of the political possibilities that emerge at the margins and through multiple social locations. Chandra Talpade Mohanty built on it to explore how social positioning informs the categories of "experience" and "difference" in cross-cultural feminist criticism. Rich's concept also informed the work of geographers like Neil Smith and Cindi Katz, and James Clifford used it "to question the totalizing operations of Euro-American theory."[184] Critics like Michele Wallace have also pointed out how Rich's concept may inadvertently recenter the white, upper-middle-class positionality it seeks to challenge.[185] Yet for all that has been said about this famous formulation, scholars have not considered its relationship to Rich's classrooms. As her teaching archives reveal, she developed not only a politics but also a pedagogy of location that invited students to take up this materialist, relational, and intersectional mode of thinking.

In the 1980s, Rich's teaching became more sporadic. After leaving Douglass, she accepted a lucrative position as Cornell University's A. D. White Professor at Large, occasionally traveling to Ithaca to deliver lectures and teach a small seminar called Difference in the Women's Movement. In 1984 she also spent a month teaching poetry workshops as a visiting professor at Scripps College, a women's college in Claremont, California. That year, she permanently relocated to California in search of weather more conducive to her health. There, she began teaching at San Jose State University (SJSU), a public university, like City College and Douglass, where a wide array of students could go to gain "greater direction of their lives."[186] She admired SJSU's commitment to educating disenfranchised students: "education for the woman who dropped out of high school as a teenage mother and is now a graduate student in history; education for the new immigrant struggling with ESL, a living bridge between two cultures; education for the grandmother and the disabled ex-GI; for the single mother poet-organizer."[187] Just as Rich had earlier defended what open admissions students brought to City College, these descriptions of SJSU students refuse to reduce them to deficits, instead emphasizing the experiential knowledge they bring to their studies.

Rich's SJSU course The Woman Novelist as Historian (1985) illustrates her pedagogy of location. The origins of this course can be found in her essay "Resisting Amnesia" (1983), which describes how contemporary Black women writers are "creating a new kind of historical fiction, writing novels which are quite consciously intended as resources in Black women's history."[188] Reflecting the global turn in her feminism, the course focused on contemporary novels depicting women resisting oppression around the world: Nadine Gordimer's *Burger's Daughter* (1979), about anti-apartheid activists in South Africa; Etel Adnan's *Sitt Marie Rose* (1978), about xenophobia during the Lebanese Civil War; Michelle Cliff's *Abeng* (1984), a semifictional autobiography and critique of British imperialism in Jamaica; and Lorde's "biomythography" *Zami* (1982), about her experiences coming of age as a Black lesbian feminist of Caribbean descent. Instead of reading these novels through liberal individualist frameworks, they considered how characters' lives were "shaped by forces beyond their control," by the particular social, historical, political, and economic conditions they inherited. They also analyzed how characters advocated for change. "What impact can these people make on the circumstances of their lives?" they asked. "How do they try to effect change? What in their lives is a source of empowerment?"[189] Though a few students disliked this emphasis on the "sociological and political ramifications of the literature . . . literature as it pertains to a cause," most found it beneficial.[190] One student describes how the course taught her to "read with a sensitivity towards the struggle of people. . . . I am more aware of injustices. I am more aware of how people individually and collectively rise above these."[191]

In addition to using novels as points of entry into the histories and experiences of women around the world, Rich invited students to use these texts to reflect on their own lives. "In which novel, or novels, do you find values close to your own?" she asked them. "Where do you find values you do not subscribe to?"[192] Through these kinds of questions, she created space for self-fashioning: to ask big questions, like what constitutes a meaningful life, and discuss what principles we want to govern our actions and choices. While affluent students have historically had access to this kind of transformative, humanistic learning, Rich's courses made this available to the working-class students and students of color at SJSU. And students appreciated how she "welcomed individual, personal responses to the material we covered."[193] In one student's words, this emphasis on their "subjective responses" seemed more "honest" than the "requests for objectivity in every other class I've taken," which, she believed, "can never be given."[194] Another expressed gratitude for Rich's "exacting . . . very reasonable and relevant" assignments that contributed to their "growth as individuals."[195]

The Woman Novelist as Historian is strikingly similar to Bambara's University of Delaware course The Text as a Rite of Recovery, which she was teaching around the same time but across the country, on the opposite coast. Both foregrounded the pedagogical possibilities of literature: the idea that texts can teach us things. Readers will recall that Bambara taught students to read novels as sites of "alternative education": the means by which "downpressed people" critique dominant ideologies and share wisdom beyond formal institutions. Similarly, Rich's opening lecture described "the novel as a kind of teaching": "a way of passing on realities that are not the focus of the dominant culture, that are obliterated by it, that we sorely need."[196] Both writers also taught students to analyze representations of education within literature. Considered in conjunction, their archives illustrate how teaching and learning affected the ways these authors read, including the details they paid attention to and the patterns they traced across texts.

Rich's pedagogy of location is also evident in her later courses at Stanford. In 1986 she made a reverse journey from the one she had made some twenty years earlier when she left Columbia for City College. After two years at SJSU (1984–86), Stanford made the fifty-seven-year-old a financial offer she couldn't refuse, and she returned to the elite universities that had shaped so much of her youth. As a professor of English and feminist studies at Stanford, she taught introductory and advanced poetry courses and interdisciplinary courses on feminist theory. A Stanford professor who taught there at the time described it as an "extremely elitist university in which pedagogy is rarely discussed."[197] Though prestige and publications may have been the coin of the realm, Rich continued developing "antihierarchical" teaching methods, regardless of whether they would be institutionally recognized.

In her lower-level Stanford course Feminist Studies 102/203 (1988), Rich developed a "family project" assignment that exemplifies her pedagogy of location. Adapted from an earlier research project at Douglass in which students analyzed "a woman-to-woman relationship" in their lives, the "family project" asked them to "locate yourself and others within your family" amid broader power structures. While the earlier version had focused on gender, the family project (later rechristened the "social geography project") also instructed them to consider class, sexuality, race, and ethnicity, as well as labor "(inside and out of home, how valued)," "money (who has it, how do they get it, how is it talked about)," and "how power is constructed within the family group as a function of some or all of the above."[198] Characteristic of Rich's pedagogy of location, this assignment asked students to use their lived experiences of difference as points of entry into material conditions and questions of power.[199] And as with many of her assignments, they presented their findings to the class so that others could learn from their experiences.

Sometimes this pedagogy of location took unusual turns. In the late 1980s, male and female symbols briefly appeared on a few assignments as Rich experimented with assigning different projects to students with different identities. One option for the final project in The Activist Roots of Feminist Theory (Fall 1989) was to use the course readings and discussions to write a position paper on sexual harassment at Stanford. However, Rich did not want the three male students in the class explaining sexual assault to the women on campus when the latter were the primary targets of harassment. Instead, she instructed the young men to "write a position paper to educate *male students*... about sexual harassment on this campus, suggesting some possible responses" (emphasis mine).²⁰⁰ While contemporary readers can certainly understand the sentiments behind such gestures, we can also imagine less prescriptive and essentialist methods of encouraging students to think critically about how their subject positioning impacts their research and the ways their work might be received by different audiences.

✳ ✳ ✳

Throughout her later years in California, Rich continued writing about education. As Alex Streim observes, several of her poems from this period dramatize the kind of "pedagogical ambivalence" evident in her earlier classroom lyrics. "The School among the Ruins," for instance, values the figure of the instructor while also "singing the limits of... [their] capacity to teach"—limits, Streim explains, imposed by the unpredictable and "accidental" nature of so much learning.²⁰¹ Other poems like "A Long Conversation," writes Behrent, can be read as forms of "political education," with pedagogical aims like explaining communism to readers.²⁰² Rich also continued writing educational essays, including two initially delivered as lectures while at Scripps. "The Soul of a Woman's College" argued that women's colleges should focus on empowerment (not become sites of refuge and retreat), and "Invisibility in Academe" criticized the erasure of lesbian experience in academia. In the latter, Rich adapts the insights she gained from City College and Douglass—about how universities suppress minoritarian histories, cultures, and experiences—into a forceful critique of the ways academia diminishes those who are not wealthy, white, male, and heterosexual.

Though Rich was teaching at Stanford, she continued to advocate for the open-admissions era dream of universal college. In the 1990s, as neoliberal policies were "shredding... the democratic vision" and consolidating power, her essays "Why I Refused the National Medal for the Arts" (1997) and "Arts of the Possible" (1997) argued that free public education, housing, and health care are necessary to restore democracy and create the conditions in which art can flourish.²⁰³ More specifically, she advocated for replacing the United States' educational tracking system, which sorts students into those worthy and unworthy of relevant learning, with "an imaginative, highly developed, educational system that would serve all citizens at every age—a vast, shared public schooling in which each of us felt a stake, as with public roads, there when needed, ready when you choose to use them."²⁰⁴ As such remarks illustrate, these teacher-poets not only "stole from" the university (redirecting educational resources away from the reproduction of privilege), they sought to increase the pot of resources from which to steal. And what began with their campus essays evolved over time into an extensive corpus of writing on subjects such as affirmative action, linguistic justice, women's colleges, women's studies, feminist pedagogy, and public education—open admissions humming, all the while, in the background.

✳ ✳ ✳

Maybe the topic of free college came up when Rich and Jordan, both now living in California, dined together at the Claremont Hotel. Classrooms had, after all, been a subject of heated discussions when the two broke bread back in Harlem. As with all friendships, theirs had shifted over the years, at times stretching from admiration and respect to include love, other times mired in silence bred from unaddressed anger. Following a fallout in the early 1980s over Israel's invasion of Lebanon, when the two finally reconciled, their friendship not only "resumed" but "deepened."[205] Often, Rich traveled across the bay to give readings and work with young poets in Jordan's Poetry for the People program at Berkeley. The two writers shared a love of global poetry, but on other subjects, they disagreed. On the legacy of Walt Whitman, Rich recalled:

>   you saying
>   he was unrecognized
>   I arguing
>   "he's in the canon!"

Years later, she conceded that there was a degree of truth in both positions:

>   (June, you were right...
>   canonization too
>   can be brutal).[206]

According to Holladay, Rich was never shy about "how much she had learned from Jordan during a friendship spanning nearly three decades."[207]

In June 1996, the two pledged to write each other a poem a day, resulting in a stunning, lyrical dialogue reflecting on what they had achieved through their writing, teaching, and activism and inventorying what remained still to be done. In a poem to Jordan, dated June 2, 1996, Rich expresses outrage over the "sick teachers" hanging on in "desolation's classroom," while "student might-have-beens / get stripsearched on the street," a reference to the University of California Board of Regents decision to end affirmative action (which Jordan fought against).[208] Rich's invocation of "Freire and Fanon" harks back to their shared experiences developing social justice pedagogies at City College. And for these former paramours, the subject of love was never far away. Both understood that who you love could endanger your life but also that love could fuel revolution. To console Rich in a moment of despair, Jordan wrote:

> Oh, Adrienne!
> This is that love
> > It's here
> > between us
> > > growing.[209]

While some of the poems they exchanged explore serious political realities, they also wrote playfully about their love of decadent foods: Jordan's haiku "For the Poet: Adrienne Rich" describes a candlelit conversation over a sumptuous pheasant, and Rich's poem "For June, in the Year 2001" wishes her dear friend the sweetness of "cinnamon vanilla melting / on apple tart."[210] In that poem, written amid Jordan's cancer treatments and declining physical condition, Rich expresses a desire to "clasp for you forever ... the world's quiver and shine" in such pleasures as "the western sunstruck water-light" of the Pacific, the smell of "budding acacias / tangled with eucalyptus," protest chants emanating from Tallahassee, and the felt memory of the two, sitting by a marina, enveloped in "pearlwhite mist," images that honor Jordan's sensual love of life as well as her politics.[211]

Few saw Jordan as clearly as Rich, especially how deeply her poetry, politics, and teaching connected. In the introduction to *Directed by Desire: The Collected Poems of June Jordan*, Rich describes how Jordan "wanted her readers, listeners, students to feel their own latent power—of the word, the deed, of their own beauty and intrinsic value; she wanted each of us to understand how isolation can leave us defenseless and paralyzed."[212] But what readers might not necessarily have seen were the classrooms across the country that lay beneath the surface of such sentiments. Indeed, Rich recognized that Jordan wanted others to understand their power because she had developed a similar philosophy over the past thirty years as a professor.

※ ※ ※

In 1988 Rich and her partner, Michelle Cliff, cotaught a course at Stanford called Women and Difference: Marginality, Art, Politics, which illustrates just how far her teaching had come. Citing the overlapping axes of difference, the course description states, "Women perceived as 'different' (spinsters, lesbians, women of color, Jewish women, women with disabilities, women without children) according to prescribed societal norms, have been variously designated as marginal, monstrous, freakish, asexual. This course focuses on the lives and works of women who made their difference serve their art and politics."[213] Unlike her previous course Images of Women in Poetry by Men, here such stereotypes were reduced to a single sentence: the mere point of departure for a semester-long exploration of women's art and feminist aesthetics. The syllabus included literature, performances, and visual art by women like Virginia Woolf, Frida Kahlo, and Billie Holiday alongside grassroots, small-press publications that highlighted the art emerging from contemporary social movements. Illustrating her ongoing commitment to disrupting power hierarchies in the classroom, Rich encouraged students "to participate, not only in [discussion] sections but in the lecture periods" as well.[214]

In their reflections on the course, Rich and Cliff allude to small group discussions that functioned as a "consciousness-raising" exercise. Some readers will hear in this term Paulo Freire's famous notion of *conscientização*: how individuals and communities work toward greater understanding of their social, political, and economic conditions in order to transform them.[215] Others will recognize the practice of consciousness-raising groups, which originated in the civil rights movement and became common within the women's movement. For middle- and upper-class white women who had previously been isolated in their homes, the practice of gathering to discuss their experiences helped them recognize their seemingly individual experiences as the collective products of a patriarchal society. In the decades that followed, Rich and Cliff were among the many scholar-teachers who brought their experiences in such groups into formal classrooms. In Women and Difference, small group discussions helped students locate their lives in relation to broader power structures and consider how their positionality shaped the possibilities available to them. Former student Sue Reinhold recalls that "good old-fashioned feminist consciousness raising" was the heart of the class, which included some "tough stuff": analysis of "privilege, family origins, points of pain, points of vulnerability."[216] As Holladay notes, for some Stanford students, especially "the children of affluent families, this was the first time they had questioned their social advantages and privileges."[217]

At the same time, perhaps even down the hall, their Stanford colleague Estelle B. Freedman was also adapting consciousness-raising techniques for her Introduction to Feminist Studies course. Though few archival records remain documenting how Rich and Cliff implemented this practice, Freedman's essay "Small Group Pedagogy: Consciousness-Raising in Conservative Times" explores some possibilities. In 1988, the same year that Rich and Cliff cotaught their course, Freedman decided to supplement her weekly lectures with "small groups" modeled on the consciousness-raising groups of the women's movement. In these groups, students discussed prompts like "How does your personal experience of race, class and ethnicity affect your response to what you are learning?"[218] She also gave instructions drawn from activist practices, such as having "a rotating timekeeper, leaderless groups, and an uninterrupted five to ten minutes for each member to speak at the outset of sessions."[219] Freedman writes, "As they did for second-wave feminists of the 1960s and 1970s, consciousness-raising groups in FS101 functioned to move students from silence to speech, from isolation to community, and sometimes from political ambivalence to . . . commitment."[220]

While it's unclear how much of this held true in Rich and Cliff's classroom, we do know that their small groups proved so effective that some continued to meet even after the semester officially ended. In addition, there's one other clue that seems to indicate some affinities between Rich's and Freedman's pedagogies. In a moment when Rich was fiercely guarding her personal writing time like an ursine matriarch, Freedman's acknowledgments indicate that Rich took time out of her busy schedule to provide feedback on an early draft of "Small Group Pedagogy." This exception illustrates how committed Rich was not only to teaching but also to sharing the stories of feminist classrooms. Doing so allows others to learn from our mistakes, build on our successes, and more effectively teach in the service of social change.

4

Sharing the Illumination
Audre Lorde's Pedagogies of Difference

On the first day of CUNY's fall 1970 semester, Audre Lorde packed up her bag with syllabi, lesson plans, and books: Gordon Allport's *The Nature of Prejudice* and Joel Kovel's *White Racism: A Psychohistory*. She carried these materials from Staten Island, across the Narrows, past subway turnstiles, and to her classroom on Manhattan's Upper West Side. We can picture her, dressed in a bright dashiki, adorned by a bold, chunky necklace, peering out at her students from behind thick spectacles. And the students staring back at her were not your average undergraduates. They were New York City Police Department officers, as well as civilians, who had signed up for her course on Race and the Urban Situation. Reflecting on this moment, Lorde writes, "In 1970, the Black Panthers were being murdered in Chicago. Here we had Black and white cops, and Black and white kids off the block."[1] Amid widespread outrage over police brutality against African Americans, teaching held out the promise that she could directly influence and improve conditions of anti-Black racism. How she taught these students to view each other and to view the world could, quite literally, save lives.

Lorde was a major author of American literature, a social and cultural theorist, and an activist in the twentieth century's feminist, Black liberation, and gay and lesbian movements. Today she is best remembered for her insights on difference. In her eleven poetry collections, the essays collected in *Sister Outsider*, her biomythography *Zami*, and two cancer memoirs, Lorde used her experiences as a "Black, lesbian, feminist, mother, warrior, poet," as the grounds to think, theorize, and imagine. In doing so, writes Rudolph P. Byrd, she transformed these marginalized identities into standpoints for progressive organizing and brought "precision and specificity" to national conversations about race, class, gender, and sexuality.[2] In fact, nearly two decades before Kimberlé Crenshaw coined the term *intersectionality*, Lorde was writing about how multiple forms of oppression overlap.[3] As scholars like Grace Kyungwon Hong, Roderick Ferguson, and Megan Obourn have demonstrated, her work countered the era's dominant ideologies of liberal multiculturalism: the idea that we are all different but equal. Instead, she explored how precarity, vulnerability, and expendability are unequally distributed along embodied axes of difference.[4] At the same time, Lorde saw the differences among us as a source of creativity and catalyst for change. Among her many contributions to American literature, feminist criticism, Black studies, and queer theory, these ideas—her reclamation of marginalized subject positions, attention to overlapping axes of power, and insistence on both the materiality and creative potential of difference—have been some of her most enduring and impactful.

Since her untimely death in 1992, at the age of only fifty-eight, Lorde's work has inspired commemorative conferences, films, a "Bio/Anthology," and community health centers and endowed chairs established in her honor. Contemporary youth, not yet born when she passed away, continue to wear T-shirts emblazoned with her words and visage. Patrisse Khan-Cullors, one of the three cofounders of Black Lives Matter, refers to *Sister Outsider* as nothing less than her Bible, a foundational text for the contemporary fight against anti-Black violence.[5]

Yet long before Lorde was named poet laureate of New York State or inducted into national monuments, she stood each week in front of a classroom full of police officers at John Jay College of Criminal Justice. There, she was Professor Lorde, the first Black faculty member in the English Department, known to many of her students simply as Audre. John Jay was, in fact, one of four CUNY colleges Lorde would teach at throughout her career. Prior to that, she had taught at City College, where she participated in the fight for open admissions and met three women who became close conspirators and friends. And these positions did not merely pay the bills to sustain her work as a writer. Put simply, she believed that "teaching and writing were inextricably combined."[6]

This chapter explores how Lorde's theories of difference emerged in reciprocal relation to her CUNY classrooms. On the one hand, it analyzes her pedagogies of difference: the methods she developed for teaching students about race, class, gender, and sexuality. We will see how she made creative use of traditional methods like lectures and essays, while also developing the kinds of interactive, student-centered assignments—daily journals, student-led discussions, creative projects, and the publication of student writing—that have been the focus of this book. More specifically, I show how she combined introspective assignments like journals with public projects in order to help students cultivate an activist consciousness: a sense of their own power to address the injustice they were studying. This chapter also considers the impact these classrooms had on her writing. Not only did they inspire many of Lorde's poems about teaching, it was there that she developed the prose writing skills and performed the research that would inform some of her most influential essays on difference.

Lessons in Courage

Similar to Toni Cade Bambara's and June Jordan's experiences, the schools of Lorde's youth were places of discipline, where her exceptional abilities and continual questioning were met not with praise but with punishment. The white nuns at her Catholic elementary school, St. Mark's Academy, ruled over their Black students with "an iron fist."[7] They sent notes home to Lorde's parents, held her after school, and beat her for even the most minor infractions.[8] In 1947, at the age of thirteen, she tested into Hunter High School, a prestigious, public all-girls school for the city's most accomplished students. Though she continued to encounter "overwhelming racism" from both teachers and students, it was there that she was first introduced to poets like the Romantics, modernists, and Beats.[9] As her biographer, Alexis DeVaux, writes, these poets gave her permission to explore "feelings for the beauty of everyday things, friendship, and love," which were seldom discussed at home.[10] At Hunter, she and a group of young women poets, including Diane diPrima, formed a literary group who called themselves the Branded. In the hours before the school bell rang, the Branded gathered in vacant classrooms to hold seances summoning the ghosts of poets past and to read their own verses aloud to one another.[11] While Lorde found the acceptance she had longed for in this "exclusively female, intensely loyal community," this inclusion came at a cost: the suppression of her identity as the sole Black member of the otherwise all-white Branded.[12]

Though Lorde was accepted to her dream college, Sarah Lawrence, she couldn't afford the elite school's tuition and ended up instead at CUNY's Hunter College.[13] With the exception of an inspiring professor or two, she was largely "dissatisfied with the absence of camaraderie, political awareness, and rebelliousness among this more conventional student body."[14] However, the degrees she earned—a BA in English followed by a master's in library science from Columbia—offered a path out of the minimum-wage jobs she was desperate to escape. Throughout her late teens and early twenties, Lorde had worked (including during college) on a radioactive assembly line, as a nurse's aide, and as a medical receptionist and had even sold her blood to pay for rent. But college opened the doors to more intellectually stimulating and less physically taxing work as a librarian. After graduating from Columbia, she spent the next seven years (1961–67) working at libraries throughout the city, sometimes engaging in stealth acts of subversion, like sliding Black teenagers the stories about Black adventurers that she had stowed away inside her desk.[15]

In 1968 Lorde published her first poetry collection, *The First Cities*. Critics hailed it as a "quiet, introspective book" of "inner weather," notable for its contrast to "urban poets who write of concrete and machines."[16] That same year, she was invited to serve as a visiting poet at Tougaloo College, a historically Black university in Jackson, Mississippi. Initially, she was terrified at the prospect of trading New York City for the South, especially a college campus continually besieged by racist groups like the Ku Klux Klan and White Citizens Council.[17] She was also wary of teaching, which she had no experience doing. "You have to do this," her husband urged.[18] Eventually, she accepted the position and began what would become a lifelong career as a teacher-poet.

Lorde's contract stipulated that she would deliver poetry readings, sit in on a class or two, and focus primarily on her writing. But she was struck by the aspiring young poets she met and decided to convene a workshop for them. As someone with no formal pedagogical training who, most often, had felt abused, excluded, and silenced as a student, she knew "I couldn't give what regular teachers of poetry give . . . nor did I want to, because they'd never served me. . . . The only thing I had to give was me."[19] She supplemented their English curriculum with poems by Black writers and discussed how poetry related to their lives. Together, in what she described as a "nurturing atmosphere" of "honesty and openness," they wrote poems about relationships, violence, race, poverty, and loneliness.[20] "I was so involved with these young people," Lorde writes, "I really loved them."[21]

Surrounded by students confronting difficult and painful realities, Lorde began to feel as if she was hiding the fact of her white husband, out of fear that she would be seen as a race traitor rather than an inspiring leader. As a working-class Black student in majority-white schools, a lesbian poet "tolerated but never really accepted" in the Harlem Writers Guild, and a Black lesbian in the predominantly white "gay girl" culture of the Village, Lorde was accustomed to suppressing certain aspects of her life in order to navigate different social worlds.[22] Yet at Tougaloo, something shifted, and she decided to bring her full self to the classroom. She admitted to students, "The father of my children is white."[23] While students were initially disillusioned, DeVaux writes, their hostility soon gave way to a more complex understanding of Blackness "as both self-constructed and historic; embracing the boundaries of identity while at the same time not being limited by them."[24]

That semester, students wrote "with great pride, excitement, and power."[25] Their poems bear titles like "Moments of Depression," "What Do I Believe?" and "Studies in Black and Gold." While some shout against white supremacy, others quietly explore longing, how a lover's kiss compares to a glass of wine against your lips. So moved by their words, Lorde wanted to do even more to affirm their voices. At the time, Black Arts Movement authors were criticizing the dearth of published Black writing for Black audiences—and there she was, surrounded by Black students writing insightful and imaginative poetry. Recognizing that others might want to read their poems as well, she abandoned the conventional feedback loop between teachers and students. At the same time that Jordan and Bambara were compiling anthologies of their New York City students' writing, Lorde engaged in a parallel act of editorial activism and obtained funds from a literary nonprofit to publish their poems in a thirteen-page chapbook titled *Pound*.[26] "POUND.... BANG Bang bang bang," the sound of bullets, shot by the White Citizens Council, aimed at Tougaloo's students.[27] It is also the sound of "a Poet-":

> It is my fist you hear
> Beating against your ear.[28]

Like Jordan's and Bambara's anthologies, *Pound* showed students that their writing could impact readers beyond their classroom. It also demonstrated to Black lesbian poet Kate Rushin "the value of putting together many such publications—rarely high-tech, never perfect."[29] Inspired by Lorde's example, she decided to use a similar approach and publish the poems that students wrote in her elementary and high school workshops.

At Tougaloo, Lorde discovered "that teaching was the work I needed to be doing."[30] These classrooms also galvanized her writing. During her time in Mississippi, she wrote nearly all the poems in *Cables to Rage* (1970), including "Martha," her first poem openly conveying her love for another woman. There, Lorde recalls, she put herself "on the line": "I began to learn about courage, I began to learn to talk."[31] As a writer who would later become famous for her unwavering courage—from her erotic poems about Black lesbian sexuality, at a time when such subjects could threaten her career and safety, to her refusal to wear a prosthetic breast after a mastectomy—those six weeks at Tougaloo were pivotal. In fact, her life partner, Gloria Joseph, went so far as to state that these classroom interactions "provided the groundwork for [Lorde] to acknowledge that the differences that exist among people—racial, sexual, economic, and political—could be used as a positive force in forging unity for progress."[32] For years to come, classrooms would continue to shape her thinking about difference.

Teaching at the End of the World

When her six weeks as a visiting poet were over, Lorde returned home to some of the most politically charged months in New York City history. Nationwide, anger was mounting over the United States' continuing involvement in the Vietnam War, now in its thirteenth year. The civil rights movement was in full force, the Black Power and women's movements were growing, and cities were experiencing aftershocks from the urban rebellions in Cleveland (1966), Chicago (1966), Newark (1967), and Detroit (1967). In February 1968, New York City's sanitation workers union went on strike for nine days, and 100,000 tons of garbage piled up in the streets before the city agreed to a better contract. Two months later, hundreds of Columbia University students occupied the campus to protest the university's racism and imperialism. Soon thereafter, a citywide teacher strike shut down public schools for thirty-six days.

Amid this turmoil, Lorde maintained contact with her Tougaloo students. In April several of them, members of the Black choir, traveled to New York City to perform a fundraiser concert with Duke Ellington at Carnegie Hall. Their performance was scheduled for what would become an infamous date in history: April 4, 1968. Lorde, unable to pass up an opportunity to support her students, was in attendance. In a confluence of events so evocative it borders disbelief, their performance of "What the World Needs Now Is Love" was interrupted by the announcement that Dr. Martin Luther King Jr. had been assassinated. Performers and audience alike were shocked. The students finished the song as a memorial to King, and the rest of the concert was cut short as the theater dissolved into tears.[33] This experience only intensified Lorde's feeling that they were living through the apocalypse. Reflecting on this era, she writes, "I have always had the sense of Armageddon and it was much stronger in those days, the sense of living on the edge of chaos. Not just personally, but on the world level. That we were dying, that we were killing our world."[34] During this period, she continues, teaching and writing "functioned to hold us from going over the edge.... [T]his was the most we could do while we constructed some saner future."[35] Through these creative acts, she managed to survive this catastrophic present and help others to do the same.

In the fall of 1968, Lorde was hired by Mina Shaughnessy as a part-time lecturer in the City College SEEK program. Given how CUNY had helped her escape night shifts and exhausting, dangerous minimum-wage work, she understood the importance of such initiatives. But despite her newfound belief that teaching was her calling, she was apprehensive about the new position. It wasn't "going back south and being shot at, but when Mina said to me, 'Teach,' it was as threatening as that was."[36] She felt she had a responsibility to these students but was worried she wouldn't be able to communicate with them in the same way she had with those at Tougaloo. "How am I going to speak to them?" she wondered, describing the fear teaching elicited. "How am I going to tell them what I want from them—literally—that kind of terror."[37] With the memory of Tougaloo fresh in her mind, Lorde knew that the answer was not to suppress her anxiety and feign confidence: "The first thing that I said to my SEEK students was, 'I'm scared too.'"[38] With this confession of vulnerability, she began creating a classroom where it was okay to express one's feelings, even when they jeopardized her image as a confident authority figure. Over time, these kinds of open admissions, started at Tougaloo and sharpened at CUNY, would become crucial to her pedagogies of difference.

That first semester, Lorde taught one basic writing class, which met on Mondays and Wednesday from four to six. She was paid $408 per month, which would amount, in 2023 dollars, to around $14,000 for the course (nearly four times as much as the average $3,500 compensation for such courses today).[39] While few archival records remain from her time at City College, we do know that her writing course was paired with another course, taught by fellow SEEK instructor Janet Mayes, that focused on grammar. Despite having two children to raise and poems to write, Lorde voluntarily took time out of her daily schedule to attend Mayes's classes and sit with their students. Mayes recalls that Lorde "often would visit my classroom, because she said she wanted to learn teaching techniques from me, which really blew my mind; I never believed I was special or particularly skilled, and Audre made me feel great about my work."[40] As Mayes's words suggest, Lorde did not see teaching as a distraction that took away from her work as a writer; instead, she dove headfirst into this challenge and began to study pedagogy. She sat in on Mayes's classes, read the work of pedagogical theorists like Paulo Freire, and collected other educators' syllabi to study their approaches.

During her time in SEEK (and perhaps inspired by Mayes's classes), Lorde became fascinated with, and began seriously studying, English grammar. Though she likely shared the sentiment, common among SEEK's earliest educators, that students' ideas should take precedence over grammar and that Standard English should not be taught in ways that devalue Black English, she was also intrigued, on an existential level, by the ways linguistic systems structure our sense of the world. "Guess what I found out last night. Tenses are a way of ordering the chaos around time," Lorde told her students, and it's easy to imagine the eye rolls—or the perking of poetic ears—this sentiment may have elicited.[41] As she prepared for her SEEK courses, she "learned that grammar was not arbitrary, that it served a purpose, that it helped to form the ways we thought, that it could be freeing as well as restrictive."[42] In fact, it was in preparation to teach remedial English that both she and Adrienne Rich, two of the era's most important writers, first learned the formal rules of grammar. Given that these two poets would later become so famous that scholars would debate the significance of a single comma or em dash, it seems crucial that they first acquired this knowledge in order to teach it to their students in SEEK.

Though Lorde spent only one year at City College, it was an important one: the year of the student strikes. She moved her classes to their pop-up Harlem University and brought them "soup and blankets," but she was concerned by what she witnessed at the occupation. There, she saw "Black women being fucked on tables and under desks... being used and abused."[43] To Lorde, the student movement reflected a belief within other factions of Black liberation movements: that Black women could best serve the revolution by standing behind Black men, rather than organizing for their needs and demands as women. This troubling experience illustrated how activist efforts can reproduce, rather than challenge, social hierarchies, which soon became a major theme within her writing.

City College also introduced her to three women who would become lifelong interlocutors. Though Lorde and Rich overlapped there only briefly, the two formed an enduring friendship that would shape the trajectory of feminist literature and criticism. While Lorde urged Rich to treat the history of Black and white women with greater nuance, Rich encouraged Lorde to write about her fear of cancer, which led to powerful essays like "The Transformation of Silence into Language and Action."[44] The two also, in Rich's words, "climbed into" each other's poems. In her poem "Hunger" (1974), dedicated to Lorde, Rich conveys the emotional complexities of a friendship across differences yet grounded in shared political will.[45] The timing of the poem suggests it may have been, in part, an apology for the National Book Award debacle, in which Rich sacrificed Lorde's personal feelings at the altar of public feminism. The poem opens with an image of their friendship as "lighted windows signifying shelter" and the promise of "desolation comforted." The subsequent lines measure the distance between the two writers, especially the speaker's sense that "I'm partly somewhere else," in a distinct social location. While honoring the differences of race, class, and religion that separate them, the poem also appeals to their intersecting experiences as teachers, lesbian mothers, and activists. As Rich imagines it, what united them was a kind of "hunger": a desire for a world without the suffering induced by racism, sexism, homophobia, and capitalism. Yet, like many friendships, theirs was sometimes uneven, and it angered both that Rich received more accolades and recognition. One notable incident occurred when prestigious publisher W. W. Norton used Rich's name recognition to introduce readers to the poetry of the lesser-known Lorde, first on the jacket cover of Lorde's poetry collection *Coal* (1976), then on *The Black Unicorn* (1978).

While scholars have recognized the literary legacy of Lorde's friendship with Rich, much less has been said about her relationships with Jordan and Bambara.[46] Prior to the City College protests, Lorde and Jordan had been, at best, acquaintances. But through their joint experiences as faculty, trying to figure out how they could best support their students, they came to recognize each other as comrades. Jordan writes of the central role that the open admissions protests played in their friendship:

> I first really recognized her special self back in 1968 when she showed up, as most teachers did not, to keep the faith with the Black SEEK students of City College who were attending Freedom Classes at Harlem's IS 201, while the College campus closed down in the name of open admissions. The generous integrity of my Sister Audre Lorde impressed me then as I will never forget: In a time of superfluous posturing and rhetoric she made real her dedication to our needs.[47]

Jordan also describes how their experiences as Black mothers fueled their involvement in these protests. In a moment when "predictable diatribes" against open admissions equated "the entry of our Black and Brown children" with the "lowering of [academic] standards," she writes, "We knew better. We had Black children."[48] Though their friendship was, at times, clouded by Lorde's jealousy over Jordan's widespread popularity, the relationships she sustained with prominent Black male intellectuals, and her "heterosexual approval," they never faltered in support for each other's writing.[49] They published each other's poems in journals and edited collections, arranged speaking engagements for one another, and introduced each other at readings. Lorde also joined Jordan's literary organization, cofounded with Alice Walker, the Sisterhood: a group of Black women who collaborated in securing publicity and publication opportunities. And it was their shared participation in the open admissions struggle—something concrete, immediate, and physical, yet much larger than either one of them—that solidified their bond.

It was also at City College that Lorde first met Bambara (she knew a kindred spirit when she saw one). In 1970 Lorde wrote a poem for Bambara depicting an intimate, conspiratorial friendship that exceeded the professional category of colleague. The poem's humorously long title, "Dear Toni Instead of Congratulations upon Your Book and Your Daughter Whom You Say You Are Raising to Be a Correct Little Sister," pays homage to Bambara's gifts as a comedic writer. Written one year after they overlapped at City College, "Dear Toni" celebrates the twinned births of Bambara's daughter and her anthology *The Black Woman*, which contained three of Lorde's poems alongside the writing of their City College students. In it, Lorde imagines encountering Bambara

> in an office down the hall from mine
> calmly studying term papers like maps
> marking off stations
> on our trip through the heights of Convent Avenue
> teaching english our children citycollege[50]

Here, Lorde catches a glimpse of Bambara at her desk in a moment of recognition that reveals as much about Lorde's own teaching as it does about Bambara's. While others might have seen a professor grading her students' papers, Lorde's vision is different. She depicts Bambara not punitively evaluating students' work—sorting correct from incorrect—but "studying" them as one would a "map" for guidance on where to go next. Whereas students are typically the ones who "study" to prepare for an exam, here Bambara, the instructor, is learning from their words, using them to proceed through unfamiliar territory. Such maps might be the syllabi for students' dream courses or the projects that Bambara's students submitted at the end of each semester. They might be maps for navigating dangerous, racist territory or blueprints for how they wanted the world to look. This image of students' term papers as "maps" suggests that for Lorde, as for Bambara, students' words and ideas determined the direction of each course. Given the dearth of archival materials from Lorde's time at City College, her poem offers a welcome glimpse of what might have been: namely, their shared practice of centering student voices, in both their classrooms and anthologies.

"Dear Toni" weaves together the activities of writing, teaching, and mothering, revealing all three to be interrelated modes of activism. Here, the subjects of their teaching are "our children": their daughters, their SEEK students, and their readers, especially of *The Black Woman*. Historically, Black women have used this kind of family language to describe what Patricia Hill Collins calls their traditions as "othermothers," a sense of mothering that encompasses but does not end with one's biological children.[51] This reference to their "children" invites us to consider teaching as an act of what Alexis Pauline Gumbs, China Martens, and Mai'a Williams call "revolutionary mothering": "nurturing" and "affirming" those whose lives are deemed expendable by racism, sexism, and capitalism.[52] "Dear Toni" thus illustrates how Lorde imagined herself in dialogue with Bambara through their joint refusals of inherited conventions: in the classroom, on the page, and as mothers of young Black girls.

Unlike the other women in this book, who, after their time at City College, went on to teach at other institutions, Lorde would spend the rest of her career teaching at different colleges within the CUNY system. In the fall of 1969, she was hired as a lecturer in the Education Department at CUNY's Lehman College in the Bronx. Whereas at City College she had taught basic writing, at Lehman she taught her first class that focused explicitly on difference: it was a course on race for students training to be middle and high school teachers. As she recalls, the students were "99 percent white" but teaching "Black children in the city schools. . . . I had all of these white students wanting to know, 'What are we doing? Why are our kids hating us . . . ?'"[53] One way she tried to address this was through class discussions of stereotypes, which she hoped would help these teachers-in-training "examine white perceptions of Black Americans."[54] She also created sample scenarios that highlighted how race impacts daily life. She asked them, for instance, to reflect on how their own experiences of traveling through New York City to arrive at their classroom might differ from those of their Black students. The students, however, "were not prepared for this self-scrutiny and responded with guilt, anger, and silence."[55] Here she encountered white women's resistance to addressing racism, a subject that would become central to her writing. This work was exhausting, "terribly costly emotionally" rather than rejuvenating, as her work at Tougaloo and City College had been.[56] "I want to teach Black students again," she told Rich.[57]

This would not be the only time that Lorde's teaching was met with resistance from white students. On the one hand, their reactions remind us that true learning—learning that challenges what we think we know—doesn't always feel good. Reflecting on our complicity in injustice rarely does. Yet as Karen Buenavista Hanna observes, if our goal is to teach in the service of social change, white comfort should not be a metric for educational efficacy.[58] It's also important to consider how educators who address injustice and inequality, especially women of color like Lorde, can face serious repercussions for doing so. While it's unclear whether students submitted evaluations of this course, if they did, we can imagine how their feelings of guilt and anger may have resulted in negative evaluations that could have jeopardized whether she would be rehired the following year and therefore, also, her salary, livelihood, and ability to support her family. In later years, tenure would allow her to pursue transgressive teaching with less risk. But as a lecturer at Lehman, she was not guaranteed reappointment the following year. Fortunately, she had other options. Nationwide, higher education was expanding, and unlike in today's academic labor market, professors were in short supply. This was especially true at CUNY, where the implementation of open admissions in 1970 resulted in an increased demand for professors across its various campuses.

That year, Lorde's desire to teach Black students brought her to the last place one might expect a Black lesbian feminist to want to teach. She was hired as a lecturer in English at CUNY's newly established John Jay College of Criminal Justice. Though the school was initially created to train police officers, open admissions brought in an influx of African American, Puerto Rican, and civilian students. Thus, it was through open admissions that Lorde, someone who would later write poems condemning police brutality and whose words would inspire the Black Lives Matter movement, found herself teaching police officers. If she had previously been scared that her SEEK students wouldn't understand her, now the threat was greater. Here her students carried guns.

Presented with this tremendous, albeit terrifying, opportunity, Lorde designed a course called Race and the Urban Situation that immersed students in the study of institutional racism. First in 1970 and then again in 1971 and 1972 (likely other times, too), they spent fourteen weeks reading texts like

Thomas Gossett's *Race: The History of an Idea* (1963), James Boggs's "Uprooting Racism and Racists in the United States" (1970), Barry N. Schwartz and Robert Disch's *White Racism: Its History, Pathology, and Practice* (1970), and issues of the *Black Scholar* on "Black Psychology" (March 1970) and "Black Culture" (June 1970). She also asked them to read excerpts of the 440-page Kerner Commission report, authored by President Lyndon B. Johnson's National Advisory Commission on Civil Disorders, an analysis of the 160 recent racial uprisings throughout the country (John Jay students would have been involved in these rebellions, perhaps on opposing sides). While mainstream media blamed angry young Black men for the violence, the report's authors found institutional racism and a lack of opportunities to be the cause. As Gumbs observes, Lorde was, to the best of our knowledge, the first educator to assign such materials and explicitly teach police officers about anti-Black racism.[59]

Though Race and the Urban Situation was listed, in the catalog, as History-Literature 210 (it was cross-listed with the Division of Government, History, and Economics), students looking for an in-depth analysis of literature were likely disappointed. Instead, the course focused primarily on recent social science texts—works of history, sociology, psychology—while works of literature (like Nella Larsen's *Quicksand* and LeRoi Jones's *Home*) were often "recommended" or "suggested." Was Lorde concerned that students might too easily dismiss literature as subjective? This seems possible, given that her lecture notes contain extensive quantifiable data, such as median income and employment statistics broken down by race and gender. Maybe she thought these statistics would prove more eye-opening to students. Or perhaps she was trying to deepen her own understanding of the historical conditions, sociological trends, and psychological forces that produced this apocalyptic present.

The syllabus for Race and the Urban Situation is organized into an outline. It begins with definitions of key terms, then proceeds to examine histories of racism in the United States, the various mechanisms by which it operates, and its effects on white and Black Americans:

Introduction—What is race?
 I Defining racism
 II Racism in America
   A Western values for "Black"
   B What is a racist society? Institutionalized racism.
 III Mechanics of Oppression
 IV Effects of Racism on White Americans
 V Effects of racism on Black Americans[60]

This ordering—studying racism's impact on white people *before* Black people—invited white students to see how racism was distorting their own worldview and dehumanizing them, too. As Lorde's notes indicate, racism leads white people to "fear & guilt: projection & acting out."[61] To confront injustice, in these terms, becomes an act of reclaiming one's humanity.

Among the assignments for Race and the Urban Situation were writing prompts that challenged students to apply history to contemporary debates about race and power. For example, after reading Lerone Bennett Jr.'s *Before the Mayflower: A History of the Negro in America, 1619–1962*, students were asked to respond to the following: "Power steps back only in the face of more power. Do you find this an accurate statement in terms of the history of black people in America? Discuss four historical occurrences from *Before the Mayflower* as examples illustrating your answer."[62] Rather than imposing her own view on students, this assignment allows them to draw their own conclusions, provided they are grounded in historical facts. It treats history not as the mere memorization of names, dates, and locations but as a form of knowledge that helps us understand the present. Such knowledge of Black history could reframe the era's political issues, making the armed resistance and militarized rhetoric of the Black Panther Party seem less like aggression and more like self-defense. Another assignment provided students with two quotes—one from Booker T. Washington and one from Malcolm X—each with a different perspective on power. Students were instructed to discuss the quotes in relation to laws and court cases like the Civil Rights Act of 1875, Jim Crow legislation in 1877–1901, and *Plessy v. Ferguson*.[63] These assignments thus explored how histories of institutional racism and legalized discrimination continue to shape the present, while also allowing students to formulate their own evidence-based perspectives on the era's political debates.

In addition to making creative use of more traditional assignments like essays, Lorde developed formally innovative journal assignments that encouraged students to apply their readings and discussions about institutional racism, Black history, and power directly to their lives. Students in Race and the Urban Situation were instructed to keep a "Weekly Journal—one page written weekly on some point or points made in class discussions," which would then be submitted to the instructor.[64] Penned in shorthand, Lorde's lecture notes indicate how she verbally explained such assignments: "2 pg typed evaluation/response of what's been happening in relation to work you've been doing/reading. What's happened in 6 hours since last [sic] . . . what experience of where you've been & are going."[65] These instructions invite students to assume a kind of radical openness toward the material—a willingness to be changed by what they were learning. They challenge them to try and unlearn established attitudes and see things differently than they did just six hours earlier.

Lorde's journal assignments created space for reflection, introspection, and potential transformation but in a way that wasn't prescriptive, heavy-handed, or authoritative. There, students could record their shifting thoughts, feelings, and reactions; raise questions; and track what they agreed with and what might feel inaccurate, oversimplified, or missing. They could also test out, rework, and refine their ideas, in dialogue with Lorde. Looking back, we can see how these assignments encouraged praxis: both the testing of ideas from readings in one's life and the generation of insights from experiences.

Lorde assigned different kinds of journals for different courses. Creative writing students, for example, kept a private notebook in which they collected "FEELINGS, DREAM MATERIAL, IMAGINGS, FOUND LINES, etc. and any other material that might later be used in their poetry."[66] At the time, these kinds of journal assignments were uncommon but not new. Since at least the 1920s, practitioners of expressivist writing pedagogy had used journals to help students gain greater control over language and cultivate a writing voice—values that Lorde, as a poet, likely shared. Journals were also a mainstay of SEEK pedagogy. Bambara, Barbara Christian, David Henderson, Mina Shaughnessy, and Rich all used them to encourage frequent writing and the expression of ideas without fear of grammatical mistakes. Though Lorde may have picked up such assignments from her colleagues, they were also inspired by her writerly practice of keeping journals where she recorded her thoughts, feelings, and reactions to current events, much of which served as source material for her published work. While journals would later become a key feature of women's studies courses, Lorde's students were far more accustomed to quizzes, exams, and the writing of themes.[67] Well into the 1980s, they would continue to remark on the novelty of such assignments. As a student from a later course recorded in her journal, "To explain how I feel is difficult and also NEW!"[68]

Though Lorde was not the first to assign journals, it is worth considering the particular context in which she used them. In this course at John Jay in 1970, helping students move beyond abstract, theoretical discussions of institutional racism and apply these lessons was a life-or-death issue. As future police officers, many of her students actually held her life, and the lives of her friends and family, in their hands. While journal assignments are typically understood as products of expressivist and feminist pedagogy, Lorde's archives reveal how they were also shaped by the era's Black liberation movements, including the fight against racialized police brutality.

It might seem that journals, submitted only to the instructor, run contrary to the public pedagogies that have been the focus of this book, but the two actually go hand in hand. Lorde's journal assignments did not exist in isolation. Rather, these more intimate assignments, where students could reflect on their lives and develop ideas free from public scrutiny, were often coupled with other writing activities and projects that asked them to take action based on what they were learning. As one undated assignment states, "In your daily living give 3 examples of actual ways in which you yourself can function to positively counteract racism. Be specific."[69] These assignments, write Miriam Atkin and Iemanjá Brown, helped students "identify their own struggles within larger political and economic structures and ... find ways in their everyday lives to move toward action."[70] But they didn't always yield the desired results. Lorde's notes convey frustration that students weren't sufficiently connecting their classroom discussions to their lives. She writes, "We talk a lot. . . . I wanted some idea of how you see yourself functioning," in relation to their discussions of race.[71] Perhaps building on the earlier prompt, she assigned a five-page "Outside Project" due two months later: "Choose a situation + enter it or evaluate one you already are in & put into practice one of the ways you counteract racism ... write up in detail."[72] These combined assignments—both journals and public projects—guided students in cultivating an activist consciousness: an awareness of their ability to address injustice. As one student notes, they taught her "to open myself to understanding the entire consequences of racism in real life and, based on this new knowledge, to develop a plan for acting against racism."[73]

Though Lorde was originally hired for a one-year lectureship, she was soon promoted to a tenure-track assistant professor position with a salary of around $30,000, or around $171,500 in 2023 dollars.[74] This livable salary allowed her time not only to write and teach but to experiment with different approaches, like incorporating student-led discussions. In the spring of 1972, she and her colleague, historian Blanche Wiesen Cook (who later became famous for her three-volume biography of Eleanor Roosevelt), designed an exciting new course, American Women in Black and White, one of the nation's first courses on women's studies and one of the few to focus on Black women.[75] As Black and "Third World" women like Lorde were criticizing racism in the women's movement, sexism in Black liberation movements, and the homophobia of both, their course took up these issues in the classroom. More specifically, it explored the distinct histories of Black and white women in the United States. Together, they read Frantz Fanon's *Black Skin, White Masks*, Gerda Lerner's *The Woman in American History*, and Bambara's landmark anthology *The Black Woman* (which included City College students' writing). The syllabus, again organized into an outline, began with a "class discussion" of "archetypes and stereotypes" and then proceeded historically from topics like "Women in the 18th century" through "The Emergence of Black Radicalism and Suffragism" and "Radical Women in the 20th century," with two class sessions devoted to "Literary Image[s] of Women."[76] The second half of the course was dedicated to contemporary "Issues of Liberation" such as "Racism and Sexism" and "Homosexuality." The final two and a half weeks of the semester were left open for students to share their own reports and lead discussions on topics of their choosing.

Why Lorde and Cook decided to turn the course over to students is not clear. Perhaps Lorde was thinking about her own autodidacticism: how much more motivated she was to learn about subjects she selected, as compared to what she'd been assigned in school. Or maybe the two instructors recognized that their heterogeneous John Jay classroom presented an unusual opportunity for radically different students to learn from one another. Initially, Cook recalls, the students in the course were "police officers and fire fighters and men."[77] But as word got out about this team-taught course, the "women in the [lesbian] bars" the two professors frequented downtown "invaded our class, and then very quickly the police students brought their wives and their mothers and their sisters and their friends, and it was the most crowded classroom imaginable."[78] While the question of where they all sat remains a mystery, in this motley class, predominantly white gay girls from the Village debated race, gender, and sexuality with "Black and white cops" and their female kin, as well as the working-class civilians, of every race and creed, who entered the university through open admissions. Surely, they learned just as much from these discussions as they did from the readings. In Cook's recollection at least one thing was certain: "We had a lot of fun."[79]

This joyful learning, however, was not without its perils. To teach such courses at a time when neither women's studies nor Black studies was recognized as a legitimate academic subject entailed personal and professional risk, especially for Lorde. In institutions where Black women were "the last hired and the first fired," it could, write Gloria T. Hull and Barbara Smith, "spell career suicide... [and] endanger... [their] situations in their schools and departments."[80]

During her time at John Jay (1970–78), Lorde also continued to teach basic writing courses. With open admissions came an increased demand for such courses, and Lorde's senior colleagues praised her willingness to teach them. One reason she may have been inclined to do so was because basic writing courses, which are required of all students, tend to be more diverse than upper-level English seminars, where a focus on canonical white, male authors can alienate students who don't share those identities. While archival records from these courses are scarce, a stray course description indicates that she taught remedial writing as creative writing, involving the arts of "observation, description, detailed reaction, and the writing of poetry."[81] This emphasis on cultivating student creativity was an act of quiet resistance to the conservative faculty throughout CUNY, who were obsessing over the need to drill this era's "new students" in grammar and sentence-level mechanics.[82] Her archives also contain an essay submitted by one of her English 101 students. In the paper, titled "On Being Blue," this student, a Black police officer, thinks through the differential life and death possibilities attached to these social positions. He writes, "On being blue: this is only possible for a Black officer when he is working (on duty) and in full uniform.... Out of uniform he is only another black or hispanic face. A threat to ... the powers that be—he must be pushed and shoved like the rest."[83] Though we can only speculate about the readings, class discussions, and assignments that led to the production of this essay, it illustrates the ways that Lorde created space for students to think through their lived, embodied experiences of difference.

Lorde brought a poetic spirit of perpetual curiosity, responsiveness, and openness to these classrooms—no small feat, given the omnipresent police uniforms that served as continual reminders of violence. As an educator, she learned as she went along, "asking the hard questions, not knowing what was coming next."[84] In her essay "Poet as Teacher—Human as Poet—Teacher as Human," she describes changing her lesson plans based on something as minor as the weather, or as grave as "the police slaughter of a Black child."[85] More than mere caprice, these sentiments illustrate her sensitivity to what was happening in the world that students carried with them into classrooms—an awareness of the learning these events enabled and foreclosed. She also recognized that teachers are not fully in charge of what, or how much, a student learns, just as an author never has the final word about how their poem will be interpreted. Rather, she saw "the learning process" as "something you can incite, literally incite, like a riot. And then, just possibly, hopefully it goes home, or on."[86] These words connect teaching to the era's social movements and remind us of the beautiful unpredictability of learning: that single, unrepeatable sentence tattooed on a student's soul, the idea that doesn't click at the time but ten years later falls into place. And in that unknowability of the future—an uncertainty embodied by her students—lay the possibility of something different, perhaps even a world more livable than the present.

* * *

As one might imagine, these experiences teaching "black and white cops and black and white kids off the block" left an indelible mark on Lorde's writing. During this period, she began drafting a novel in which the main character is, like herself, a professor, working with students to fight for open admissions and the implementation of "a relevant Black education." These classrooms also inspired a number of poems about teaching: not only "Dear Toni" but also "Teacher," "The Bees," "The Classrooms," and "Blackstudies." "The Bees," for instance, echoes the history lessons of Race and the Urban Situation. Like the essay prompt asking students to apply their knowledge of Black history to contemporary debates over power, the poem's apian allegory thematizes how history provides a more accurate understanding of current events. The poem takes place "in the street outside a school," where a group of young boys throw rocks at a beehive, proceed to get stung, and are avenged by the school's security guards, who destroy the beehive and its inhabitants. From the guards' perspective, the boys are victims who have been attacked by the aggressive bees. Yet the poem provides readers with a broader understanding of the sequence of events that led up to the boys' tears. As readers, we witness that they threw the first stone. The bees, "buzzing their anger," were merely defending their fortress, but they were the ones whose life, labor, and love got destroyed.

"The Bees," however, did not merely reflect Lorde's classroom conversations; it also generated distinct ideas and questions that she would later take up in her teaching. While the first stanza focuses on the boys and the guards, the second takes a step back, positioning the reader alongside a group of girls who stand at the periphery and bear witness to the massacre:

> Curious and apart
> four little girls look on in fascination
> learning a secret lesson
> trying to understand their own destruction.
> One girl cries out
> "Hey, the bees weren't making any trouble!"
> . . .
> "We could have studied honey-making!"

From their vantage point along the margins, the girls—one of Lorde's many invocations of the four girls murdered in the 16th Street Baptist Church bombing—observe that the bees were defending their "almost finished rooms of wax" and "new tunnels," not attacking the boys. They identify with the nameless and faceless bees, rather than sympathizing with their crying classmates. Here we can glimpse what feminist scholars in the 1980s would call "standpoint theory" and "situated knowledge": the idea that knowledge is grounded in particular perspectives and related to one's social location amid intersecting axes of power.[87] In the poem's final line, the girls mourn not only the death of the bees but also all of the joy they could have brought into the world by teaching others "honey-making": sharing their knowledge of how to create something sweet. The poem thus frames learning as increasing our ability to experience pleasure and to live a sweeter, more joyous life. If we think of honey-making as an art form, we might read this as a gesture toward all that can be learned from the art of those who are marginalized, exploited, and rendered vulnerable by the social order. In the years to come, Lorde would take up these questions about outsider art in her classes at Hunter College.

Teaching also gave Lorde new perspectives on her writing. Like Bambara, who described her stories as a way to "dramatize lessons learned," and Rich, who considered poetry "a kind of teaching," Lorde saw her poems as "learning devices," acts of "teaching—touching—really touching another human being," making an impression, however small, that alters someone's life.[88] While the term *didactic* is often used to disparage a poem or story, these women (like many writers) embraced the pedagogical possibilities of literature: the ways texts can prompt us to think and feel differently, reframe events in a particular light, and imagine what does not yet exist.[89]

There are also subtler ways that classrooms may have left an imprint on Lorde's work. Though it requires a bit of imagination, we can think about the ways that her journal assignments may have influenced her thinking about literary form. During Lorde's tenure at John Jay, she published *The Cancer Journals* (1980), a memoir composed of poetry, essays, and entries from the journals she kept throughout her journey with breast cancer. Today it is recognized as a key text of the women's health movement and an enduring Black lesbian feminist critique of the medical-industrial complex.[90] It was also one of the first cancer memoirs, paving the way for what has now become a popular genre. Lorde's teaching archives—full of journal assignments (and in some instances students' actual journals)—invite us to consider the role that classrooms may have played in the production of that groundbreaking text. Unlike the ineffective assignments that disappear from teaching archives, Lorde continued assigning journals from some of her earliest courses to her last. By 1980, when *The Cancer Journals* was published, she had been reading students' journals for at least ten years (she would ultimately read hundreds throughout her career). We can imagine how, had she not spent so many hours with students' journals, she might have continued to see her own diaries merely as source material to be woven into more traditional formats like essays. Instead, she chose to maintain this quotidian, diaristic format in *The Cancer Journals* (and later *A Burst of Light*), signaling to readers everywhere that their everyday experiences as patients mattered.

In addition to inspiring her poetry (and perhaps the form of her cancer memoirs), it was in Lorde's open admissions classrooms that she developed some of her most influential theories of difference. Though she had previously explored race and gender in her poetry, it wasn't until she began teaching that she started writing essays like "Poetry Is Not a Luxury" (1977) and "Age, Race, Class, and Sex: Women Redefining Difference" (1980). This was because, as Lorde explained, the experience of teaching basic writing was "how I taught myself to write prose."[91] And it was her prose that expanded her readership from small poetic communities to global social movements. In addition, creating courses like Race and the Urban Situation and American Women in Black and White allowed her to earn a living while simultaneously performing the research that would inform her theories of difference. It's important to note that she was developing these courses between 1970 and 1972, five years before she penned her famous essays. In her own words, they represented not subjects she was already an expert in but ones that she and her students needed to learn more about in order to survive this apocalyptic present. She writes, "We teach best those things we need to learn for our own survival. So, as we learn them, we then reach back and teach, and it becomes a joint process."[92] Like most professors, Lorde engaged in extensive self-education in preparation to teach these courses. She studied sociological research on race and gender; the different histories of Black and white women; the ways past injustices continue to structure the present; and the psychology of oppression, in both the oppressor and the oppressed. And Lorde was the first to admit that these courses were part of her own education. "I teach myself in outline," she writes in her poem "The Classrooms," indicating that preparing these materials—organizing information in a way that would be intelligible to others—was part of her own continual learning. While she has since become renowned for her insights on difference, her teaching archives reveal how these ideas were molded five years earlier within her CUNY classrooms.

Though teaching was a source of inspiration, there was nothing romantic about the institutional racism, sexism, and homophobia Lorde experienced in universities. In 1971, when she posted her erotic "Love Poem," addressed to a woman, on the English Department bulletin board, it was met with homophobic panic from her colleagues. She also faced violent backlash for her curricular activism. She was vilified by both conservative and progressive faculty members for her allegedly radical stance that there ought to be separate departments of Black and Puerto Rican studies. Her desk was searched without permission, she received phone calls threatening her children, and angry faculty members used her status as an out lesbian to try and dissuade students from working with her.[93]

Lorde's poem "Blackstudies" (1974) explores the complicated and messy experience of teaching under these conditions.[94] The poem depicts a nightmarish scene of teaching and learning on the chilling, windy seventeenth floor of an unnamed building.[95] The speaker, a teacher, describes the stereotypes of Black women that students bring with them to the classroom. These stereotypes replay in the speaker's mind, pinning her down, distracting her, and stifling her creativity and ability to work.[96] As her archives indicate, this concern with stereotypes speaks to Lorde's actual experiences in classrooms: in courses like Race and the Urban Situation, she and her students examined the histories and detrimental effects of Black stereotypes. While helping a room full of police officers unlearn inherited biases and prejudices held lifesaving possibilities, her students may have resisted this unlearning, as we saw with those at Lehman. Though we can only guess how Lorde might have felt facilitating these discussions, "Blackstudies" suggests the ways that a Black, lesbian, feminist teacher might have to steel herself against the blows of their words, as they engaged in this important but emotionally exhausting work.

Through its extended metaphor of a court trial, "Blackstudies" suggests that social justice was at stake in these classrooms. The class is described as a "trial on the 17th floor" in which students wait outside the accused speaker's door, "searching condemning listening" with "questions that feel like judgments." Whereas in a traditional classroom, the teacher evaluates the students, here this relationship is reversed—a reminder that these police officer students held Lorde's life in their hands. Another layer of the classroom courtroom is the 1973 trial of white police officer Thomas J. Shea. One year prior to the poem's publication, Shea shot and killed a ten-year-old Black child, Clifford Glover, in Queens. Shea was later acquitted by a jury of eleven white men and one Black woman. Glover's murder became the subject of several of Lorde's poems, including "Power," "The Same Death Over and Over or Lullabies Are for Children," and "A Woman/Dirge for Wasted Children" (marked with the dedication "for Clifford").[97] She was infuriated by the idea that Shea may have attended John Jay and that she might have seen him in the hallways. In courses like Race and the Urban Situation, she aimed to increase students' awareness of the historical conditions that had resulted in Glover's murder and Shea's acquittal. Read in relation to Shea's trial, "Blackstudies" imagines the classroom as a space to do justice for Clifford while also expressing skepticism toward that very possibility, especially given how central education has been to the reproduction of white supremacy.

The poem's concluding lines enter an almost mythic register, in which survival is at stake. Referring to her students, the speaker wonders:

> what shall they carve for weapons
> what shall they grow for food

The pronoun *they* is telling. In contrast to "Dear Toni," which depicted Lorde's and Bambara's City College students as "our children," here the line between students and instructor is more pronounced. Like many of Lorde's teaching poems, these lines depict food and scenes of eating—something one might not necessarily expect to find in poems about education. On the one hand, these recurring images of food remind us that teaching was Lorde's occupation: how she, quite literally, put food on the table. And for a lesbian of color in racist, sexist, homophobic America, this was not trivial. "I am a lesbian woman of color whose children eat regularly because I work in a university," she wrote.[98] Questions of nourishment were also at the heart of her pedagogy, which taught students to analyze how differences—of race, gender, and sexuality—affect people's access to food and other material resources like safety, shelter, education, and health. These invocations of food also critique the era's liberal discourses surrounding education as a means of addressing racialized poverty. Rather than redistributing resources to ensure everyone had nourishing food, health care, and housing, policymakers looked to education as a great equalizing force that was supposed to help communities of color lift themselves out of poverty. Yet the nightmarish world of "Blackstudies" highlights the perversity of political thinking that sutures students' educational success to their ability to access what they need to survive.

Like Rich's poem "The Burning of Paper Instead of Children," "Blackstudies" is a classroom lyric that is similarly ambivalent about the political possibilities of teaching. While the majority of the poem describes how lonely, cold, and dangerous it felt to teach in the belly of the beast, at a school for police officers, it concludes with a tentative sense that if the speaker is able to navigate these conditions—make it through without compromising her health and well-being—the classroom could become a site of nourishment. In the final line, students sow the seeds of a new society, suggesting, like Rich's poetic fragment, how classrooms both reproduce the status quo and create space for alternative worldmaking.

Though we often think of feminist poetry as addressing themes like marriage, motherhood, and anger, Lorde's and Rich's classroom lyrics illustrate how teaching was also a major preoccupation. For both authors, poetry provided a space of overflow where they could explore the ideas and feelings that couldn't otherwise find a home in faculty meetings, reappointment portfolios, or conference presentations. Wrapped in poetic language ambiguous enough to protect their jobs, these poems bear witness to institutional injustices against people of color and question whether education can really address deep-seated inequities. If they needed to bracket their doubt and skepticism in order to prepare lesson plans and assignments, such sentiments found a place in poems like "Blackstudies." It's possible that poetry provided a release valve that allowed them to return to work each day. But the opposite could be true, too: writing classroom lyrics may have allowed them to explore the depths of their doubt, creating space for it to breathe, incubate, blossom, and proliferate.

Although Lorde's experiences at John Jay could be downright harrowing, she continued to advocate for free college. In 1976, when CUNY's open admissions policy ended, she criticized the negative impact this would have on women, especially women of color, and on society more broadly. In fact, "Poetry Is Not a Luxury" (1977), one of her most celebrated essays, can be read as a trenchant, nuanced critique of the neoliberal ideologies that were dismantling public higher education both at CUNY and throughout the country.[99] First published in the women's magazine *Chrysalis* during Lorde's tenure as poetry editor, the essay argues that, for women, poetry cannot be dismissed as a mere luxury, for it serves as a means by which they have given language to their experiences, confronted their fears, and imagined a better world. In doing so, writes Roderick Ferguson, it emphasizes the importance of poetry for both personal and social transformation.[100] Penned one year after CUNY's implementation of tuition, the essay can also be understood as a rebuttal to the era's neoliberal education policies, including the withdrawal of state funding from higher education, the end of open admissions, and an increasing emphasis on vocational training.

In "The Day the Purpose of College Changed," Dan Berrett traces the onset of this ideology to a 1967 press conference delivered by then-Governor

Ronald Reagan.[101] At the time, greater numbers of women, people of color, and working-class individuals were gaining access to colleges and universities. This era also saw an increase in student activism, dissent, and political organizing, including the growth of the Black student movement and protests against the Vietnam War. At a press conference in Sacramento, Reagan gave older, conservative white voters who feared this unrest, a culprit—the humanities—which he promised to attack in a way that would also lower their taxes. In a statement that Lorde directly challenges, he framed the humanities as a frivolous "intellectual luxury" and argued that American taxpayers should not be "subsidizing intellectual curiosity."[102] When asked what he meant by an "intellectual luxury" the future president answered, "repairing bad instruments" and "learning how to demonstrate, organized demonstrations.... I figure that carrying a picket sign is sort of like, oh, a lot of things you pick up naturally, like learning to swim by falling off the end of the dock."[103] Setting aside the fact that Reagan's version of swimming lessons are a recipe for drowning, this notion that education in art, music, and politics is expendable would lay the foundations not only for his defunding of higher education but for broader neoliberal reforms that continue to play out today.[104] (As recently demonstrated by events at West Virginia University, when budgets fall short, the humanities are often the first to go.)

By 1977, the year Lorde's essay was published, such reforms had drastically reduced the students of color enrolled throughout CUNY's campuses. Her classes on Afro-American Literature and American Women in Black and White, once filled with students who reflected New York City's racial and class demographics, were now increasingly affluent and white. Considered in this context, Lorde's essay refuses Reagan's rhetoric by emphasizing the negative effects of these austerity policies on the many women, especially working-class women of color, who disappeared from her classrooms: how the withdrawal of state funding and implementation of tuition curtailed their ability to study poetry and flourish. Such policies also shrank the amount of societal space for imagining a better world, thus diminishing possibilities for all of us.

Aesthetics of the Outsider

In the late 1970s, Lorde's political involvement intensified. This was prompted, in part, by a 1978 cancer diagnosis and subsequent mastectomy, which gave her life a new sense of urgency. As Black women were being murdered in Boston and Black children in Atlanta, Lorde doubled down in her fight for justice. In October 1979, she spoke at the widely publicized Gay and Lesbian March on Washington. Standing in front of a sea of 100,000 people, her largest audience yet, she delivered a speech insisting that acts of violence against Black women and children should be of concern to the gay and lesbian movement: "For lesbians and gay men have always been at the vanguard of struggles for liberation and justice . . . for a world where all our children can grow free from the diseases of racism, sexism, and classism, and of homophobia."[105] Amid a society that distributes precarity both widely and unevenly, "the question always is, what kind of a world do we want to be a part of?"[106] And that philosophical, ethical, and creative question—the kind of question we can sometimes feel too exhausted to ask—was at the heart of Lorde's classrooms.

As Lorde's reputation as a writer and activist increased, more students wanted to take her courses and spend time debating, "What kind of a world do we want to be a part of?" Although she received tenure at John Jay, she was repeatedly underpaid despite her popularity among students.[107] In 1981 she left John Jay to teach at another school in the CUNY system: her alma mater, Hunter College, located on Manhattan's Upper East Side. As a full professor in English, she directed the Poetry Center and taught literature courses and poetry workshops, like the one depicted in the documentary *A Litany for Survival*. There, we see her light up a small creative writing seminar, chatting casually with several students before the serious work of poetry begins. Sometimes positioned at the head of a long table, other times at the center of a circle, Lorde looked students in the eye and read their writing aloud with the same gravitas as her own work. "To wrench havoc . . . to wrench havoc," she repeats, reading a student's poem aloud as the class listens in rapt attention, hanging on her every word.[108] "It doesn't sit right," she proclaims, turning the student's poetic line over and over again, hands twirling as she speaks, a true New Yorker. "Whenever you don't trust what you're doing, you use language like that. And I don't think you need that line," she concludes with conviction. According to her former student Jacqueline Brown, "She made you feel, when you were talking to her, that there was no place she'd rather be."[109]

In contrast to the emphasis on social science in earlier courses like Race and the Urban Situation, Lorde's later courses illustrate the central role that literature played in her pedagogies of difference. In 1981, when asked to teach a course on post–World War II writers, the sample description she was given included nine male authors, two women, and not a single writer of color. She retitled the course The Poet as Outsider and assigned writing by women, Black people, gays and lesbians, and Native Americans. As her lecture notes indicate, Lorde and her students discussed how canonical art and literature constitute what she called "the aesthetics of changelessness."[110] It reflects what we already know: the perspectives of those in positions of power who have historically controlled schools, museums, journalism, and publishing agencies. They also discussed how the academic study of art neutralizes literature's power and obscures the myriad roles it plays in people's lives and communities beyond academic institutions. Perhaps scribbled with haste, Lorde's fragmentary lecture notes distill key points for her to riff on:

> status quo approach separates it [art] from life
> "art for art's sake"
> ivory tower
> artist withdraws.[111]

(They start to sound like poetry the more you read them.) By contrast, their course focused on "the aesthetics of the outsider": the art, ideas, and perspectives that emerge from the margins of society. "Isn't literature about change?" Lorde asked her students, and we can imagine the dramatic pause she let hang in the air. "The function of any art is to make us more what we wish to be," she told them. "Real change happens at the periphery."[112]

This belief in the power of an outsider's perspective was shaped by Lorde's own life, throughout which she was continually "defined as other in every group": an outsider in the women's movement because she was working-class, Black, and a lesbian; in Black liberation movements because she was a lesbian; in the gay and lesbian movement because she was Black, working-class, and of Caribbean descent.[113] Over time, Lorde learned to use her marginalization within these communities as a source of knowledge, to critique the politics of exclusivity. While those at the periphery are vulnerable, exposed to violence, and deprived of resources, they can also see what an insider cannot. When a world—a classroom, a school, an institution, a city—is set up for you to flourish, it's easy to assume that it's working well for everyone. You might not even think of it as structured at all, just the way things are. But when society is not working for you, when it is organized in a way that makes every day feel like the apocalypse, it's much easier to see the flaws in the design. In fact, your life might just depend on learning how things got to be that way in order to navigate and change them. Especially following her mastectomy and decision not to wear a prosthetic breast, Lorde came to see her position of "Sister Outsider" as "both strength and weakness."[114] As DeVaux writes, Lorde "invented a compelling persona as 'outsider' from which she derived strength, status, and a public platform."[115] And rather than checking these experiences of exclusion at the classroom door, she used them to inform her pedagogies of difference.

In 1985 Lorde designed a course that focused on one particular tradition of outsider aesthetics: lesbian literature. At the time, such courses were new, and she undertook extensive research in order to prepare for it, including tapping into her network of feminist professors to solicit syllabi for similar courses. As in the SEEK program, where educators recognized the sharing of teaching materials as part of larger movements for change, professors responded to her request. In Lorde's archives, alongside her own syllabi, lesson plans, and assignments, are similar materials from other educators that she collected. These include syllabi from Julia Stanley, who taught a course on lesbian novels at the University of Nebraska in 1978, and Barbara Smith, who taught The Invisible Woman in Literature in 1983.

The result of Lorde's careful research and planning was The Other Woman: Lesbian Voices in 20th Century American Literature (1985).[116] While Race and the Urban Situation thematized debates over nonviolent and violent protest, and American Women in Black and White interrogated the erasure of difference in the women's movement, Lesbian Voices focused on the particularities of lesbians' experiences, especially in relation to the era's male-dominated gay rights movement.[117] The syllabus is again organized as an outline, with required and recommended readings for each category:

I Contexts of Contemporary Lesbian Feminist Writing
- A Questions to be considered
  - a What defines lesbian literature
  - b What does it have in common with other literatures of the outsider
  - c What differentiates lesbian literature
  - d How do lesbian differences of identity affect how we create and define lesbian literatures

II Foremothers

III Issues of Difference (Racism[,] Anti-Semitism, Ageism, Class)
- A Lesbians of Color
- B Jewish Lesbians
- C Working Class Lesbians
- D Older Lesbians

IV   Ethical Questions
V   Class Topic: DISCUSSION OF TOPICS AGREED UPON BY CLASS MEMBERS
VI   What Have We Done; Lesbian Literatures of the Futures; Visions and Evaluation[118]

Lesbian Voices began with contemporary readings including Barbara Smith's "Towards a Black Feminist Criticism" and Elly Bulkin's introduction to *Lesbian Fiction*, which introduced the course's themes, then considered its "foremothers": early novels like Radclyffe Hall's *The Well of Loneliness* (1928) and Patricia Highsmith's *The Price of Salt* (1952). As they moved on to "Issues of Difference," they discussed new books like Cherríe Moraga's *Loving in the War Years* (1983)—a memoir of Moraga's coming of age as a lesbian Chicana and critique of the ongoing violence of colonialism—and the section on Black lesbians from Smith's *Homegirls: A Black Feminist Anthology* (1983). These texts are steeped in political consciousness, deftly weaving personal experiences and structural critique, and modeling embodied ways of thinking that students could emulate.

In Lesbian Voices, Lorde's earlier practice of student-led discussions took on new urgency. That semester, they discussed how society sanctions heterosexual desires and devalues, or even persecutes, other pleasures. And Lorde seemed attuned to the parallel ways that hierarchical teaching methods center the professor's intellectual interests over students'. Instead of deciding, ahead of time, all that they would study, the fifth portion of the course focused on topics selected by the students (many of whom identified as lesbians). In doing so, Lorde reoriented the learning environment around students' desires to know: the distinct curiosities that each one brought to the classroom. We might even think of this as an act of queer pedagogy insofar as it introduced greater joy and a range of intellectual desires into what is often a narrowly professor-centered space.

With these later courses like Lesbian Voices, Lorde also added group projects to her repertoire of assignments. In some instances, these were as broadly defined as "Do a group project: an evening given over to something we've worked on."[119] This vague assignment suggests that the final product, the project itself, was of less importance than the act of students working together, navigating each other's different schedules, needs, desires, perspectives, and access to material resources. Lorde's archives contain one such project undertaken by three Black women students. It was inspired by Lorde's essay "Eye to Eye: Black Women, Hatred, and Anger," which traces the social, cultural, and political conditions that incentivize antagonism among Black women. After reading the essay in class, the student leading the project wanted to better understand "her problems relating to Black women," and Lorde suggested that she discuss this "with other Black women."[120] The resulting project took the form of a recorded and transcribed conversation in which the three young women discuss their responses to the essay. In doing so, they engage in a kind of creative mimicry, revisiting, as Lorde does, incidents from their childhoods to examine how their feelings toward other Black women were, in part, the products of a racist, sexist, and capitalist society. One interviewee was struck by Lorde's examples of Black women ignoring each other "in the library . . . across the counters, at delicatessens—and if someone else were to come in—a white male, a Black man the response would be altogether different."[121] Another describes how Lorde's analysis of this "automatic hostility" gave her language and historical context for "something I knew instinctively was going on, but I never had words for." As the assignment deadline approached, the interviewer hand-delivered a note to Professor Lorde: "Audre: I'm still typing—I'll slide the rest under your door."[122]

This project illustrates three facets of Lorde's pedagogies of difference. First, it highlights how she, like all of the teacher-poets, used literature to encourage students' reflections on their own lives. Second, it demonstrates how she taught students to think about difference through the sharing of experiences. As was the case with feminist consciousness-raising groups, the sharing of seemingly personal or idiosyncratic experiences deepened their understanding of racism, sexism, and homophobia. Third, Lorde taught students to use their embodied experiences as the grounds from which to analyze the world—a version of what Moraga calls "theory in the flesh."[123]

Though few archival documents remain from Lorde's classrooms, the materials she collected from other educators provide a glimpse of what might have been. I want to pause for a moment to travel cross-country and peek into a women's studies class, the syllabus of which is preserved in Lorde's archive. Titled Women as Creative Artists, the course was taught by Paula King and Melanie Kaye at Portland State University in 1978.[124] It was organized around feminist calls for action of the 1970s: interrogating the lies of patriarchy; reclaiming women's art, history, and culture; and forming feminist communities. Each week, readings in feminist criticism were paired with a small, creative research and writing task that asked students to test out a particular theory or concept. Several of these involve creative mimicry. For example, when they read Virginia Woolf's "A Room of One's Own," which invites readers to imagine what would have happened if William Shakespeare had an equally "adventurous" and "imaginative" sister, the accompanying writing assignment asked students to engage in the kind of radical speculation modeled in Woolf's essay. They were told to "recreate a woman-historical, someone you know, someone you imagine—who didn't get to say what she knew & try to answer: what do you need to know from her, what are you deprived of by her silence[?]"[125] Similar to many of the assignments in this book, Kaye and King's encouraged praxis: testing out and generating ideas through actions and experience. One such assignment asked students to attend an art museum, performance, or festival and count the number of women represented as artists and in the audience. Another asked them to keep a journal for three weeks, focusing on "women & something, you fill in the blank."[126] Through these assignments, students used the methods of Woolf, Rich, Judy Chicago, and Barbara Smith to research and write about the silencing of women in the literary, historical, and cultural record.

We can't say with any degree of certainty whether Lorde used the assignments on Kaye and King's syllabus. All we know is that she collected and saved it. What such materials do remind us is that the four teacher-poets in this book were part of broader networks of educators who saw their classrooms as sites of social change.

Like many feminist professors, Lorde's activist teaching extended beyond the classroom. At Hunter, for instance, she led a faculty seminar on racism. The proposal includes examples of "Racism at Hunter Today," such as professors discouraging students of color from pursuing difficult career paths and the erasure of Black history in the curriculum. These, she notes, will only "change when we begin to recognize that . . . distortions around race are realities in American consciousness and when we as educators, dare to examine the ways in which these distortions affect our teaching, and imprint themselves upon our students."[127] As a tenured professor, educating her colleagues was one way she used her position of power to advocate for change.

At Hunter, Lorde continued to collaborate with the three writers she had met at City College. Whereas her poem for Bambara, "Dear Toni," had recounted their peregrinations down Harlem's Convent Avenue, the 1980s provided opportunities to venture further. In 1981 Lorde, Bambara, and Rich traveled to the St. Croix Women Writers Symposium on the tropical, palm-lined, salt-swept campus of the College of the Virgin Islands, along with Michelle Cliff (Rich's partner) and Gloria Joseph (Lorde's partner). That same year, all three journeyed to the foliage forests of Hampshire College to speak at a course Joseph was teaching called Insurgent Sisters. The year 1985 brought Bambara and Lorde to Cuba's cerulean seas as part of a delegation of Black women writers sponsored by the *Black Scholar*.[128] As fellow attendee Alexis DeVaux recalls, the writers sunbathed and sipped cocktails on the Havana Hotel roof deck, debating "whether the Cuban revolution had truly challenged racism, and what was the real status of lesbians and gays there."[129]

In addition to these physical intersections, the four remained connected in each other's imaginations. During the open admissions era, they had confronted the crushing impact of silence: the ways schools suppressed minoritarian art and knowledge and stifled students' voices and potential. Knowing that these silences were not absences but the effects of power hierarchies, they challenged the institutional structures that maintained them. Nearly two decades later, Bambara instructed students in her University of Delaware course The Text as a Rite of Recovery to prepare for their midterm by reviewing their class notes on the theme of "silence . . . silence as madness, as weapon, as tool, as punishment. See—slave narratives, Adrienne Rich, Audre Lorde, June Jordan, Warrior Woman." It was as if they were all still writing one larger story that began at City College but extended far beyond it.

Differences among them notwithstanding, these women found in each other both shared outrage and shared revolutionary love—a will to teach, write, and organize that mirrored their own.[130] At City College, they forged the unique kind of bonds that emerge from political action, when people come together, devoting their time and energy to fighting for a better world. Long after they left, they continued working together to challenge the silences imposed by dominant institutions. And when arguments or affairs threatened their friendships, these overlapping experiences constituted an unshakeable foundation that withstood the weight of distance and disagreements, be they fleeting or sustained. One could even say that such friendships helped save Lorde's life. As she battled breast cancer, she was buoyed up by a life preserver, a "ring of women" who kept her "afloat upon the surface of that sea."[131] Together, they restored her "volition": "energy . . . that I converted into power to heal myself."[132] In short, she believed that "the love of women healed me."[133]

Sharing the Illumination

In 1984 Lorde took a sabbatical from Hunter and accepted an invitation from sociologist Dagmar Schultz to teach for a semester at the Free University of Berlin. An avid traveler, she was especially excited to work with the Black women students Schultz had mentioned. "Who are the German women of the diaspora?" she wondered. "Where do our paths intersect as women of color and where do they diverge?"[134] That spring, she taught two courses at the university's John F. Kennedy Center for North American Studies.

In Contemporary Black Women's Poetry, as in many of her courses, it was not only literature but students' lives that were placed under the microscope. That semester, they studied poems by Nikki Giovanni, Pat Parker, Mari Evans, and Sonia Sanchez in relation to both "the lives and consciousness" of their authors and students' own experiences.[135] And for many German students, this was an entirely new way of learning. On the first day, Lorde gave a straightforward prompt: to introduce themselves and talk about what they hoped to get out of the course. The students, however, were shocked. One wrote, "In all the other classes each of us students including myself sat there ready to participate passively, but that didn't work this time. After Audre Lorde had introduced herself she expected us to do the same plus to tell the group why we came to this class."[136] Wasn't it obvious that they were there to learn more about Black women's poetry? No one knew what to say, and it took a long time for anyone to speak. The air was thick with tension, anxiety, and confusion. Another student noted that they were "not used ... to that kind of lesson or teaching—it's too personal."[137]

That semester, Lorde assigned journals to help students move beyond the illusory ideal of a detached, neutral observer's perspective and instead engage in the more messy, challenging, and self-reflexive mode of reading that she called "entering a relationship with the poem."[138] Most of the students in the course were white women, and their journals initially focused on what was recognizable in the poems: themes like love and what appeared to be shared experiences of patriarchal oppression. In an early journal entry, one student wrote:

> don't we all have the same basic problems?
> the want for love
> the struggle for truth
> equality HAPPINESS[139]

But Lorde urged them to move beyond "cheap identification" and instead consider the "taste and feel" of each "poet's particular consciousness," "the emotional textures of the poem," and the ways their reactions were filtered through their distinct racial, ethnic, national, and sexual identities.[140] Several weeks later, the same student who had asserted that women share identical problems wrote:

> Lesbian poets don't want straight women to identify directly with their experiences and thus with their poems. By doing that we deny an essential part of the women's life—their love to women... by thinking that deep deep down we are all the same sharing the same problems—which in fact isn't so—I miss the wonderful, important and exciting experience to learn about the other woman's very own life.[141]

For another white student, tracing her shifting reactions to the poems in her journal helped her realize how her prior assumption that "we're all the same" essentially "invalidat[ed] other women's... goals, hopes, and fears."[142]

Gradually, over time, and with some obstacles along the way (namely, students' feelings of defensiveness and guilt), they began to take up Lorde's challenge to use the assigned poems to reflect on their lives. One student used the ambiguous pronouns *they* and *we* in Pat Parker's poem "Where Will You Be?" to meditate on German history, politics, and current events, especially her fear of a new rising fascism.[143] Others wrote about their experiences teaching in prison or having an abortion, or their relationships with other women, with attention to the underlying forces of racism, patriarchy, and heterosexism—a method modeled by the poems. And Lorde welcomed these revelations. "Gut" and "Sehr Gut" are scribbled throughout their journals (German for "good" and "very good") in her swooping, billowy cursive.[144]

As in Race and the Urban Situation, these journal assignments weren't an end in and of themselves; rather, they were a means to help students connect their discussions of poetry and power to their own advocacy for change. That semester, Mari Evans's poem "Vive Noir!" and Lorde's poem "Power" sparked intense debate over what it means to have power. "Power" describes how, in the trial of Clifford Glover's murderer, a jury of "eleven white men... and one Black Woman" acquitted the "policeman who shot down a ten-year-old in Queens."[145] While some students thought that the Black woman juror in the poem had no power, others disagreed: "Power is not only something you use or have when there are obvious changes caused by your voice or oppinion [sic]. Power is also the ability to speak up, to express what you like and what you dislike, to lead your own life."[146] Lorde wanted students to extend these conversations beyond the context of Black women's poetry and examine how they could use their own power to make changes in the world. Journals facilitated these connections. There, one student described how these discussions helped her understand that "every day I have the choice of remaining silent about what I think is wrong or saying something about it."[147] She recounted her recent efforts to "start small" by explaining to an anti-feminist woman "what the feminists are moving towards in the university."[148] Another pledged to "work against that what hurts me" and take advantage of the "chances every day, which I can use to speak up."[149] "I'm so glad! Good luck to you," Lorde wrote in the margins.

It was also in the pages of her journal that Katharina Oguntoye, the only Black woman in the class, observed how her feelings of isolation were connected to the absence of Black German women's histories, literature, and experiences within her education. After identifying this omission, Lorde then guided Oguntoye and several other Black women students at the university in researching these overlooked perspectives. They reread colonial histories; interviewed other Black Germans; analyzed the stereotypes and racist caricatures in the stories, coloring books, and songs of their youth; and drafted poems and personal narratives reflecting on their histories and experiences. But the learning did not stop there. Lorde believed that "real learning... does not happen in some detached way of dealing with a text alone, but from becoming so involved in the process that you can see how it might illuminate your life, and then how you can share that illumination."[150] Thus, the process that began with students reading Black women's poetry, then reflecting on their lives and researching the missing information, was not complete until they "shar[ed] the illumination" and used what they had learned to benefit others. In Berlin this meant sharing their research on the untold histories of Black German women with audiences beyond the classroom.

In 1986 Oguntoye and fellow student May Ayim, along with Dagmar Schultz, published *Showing Our Colors*, an edited collection of historical essays, personal narratives, interviews, and testimonials describing the history of Black women in Germany, dating back to the Middle Ages: from the first Africans in Germany and German women in the colonies to Afro-German women in the Weimar Republic, eugenics and forced sterilization, and racism in children's books. It included the work of eleven authors, many of whom were students, and introductions by Lorde and Schultz. Not only did the anthology coin the term *Afro-German*, it inaugurated the Afro-German movement, which continues to advocate for refugees and other vulnerable populations in Germany to this day.[151]

Showing Our Colors is an anthology of student writing: a form that Lorde had explored nearly twenty years prior with her students at Tougaloo College. A lot had happened since she had compiled their poems in *Pound*, including the publication of Bambara's and Jordan's anthologies of student writing. As we saw in "Dear Toni," Lorde celebrated that these collections challenged literary and educational hierarchies by including student writing. While we can only speculate, it's easy to imagine how such anthologies might have influenced Lorde's efforts to support her German students' publication. In this sense, *Showing Our Colors* is a testament to the afterlife of open admissions and the literary genres it gave rise to. We can also read these anthologies as kinds of final projects to emerge from these writers' classrooms. They are the material artifacts that allow us to apprehend the broader pedagogical project of student knowledge production that extends not only through Lorde's work but Jordan's, Bambara's, and Rich's as well.

This pedagogy of student knowledge production began at the level of course design. These writers devised courses that taught students to think beyond dominant liberal ideologies and interrogate the unequal power structures of capitalism, racism, patriarchy, colonialism, and imperialism. As humanities professors, they highlighted the roles that language, art, history, education, and culture play in perpetuating and altering these conditions. Though they foregrounded the tremendous scale of what we're up against, they did not allow students to despair or feel powerless. Instead, they helped students identify what Jordan called "routes to power": ways they could use their knowledge, resources, and skills to advocate for change. Though we tend to think of such actions in grand terms, such as organizing a protest or staging an occupation, these usually took smaller, more local forms. Often, it meant getting better books into the hands of readers who needed them.

Organizing a course so that it concludes, not with an exam, but with the creation of something impactful is no easy task. To facilitate this, their courses explored the gaps and distortions in dominant narratives: claims for "Black Power" and "Sisterhood" that erased the realities of Black women's experiences, reductive rhetoric around "ghettos" that homogenized urban communities of color, a patriarchal curriculum that devalued embodied knowledge, depictions of women's studies as mere "therapy" that does not "belong in a university," xenophobic nationalism, critical neglect of relationships between women, and the erasure of Black German women's histories. They also created opportunities for students to address these. Throughout the semester, they incorporated smaller assignments, like daily journals or creative mimicry exercises, that encouraged students to apply the readings and discussions to their lives and draw lessons from their experiences. These low-stakes assignments allowed them to brainstorm ideas that might lead to public interventions. In addition, these teacher-poets used their networks to connect students to broader audiences through editors, media outlets, radio stations, and publication venues.

For years to come, Lorde continued teaching others to share the illumination. In the last years of her life, as she retired to the azure waters of St. Croix to pursue hobbies like beekeeping, she continued visiting local high school classes, where she used historical folktales and writing exercises to help young people understand the "racist, sexist, and classist apartheid policies" in South Africa. There, writes Chenzira Davis Kahina, Lorde "encourage[d] each and every one she talked with, taught, read to and interacted with to positively transform and honor the differences amongst humanity—no matter what."[152] Kahina recalls that Lorde's ability to teach young people "to move beyond an apathetic acceptance of things and resort to protest was amazing."[153] Indeed, Lorde taught hundreds of students across multiple continents that "it is better to speak... knowing we were never meant to survive."[154]

The Art of Useful Learning

Lorde lived an intensely outward-facing life, often sharing what she learned, including through painful experiences, in hopes that it might be useful to others. When she was diagnosed with cancer, she needed survival strategies from "a Black lesbian feminist" but then realized, "Hey, honey, you are it, for now."[155] Following her mastectomy, one of the questions at the front of her mind was how she could make the experience useful to others: "What can I learn & how shall I teach it?"[156] The answers can be found in *The Cancer Journals* and *A Burst of Light*. She thought "that if this work were useful to just one woman, it was worth doing."[157] As her cancer returned and her prognosis worsened, prompting an acute sense of mortality, this desire to be useful only intensified. Given that "we all have to die at least once," she felt that "making that death useful would be winning for me."[158]

As educators, Lorde, Bambara, Jordan, and Rich all sought to make learning useful, both to their students and to the world beyond the classroom. They helped the individuals enrolled in each class find joy amid a radically unequal society, while also equipping them to challenge those structures and build better alternatives. In doing so, their teaching also benefited strangers that they might never meet but whose lives would, nevertheless, be impacted by students' actions, as well as the cultural productions—radio broadcasts, short stories, poems, and anthologies—they created.

In the intervening years, the privatization of higher education has narrowed how we think about the utility of college. Today exorbitant tuition has reduced our understanding of college to a commodity: an investment that individuals make in their future, the utility of which is measured in terms of financial return. Yet these writers remind us of the dream of the open admissions era: that a college education should be freely available to all because what students learn there benefits not just them—it contributes to the public good.

Conclusion

An Education Worth Fighting For

In this book, we saw how Toni Cade Bambara, June Jordan, Audre Lorde, and Adrienne Rich transformed CUNY's free and open classrooms into sites of liberatory learning. As educators, they drew on the critiques of power emerging from the era's social movements and their literary sensibilities to develop teaching methods that redistributed classroom power and facilitated student knowledge production. We observed, too, how their multimodal assignments countered white supremacy by valuing multiple, distinct ways of knowing and how group projects presented opportunities to think beyond liberal individualism. These approaches honored students' desires for relevant learning and equipped them with useful life skills. And though they were initially developed in response to the specific conditions of the open admissions era, these writers found, as they went on to teach in other sites (and as many a CUNY professor has since discovered), that these methods were useful for a wide range of individuals. Revisiting their work today, one finds transgressive teaching that prepared students both to navigate the world and to change it.

Though these pedagogies may be new to some, for others—especially at teaching-focused institutions—they are all around us. Walking through the halls of my own regional, comprehensive state school, you will encounter students researching material artifacts from Native American boarding schools to learn about histories of state-sanctioned violence and dispossession, as well as the creative responses to this devastation from an array of Indigenous writers. You will stumble, too, on students debating how the horror film *Get Out* challenges prevailing ideas about race, class, gender, and sexuality.[1] And that's just in my small corner of a modest campus in a snowy pocket of Central New York. Scroll through one of many online education networks or academic communities on social media, and you will read about students creating video archives to preserve activist stories and coauthoring digital anthologies inspired by *This Bridge Called My Back*.[2] (If historical archives remind us of the invisible collaborations behind classrooms, such exchanges now thrive online.) Every day, professors and students are working together to eradicate oppression and build a more livable future.

One of my favorite recent examples of transgressive teaching is from Hiʻilei Julia Hobart's course Race and Indigeneity in the Pacific at the University of Texas at Austin. At the end of the semester, students in Dr. Hobart's class create decolonial postcards that highlight how the tourism industry obscures ongoing conditions of settler colonialism.[3] For the assignment, she brought in a graphic designer to teach students some basic principles they could use to make visually impactful projects. The students then used photo manipulation and collage techniques to create stunning postcards that reveal the material realities obscured by dominant narratives. For instance, while New Zealand boasts about its biodiversity, one student, Kennedy, designed a postcard that foregrounds how European travelers have introduced invasive species like German wasps that are contributing to the extinction of native birds. Another student, Rachel, created a postcard illustrating how popular photographs of Bondi Beach, Australia, erase the ongoing struggle of Aboriginal groups to regain sovereign control of this area. Rachel superimposed a group of Indigenous activists on the more common image of colorful umbrellas and bikini-clad loungers on the white sand beach. Rachel writes, "I juxtaposed the Aboriginal Embassy within this landscape to showcase the complex and layered histories of possession and dispossession that Aboriginal people face amongst the tourist landscape."[4]

This assignment exemplifies the kind of pedagogy these writers championed. It asks students to use what they have learned to spotlight perspectives missing from mainstream media, the curriculum, and the culture industry. It encourages creativity, allowing students to pursue their intellectual interests and develop projects that are meaningful to them. It also teaches them to think in increasingly complex terms about the relationship between texts and images, a valuable skill that will serve them well the next time they want to deliver a presentation, create a zine, or design an eye-catching poster—perhaps one they will brandish overhead at a protest. Indeed, these knowledges and skills can enrich students' lives as activists, artists, community members, and engaged participants in society.

At the same time that we draw inspiration from the teacher-poets in this book, it's important to acknowledge that part of what made their work in SEEK and open admissions so significant was that they were making transformative learning available to working-class students and students of color—those to whom it has historically been denied. For years to come, long after they left City College, they continued to fight for the downward redistribution of educational resources. They advocated for reduced class sizes and lower teaching loads; support for minoritized knowledges like Black studies, ethnic studies, and women's, gender, and sexuality studies; and increased funding for initiatives like remedial education, opportunity programs, and open admissions that would expand access to life-changing learning. Indeed, like many feminist, and especially Black feminist, educators throughout history, these women understood classroom teaching as connected to broader questions of educational access, admissions policies, and funding.[5] Considered together, their work reminds us that social justice pedagogies must extend beyond the classroom to the material conditions that enable (or foreclose) learning.

Since the end of the open admissions era, those conditions have shifted. In the 1970s, Congress decided that instead of providing funds directly to universities, they would make loans to student borrowers, which they would put toward the cost of tuition. This set in motion a debt-fueled higher-education system that relies on increasing costs for its survival. It has also allowed states to drastically reduce funding for public universities.[6] Whereas in the late 1960s and early 1970s taxpayer dollars covered around 60 percent of our nation's higher-education costs, they now cover around half that amount—a mere 34 percent.[7]

Since their implementation, these neoliberal education policies have continually decreased access to transformative learning. While college enrollment has increased, disparities in the *kinds* of institutions students attend, the *subjects* they study, and their *educational experience* have intensified along the lines of race and class.[8] Today wealthy students are ushered into elite, exclusive, and well-funded institutions (private colleges or the flagship universities within state systems) where they have access to small class sizes, personalized instruction, and a well-rounded education that includes the humanities. By contrast, working-class students and students of color are channeled into massively underfunded public institutions with fewer full-time instructors, larger class sizes, and an emphasis on vocational training.[9] Of course, our nation's poorest students don't attend college at all.

Left to foot the bill, students select courses and majors that they believe will lead to lucrative careers, a worthwhile return on their investment, and the ability to pay off their loans. Unsurprisingly, people of color and white women take on the greatest amounts of debt to fund their education, and that debt shapes the choices they make.[10] "Don't take art classes" is the message tuition sends to students. "Don't take classes that pique your curiosity," debt whispers in their ears. Whereas in 1970, 70 percent of students said they attended college in hopes of crafting a life philosophy, that figure has now dropped to 30 percent.[11] And who could blame them? When college is free or low-cost, such contemplation of the self and the world feels more possible.

These policies have also attenuated faculty working conditions, especially at campuses that serve low-income students of color.[12] In response to decreased funding, many colleges have replaced full-time, tenure-track positions with a precarious, temporary, part-time adjunct labor force. Forty years ago, 70 percent of academic employees were tenured or on the tenure track, but now that figure has flipped.[13] Today 70 percent of college professors are woefully overworked and underpaid adjuncts, lecturers, graduate students, and instructors who spend their lives teaching multiple courses, grading hundreds of papers, and commuting between different campuses to make ends meet, often without health care, benefits, or job security. Adjunct instructors make, on average, less than $3,500 per course—a far cry from the $12,500 recommended by professional organizations like the Modern Language Association.[14] They teach an average of eight courses per year, leading to only $28,000 in annual income.[15] Nearly one-third live below the poverty line, one-quarter rely on public assistance, and 40 percent can't cover basic household expenses.[16]

Today's academic labor conditions are thus quite different from those of the teacher-poets in this book. If we're to draw inspiration from them, we must also understand that they were teaching at a different historical moment, before the structural changes of neoliberalism produced the threadbare austerity landscape we now inhabit. On average, these writers were paid three (and often closer to four) times as much, per course, as current instructors. They typically taught only one or two courses per semester. They also had greater access to the public resources of the welfare state, so their health, housing, security, and livelihood would have been at least somewhat less dependent on their employment. For Bambara, Jordan, Lorde, and Rich, their livable academic salaries and low course loads allowed for the development of creative teaching methods, as well as activism and writing. Today a comparable career path would leave little time for such pursuits.

Yet things did not always look this way. As we have seen, liberatory learning was once widely available, and it can be again if we, as a society, decide to make that a priority. In fact, the early years of the SEEK program offer a useful vision of what we might want the future of higher education to look like.[17] Both SEEK and open admissions granted students access to a full liberal arts education—one that they would help to radically transform. Of the two initiatives, SEEK was more successful because it invested in the material conditions that support learning: not just free tuition but money for books, travel stipends, and on-campus housing.[18] In SEEK, class sizes were small, and students received personal attention from professors, tutors, academic advisors, and career counselors.[19] The program thus provided what is readily available at elite institutions to the students most marginalized by the social order. Faculty were also encouraged to experiment with teaching methods and given the professional latitude to do so. They even had time to collaborate: they sat in on each other's classes; exchanged syllabi and assignments; and read, wrote, and dialogued about pedagogy. The result was transgressive teaching that improved students' lives and contributed to the public good.

At present, our nation's tiered higher-education system is teaching affluent white students that they deserve transformative learning, while overworked faculty, crowded classes, giant lecture halls, standardized tests, antiquated facilities, prehistoric technology, and preprofessional training are good enough for everyone else. In these pages, we've followed the stories of four women who fought for something better. Continuing their work means not just changing our classrooms but demanding tuition-free, robustly funded higher education for all. It means demanding that the things Ivy League students have access to—small class sizes, student-centered teaching, counselors, advisors, extensive libraries, quiet learning spaces, cutting-edge technology—are available to all. It means abolishing the exploitation of adjunct labor and providing all professors a living wage: one that will allow us to undertake the engaged teaching that drew so many of us to universities in the first place. It means changing policies that allow resources to accumulate in the hands of a select few and redirecting the funds currently used for policing, mass incarceration, and war toward free, universal health care, housing, and education. It means committing to a vision of educational abundance: a world in which anyone can wander into their local university and take a class on poetry or racial capitalism (ideally both). It means deciding that we want to live in a world where the person sitting next to us on the bus is likely to have conducted oral histories with local activists, studied how *A Raisin in the Sun* critiques the American dream, or created a decolonial postcard.

I leave you, then, with June Jordan's call to arms: "How will the university teach otherwise?"[20]

NOTES

Preface

1. While this quotation is generally attributed to Cooper, Samuel Holleran suggests that it was actually Cooper's son-in-law, Abram Hewitt, who coined the mellifluous phrase. Holleran, "Free as Air and Water."
2. Backer et al., "Horizontal Pedagogy."

Introduction

1. Toni Cade Bambara, in "Report on the Summer Seminar, Pre-baccalaureate Program, City College," 1968, folder 385, Adrienne Rich Papers, Schlesinger Library, Radcliffe Institute, Harvard University, Cambridge, Massachusetts.
2. Bambara, in "Summer Seminar."
3. J. Jordan, "Black Studies," 45.
4. J. Jordan, introduction to "Tomorrow in English," 1967, box 76, folder 13, June Jordan Papers, Schlesinger Library, Radcliffe Institute, Harvard University, Cambridge, Massachusetts.
5. J. Jordan, "Notes toward a Black Balancing," 84.
6. Rich, "Teaching Language," 53.
7. McGurl, *Program Era*, 2.
8. Nabokov, quoted in McGurl, *Program Era*, 1.
9. Bourdieu and Passeron, *Reproduction in Education*, 10–11.
10. hooks, *Teaching to Transgress*.
11. Givens, *Fugitive Pedagogy*, 13.
12. Evans, *Black Women*.
13. Freire, *Pedagogy of the Oppressed*, 72, 80, 83.
14. As Hines writes, in the 1940s and 1950s, Black leftist artists and intellectuals excluded from, or censored by, historically white universities utilized communist labor schools to pursue the study of Black culture and questions of

politics, economics, and justice. Hale shows how the Mississippi Freedom Schools taught Black students to advocate for change. Rickford illustrates how the Black Power movement led to the establishment of dozens of Pan-African Nationalist schools, where anti-imperial, anticapitalist, and radically internationalist teaching cultivated critical consciousness and self-determination. Hines, *Outside Literary Studies*; Hale, *Freedom Schools*; and Rickford, *African People*. See also Murch, *Living for the City*, 182; and Kelley, "Black Study, Black Struggle."

15. See hooks, *Teaching to Transgress*; Neville and Cha-Jua, "Kufundisha"; Boxer, *When Women Ask*; Kynard, *Vernacular Insurrections*, 133; and McWorter and Bailey, "Black Studies Curriculum Development."

16. City College of New York, "Our History."

17. Webster, quoted in Lavin, Alba, and Silberstein, *Right versus Privilege*, 2.

18. Kriegel, "Surviving the Apocalypse," 54.

19. While City College's admissions criteria claimed to be meritocratic, a 1964–65 study by political scientist Allen B. Ballard found its standards made admission almost impossible for minority students. Traub, *City on a Hill*, 45.

20. Lavin, Alba, and Silberstein, *Right versus Privilege*, 3.

21. The Servicemen's Readjustment Act of 1944, colloquially known as the GI Bill, and Lyndon Johnson's National Higher Education Act (1965) increased federal funding for college. This era saw the emergence of what Christopher Newfield calls "a midcentury consensus" around the notion that higher education was a public good that benefited all of society and the economy, not just those individuals who attended college: "Society was therefore justified in bearing the cost of public colleges itself." Newfield, *Great Mistake*, 37–38. Though the GI Bill provided a free university education to thousands of World War II veterans, the legislation was strategically crafted so that these provisions would bypass low-income communities of color and primarily benefit white people.

22. In 1952 City College admitted 17 percent of New York City high school graduates; by 1960 that number was down to 13 percent. Molloy, "Convenient Myopia," 45–46.

23. Molloy, "Convenient Myopia," 40.

24. Molloy, "Convenient Myopia," 42, 63.

25. Molloy, "Convenient Myopia," 392.

26. Dinkins, quoted in Hershenson, "Second Chances."

27. Bernard Levy, Leslie Berger, and Allen B. Ballard established the SEEK program.

28. Ballard and Berger designed a program that was technically race neutral but would, in effect, admit and support more Black and Puerto Rican students. To qualify for SEEK, "students had to have a high school diploma, live in a deprived area in New York City, be under age 30, and not have attended college before." Reeves, "Mina Shaughnessy," 118. They received a weekly stipend of $50.

29. Molloy, "Convenient Myopia," 114.

30. Arthur O. Eve used SEEK as the model for the Educational Opportunity Program at the State University of New York (SUNY), which was later extended to private universities like Cornell, where it was known as Higher Education Opportunity Program.

31. Traub, *City on a Hill*, 112.

32. Gumbs, "Nobody Mean More," 241, 243.

33. Harney and Moten, *Undercommons*, 9.

34. Rich described being hired as a "poet-teacher." Rich, "Teaching Language," 55. Though Bambara primarily wrote fiction and prose, I use *poet* to denote their shared creative use of language.

35. Gayle, "Quiet Revolution."

36. Dyer, "Protest and the Politics," 1.

37. As W. E. B. Du Bois argues, Black activists have historically led struggles for universal public education. Du Bois, *Black Reconstruction*, 638. During Reconstruction, the Freedmen's efforts made schools available to both Black and white Southerners. At HBCUs, the mission of Black education necessitated a focus on access rather than exclusivity. Kynard writes, "HBCUs had long ago established open admissions programs, provided for the education of African Americans, and heralded in an educated, professional class who would challenge . . . segregation and racial oppression." Kynard, *Vernacular Insurrections*, 177.

38. Lavin, Alba, and Silberstein, *Right versus Privilege*, 19–20.

39. Lavin and Hyllegard, *Changing the Odds*; Lavin, Alba, and Silberstein, *Right versus Privilege*; and Attewell and Lavin, *Passing the Torch*.

40. In their first twenty years, SEEK and College Discovery (its sister program in the community colleges) provided 100,000 students access to college. Reagan, "National SEEK and College Discovery Day."

41. Winslow, "Shirley Chisholm."

42. Reagan, "National SEEK and College Discovery Day."

43. Though open admissions benefited all major ethnic groups in the city, including many students of color, white students disproportionately reaped the benefits, and thus it actually preserved racial inequality. Lavin, Alba, and Silberstein call this "the paradox of open admissions": "While benefits do flow to those targeted to receive them, they also flow unintentionally to others, and often the latter, possessing more resources than the former, are better able to take advantage of the new opportunities." Lavin, Alba, and Silberstein, *Right versus Privilege*, 284.

44. Lorde, "Excerpt from Deotha," 49.

45. Evans, *Black Women*; and Perlow et al., *Black Women's Liberatory Pedagogies*, 2.

46. The identity of full-time faculty varies by academic rank such that white people, especially white men, are disproportionately represented among higher-ranked, research-focused positions that involve less teaching. For instance,

79 percent of full professors are white, and 51 percent are white men. National Center for Education Statistics, "Race/Ethnicity of College Faculty." White women and people of color are overrepresented among adjuncts. American Federation of Teachers, "Army of Temps."

47. Christian, "Race for Theory," 52.

48. Bambara, *Realizing the Dream*; Lorde, *"I Teach Myself"*; and J. Jordan, *"Life Studies."*

49. Hartman, "Venus in Two Acts," 11, 8.

50. Rich, "Resisting Amnesia," 148.

51. These classrooms supported what Michel Foucault calls the "insurrection of subjugated knowledges": historical and popular knowledges "that have been buried and disguised," not recognized by authority, marginalized, and "disqualified as inadequate ... or insufficiently elaborated: naive knowledges, located low down on the hierarchy, beneath the required level of cognition or scientificity." Foucault, "Two Lectures," 81, 82.

52. Gumbs, "Nobody Mean More," 242.

53. Tomás Reed, "Early Developments." See also Tomás Reed, *New York Liberation School*.

54. In *Democracy and Education* (1916) and *Experience and Education* (1938), Dewey argued that learning should emerge from students' observations and experiences. He advocated for problem-solving, hands-on activities, projects, and critical thinking.

55. Evans, *Black Women*. See also Givens, *Fugitive Pedagogy*, 182. Some aspects of student-centered pedagogy extend back even further. Perlow et al. have found that teaching methods grounded in "collective responsibility" were present in precolonial Africa, Asia, and the Americas. Perlow et al., *Black Women's Liberatory Pedagogies*, 5–6.

56. Zimmerman, *Amateur Hour*. Research has found that learner-centered methods are more effective than lectures in helping students process and retain new information. These methods promote deep and meaningful learning rather than surface learning (learning that doesn't fade when the semester ends); they improve students' abilities to apply what they're learning to other contexts and situations; and they increase students' motivation. Weimer, *Learner-Centered Teaching*.

57. Buurma and Heffernan, *Teaching Archive*.

58. Critical pedagogy treats schools within the social and political fabric of a class-driven society, rejects the neutrality of knowledge, analyzes teaching as an inherently political act, and challenges practices of education as domination.

59. Omolade, "Black Feminist Pedagogy"; Joseph, "Black Feminist Pedagogy"; and hooks, *Teaching to Transgress*.

60. See also Henry, "Black Feminist Pedagogy."

61. Schumach, "50% of Freshmen."

62. "Report from Ann Cook to Dean Robert Young and the SEEK Faculty Re: Evaluation and Recommendations," 1968, City College, folder 385, Rich Papers.

63. Gross, "How to Kill a College."

64. J. Jordan, reflections at memorial service for Audre Lorde, February 18, 1993, box 58, folder 2, Jordan Papers.

65. Wheeler and Gavaler, "Imposters and Chameleons"; and Hines, *Outside Literary Studies*, 132–33, 151–52.

66. Buurma and Heffernan, *Teaching Archive*; and Brim, *Poor Queer Studies*.

67. McGurl, *Program Era*, ix.

68. McGurl, *Program Era*, xi, 34, 4.

69. See Ferguson, *Reorder of Things*; Harney and Moten, *Undercommons*; Chatterjee and Maira, *Imperial University*; Kelley, "Black Study, Black Struggle"; and Boggs et al., "Abolitionist University Studies."

Chapter One. Toni Cade Bambara's Community-Controlled and Multimodal Pedagogy

1. Toni Cade Bambara, "Working at It in Five Parts," 2 drafts, 1980?, box 4, Toni Cade Bambara Papers, Spelman College Archives, Atlanta, Georgia.

2. Bambara, interviewed in Chandler, "Voices beyond the Veil," 350.

3. Bambara, quoted in Holmes, *Joyous Revolt*, 10.

4. Bambara, quoted in Holmes, *Joyous Revolt*, 10.

5. Bambara, quoted in Holmes, *Joyous Revolt*, 10.

6. Holmes, *Joyous Revolt*, 11.

7. Toni Cade Bambara, "What Is It I Think I'm Doing Anyway?," draft and proof, 1979?, box 4, folders 80–82, Bambara Papers, Spelman College Archives.

8. Bambara, quoted in Holmes, *Joyous Revolt*, 1.

9. Holmes, *Joyous Revolt*, 35.

10. Bambara, quoted in Holmes, *Joyous Revolt*, 39.

11. Holmes, *Joyous Revolt*, 36.

12. Holmes, *Joyous Revolt*, 40.

13. The pilot year of SEEK (1965–66) was funded by a $125,000 federal antipoverty grant, $60,900 of which went toward the salaries of its seven lecturers. Molloy, "Convenient Myopia," 64–65, 186. These figures assume that funds were distributed equally. All 2023 dollars were calculated using the US Bureau of Labor Statistics CPI Inflation Calculator.

14. Bambara, "Realizing the Dream."

15. Molloy, "Convenient Myopia," 18.

16. Bambara, "Children Who Got Cheated," 65.

17. Toni Cade Bambara, in "Report on the Summer Seminar, Pre-baccalaureate Program, City College," 1968, folder 385, Adrienne Rich Papers, Schlesinger Library, Radcliffe Institute, Harvard University, Cambridge, Massachusetts.

18. Bambara, in "Summer Seminar."
19. Molloy, "Convenient Myopia," 209.
20. Bambara, in "Summer Seminar."
21. Bambara, in "Summer Seminar."
22. Bambara, in "Summer Seminar."
23. In "Do-It-Yourself: Writing a Novel in a Literature Class," John J. Dunn found that experimenting with literary techniques improves students' analytic reading abilities.
24. Holmes, "Lessons in Boldness," 154.
25. White, "Oral History."
26. Molloy, "Convenient Myopia," 8–9.
27. Berlin, *Rhetoric and Reality*, 58.
28. Covington, "Oral History."
29. Molloy, "Convenient Myopia," 189, 201–2, 342, 215. Kynard has demonstrated how many of the era's "innovations" in writing pedagogy, by Shaughnessy and others, were fundamentally shaped by Black freedom struggles. Kynard, *Vernacular Insurrections*.
30. Berlin, *Rhetoric and Reality*, 71, 107–8.
31. Gayle, "Racism and the American University," 55.
32. Bambara, quoted in Holmes, *Joyous Revolt*, 92.
33. Molloy, "SEEK's Fight."
34. Bambara, "Realizing the Dream."
35. Bambara, in "Summer Seminar."
36. Ferguson, *Reorder of Things*, 223.
37. Bambara, in "Summer Seminar."
38. Bambara, in "Summer Seminar."
39. Givens, *Fugitive Pedagogy*, 123.
40. Bruffee writes, "For American college teachers the roots of collaborative learning lie neither in radical politics nor in research. They lie in the nearly desperate response of harried colleges during the early 1970s to a pressing educational need." Bruffee, "Collaborative Learning," 637.
41. Bambara, in "Summer Seminar."
42. Bambara, *Salt Eaters*, 114.
43. Bambara, "Summer Seminar."
44. Molloy writes, "Beginning in 1966, SEEK received only single-year annual funding grants from Albany," leaving this "already politically sensitive program... in constant jeopardy." Molloy, "Convenient Myopia," 119.
45. Busia, "Teaching Toni Cade Bambara Teaching," 188.
46. Givens writes, "While many progressive educators pushed for contextual learning, encouraged social transformation and anti-indoctrination, and stressed communal values... the movement offered no critical social analysis of whiteness or antiblackness, of power and domination... [thus] negat[ing] the violent experiences of black people in relationship to the American

School." Woodson, in particular, criticized how progressive education theories failed to help Black people understand their experiences. Givens, *Fugitive Pedagogy*, 122–24.

47. Rickford, *African People*.
48. Bambara, quoted in Busia, "Teaching Toni Cade Bambara Teaching," 188.
49. H. Lewis, *From Brownsville to Bloomberg*, 4.
50. Brier, "Community Control."
51. Bambara, "Children Who Got Cheated," 65.
52. Bambara, in "Summer Seminar."
53. While *community control* usually refers to a specific, short-lived set of historical events, Heather Lewis argues that the movement's demands for professional accountability, equitable opportunities, and creative education impacted ideas about education far beyond this immediate context. H. Lewis, *From Brownsville to Bloomberg*.
54. Bambara, in "Summer Seminar."
55. Bambara, in "Summer Seminar."
56. Bambara, in "Summer Seminar."
57. Kendi, *Black Campus Movement*, 123.
58. Bambara, interviewed in Tate, *Black Women Writers*, 18.
59. Bambara, in "Summer Seminar."
60. Bambara, in "Summer Seminar."
61. Bambara, in "Summer Seminar."
62. Bambara, in "Summer Seminar."
63. Toni Cade Bambara, syllabus for Introduction to Third World Literature, fall 1974 Duke University B.S. 150, box 1, folder 13, Bambara Papers, Duke University Archives, Durham, NC, https://archives.lib.duke.edu/catalog/uaafro_aspace_ref27_tod.
64. Holmes, remarks.
65. Blum, *Ungrading*.
66. Molloy demonstrates how the SEEK program developed socially just approaches to writing assessment at a programmatic level. Molloy, "'Human Beings.'"
67. Bambara, in "Summer Seminar."
68. Bambara, in "Summer Seminar."
69. Bambara, in "Summer Seminar."
70. Bambara, in "Summer Seminar."
71. Bambara, in "Summer Seminar."
72. Bambara, interviewed in Tate, *Black Women Writers*, 19.
73. See Molloy, "Convenient Myopia," 192.
74. Bambara, "Lesson," 94.
75. Bambara, "Lesson," 95.
76. Bambara, "Lesson," 95.
77. Bambara, "Lesson," 94.

78. As Holmes writes, Bambara's story "Geraldine Moore" is "as much a cultural competency lesson for teachers on how to see the strengths and beauty in a challenged student's writing as it is an empowering story for young readers." *Joyous Revolt*, 45.

79. T. Lewis, "Black People," 32.
80. T. Lewis, "Black People," 32.
81. Busia, "Teaching Toni Cade Bambara Teaching," 189.
82. Morrison, preface to Bambara, *Deep Sightings*, ix.
83. Bambara, "Working at It," 19.
84. Holmes, *Joyous Revolt*, 42.
85. For examples, see Molloy, "Convenient Myopia," 86–87.
86. "Five Demands."
87. "Five Demands."
88. Bambara, "Realizing the Dream."
89. Lavan and Tomás Reed, introduction to Bambara, *Realizing the Dream*, 8.
90. Kelley, *Freedom Dreams*; and Nash, "Practicing Love."
91. Kendi, *Black Campus Movement*, 112.
92. Bambara, "Realizing the Dream."
93. Bambara, "Realizing the Dream."
94. Bambara, "Realizing the Dream."
95. Bambara, "Realizing the Dream."
96. Bambara, "Realizing the Dream."
97. Dyer, "Protest and the Politics," 110.
98. Jiménez, "Puerto Ricans and Educational Civil Rights"; Tomás Reed, "'Treasures That Prevail,'" 50.
99. Dyer, "Protest and the Politics"; Molloy, "Convenient Myopia," 256; and Tomás Reed, "Early Developments," 51.
100. Lavin, in Hershenson, "Second Chances."
101. Rivera, in Hershenson, "Second Chances."
102. Ballard, in Hershenson, "Second Chances."
103. Gerald Graff argues that freshman composition courses introduced students to the social criticism of writers like George Orwell, Henry David Thoreau, and James Baldwin and taught them "to contemplate the gap between hypothetical American ideals of justice and equality and the observable realities of racism, exploitation, and militarism." Graff, *Professing Literature*, ix.
104. The movement for community control inspired the students' third demand, for greater involvement in decisions regarding SEEK. Dyer, "Protest and the Politics," 100.
105. Biondi, *Black Revolution on Campus*, 8.
106. Biondi, *Black Revolution on Campus*, 8.
107. Gross, "How to Kill a College," 15.

108. Holmes, *Joyous Revolt*, xviii.
109. Holmes, *Joyous Revolt*, 158.
110. Bambara, *Deep Sightings*, 231.
111. Bambara, in "Summer Seminar."
112. Holmes, *Joyous Revolt*, 103.
113. National Council of Teachers of English, "Multimodal Literacies." See also Yancey, "Made Not Only in Words"; and Shipka, *Towards a Composition Made Whole*.
114. Mendelsohn and Walker, "Agents of Change," 33–34.
115. Palmeri, *Remixing Composition*, 11.
116. Walker, "Our Mothers' Gardens," 239
117. Christian, "Race for Theory," 52.
118. T. Lewis, *"Black People"*; Waller-Peterson, "'Are You Sure, Sweetheart'"; and Collins, "Generating Power."
119. Bambara, *Salt Eaters*, 3.
120. There are some biographical parallels. Bambara was exhausted from being a doula to everyone else's creative projects, which often left her little time to work on her own.
121. Bambara, *Salt Eaters*, 264.
122. Bambara, *Salt Eaters*, 107.
123. Benjamin, *Half in Shadow*, 14, 31, 47.
124. Hill Collins, *Black Feminist Thought*; and F. Griffin, "That the Mothers May Soar," 485.
125. Kelley, *Freedom Dreams*, 143–44.
126. C. Franklin, *Writing Women's Communities*, 5; Mirikitani, *Third World Women*; Moraga and Anzaldúa, *This Bridge Called My Back*; Hull, Bell-Scott, and Smith, *All the Women Are White, All the Blacks Are Men, but Some of Us Are Brave*; Smith, *Home Girls*.
127. A search on the Open Syllabus Explorer (https://explorer.opensyllabus.org/) indicates that *The Black Woman* appears on 95 syllabi.
128. Bambara, *Deep Sightings*, 228.
129. Covington, in Bambara, *Deep Sightings*, 229.
130. Gayle, in Bambara, *Deep Sightings*, 229.
131. Bambara, interviewed in Tate, *Black Women Writers*, 29.
132. Clark, "Motherhood," 65, 66.
133. Clark, "Motherhood," 70.
134. Hill Collins, *Black Feminist Thought*, 187–88.
135. See Holmes, *Joyous Revolt*, 45.
136. Traylor, "ReCalling the Black Woman," xv–xvi.
137. Lavan and Tomás Reed, introduction to Bambara, *Realizing the Dream*, 9.
138. Bambara, *Deep Sightings*, 230.
139. Holmes, *Joyous Revolt*, xix.

140. Buurma and Heffernan, *The Teaching Archive*; Brim, *Poor Queer Studies*.

141. Shesgreen, "Canonizing the Canonizer," 303.

142. Molloy, "Convenient Myopia," 196.

143. Molloy, "Convenient Myopia," 285.

144. Molloy, "Convenient Myopia," 196.

145. Molloy, "Convenient Myopia," 196.

146. Christian's *Black Women Novelists* (1980) established the idea of an African American women's novelistic tradition stretching back to the nineteenth century.

147. One of Christian's critiques of literary theory is its opaque jargon and "lack of clarity... it is the kind of writing for which composition teachers would give a freshman a resounding F." Christian, "The Race for Theory," 56. This is a direct invocation of her experiences teaching basic writing in SEEK.

148. Bowles, Fabi, and Keizer, introduction to *New Black Feminist Criticism*, xi.

149. McCormick, *Black Student Protest Movement*, 30.

150. "Livingston College, 1969–1970," cited in Clemens and Yanni, "Early Years of Livingston," 84.

151. Murray, "1974 Graduate's Memories."

152. Holmes, "Lessons in Boldness," 154.

153. Holmes, *Joyous Revolt*, 58.

154. Bambara, "Working at It," 3.

155. Traylor, "ReCalling the Black Woman," xvii.

156. Giovanni, "We Drove Together," 151.

157. Giovanni, "We Drove Together," 151.

158. Giovanni, "We Drove Together," 153.

159. Bambara, interviewed in Tate, *Black Women Writers*, 22.

160. Bambara, interviewed in Tate, *Black Women Writers*, 22.

161. Bambara, interviewed in Tate, *Black Women Writers*, 22.

162. Bambara, interviewed in Tate, *Black Women Writers*, 22.

163. Bambara, interviewed in Tate, *Black Women Writers*, 22.

164. Bambara, interviewed in Tate, *Black Women Writers*, 22.

165. Bambara, interviewed in Tate, *Black Women Writers*, 22.

166. Holmes, *Joyous Revolt*, 68, 148.

167. Bambara and Powell, "Three Little Panthers," 140.

168. *Kirkus Reviews*, "Tales and Stories."

169. Bambara, *Deep Sightings*, 230.

170. Vazquez, *Listening in Detail*, 59.

171. Bambara, quoted in M. Patterson, "Bambara Teaches," 13.

172. Bambara, syllabus for Introduction to Third World Literature.

173. Bambara, syllabus for Contemporary American Novel, fall 1987, University of Delaware, box 5, Bambara Papers, Spelman College Archives.

174. Toni Cade Bambara, take-home exam for The Text as a Rite of Recovery, Fall 1987, 2 versions, box 5, Bambara Papers, Spelman College Archives.

175. Toni Cade Bambara, lecture notes for History Through Literature n.d., Bambara Papers, Spelman College Archives.

176. Bambara, syllabus for Contemporary American Novel.

177. Bambara, syllabus for Contemporary American Novel.

178. Bambara, syllabus for Contemporary American Novel.

179. Holmes, *Joyous Revolt*, 58.

180. Brier and Fabricant, *Austerity Blues*.

181. Bambara, quoted in Holmes, *Joyous Revolt*, 92.

182. Holmes, *Joyous Revolt*, 107.

183. Bambara, *Deep Sightings*, 124.

184. Beckman, "Black Media Matters."

185. Scribe Video Center, "Mission and History."

186. Scribe Video Center, "Mission and History."

187. Scribe Video Center, "Mission and History."

188. See Massiah's forthcoming documentary *The T.C.B. School of Organizing*.

189. Toni Cade Bambara, notes for Video for Social Change, 1994, Scribe Center Workshop, box 5, Bambara Papers, Spelman College Archives.

190. Bambara, notes for Video for Social Change, 1994.

191. Holmes, *Joyous Revolt*, 172.

192. Thabiti Lewis illustrates how Bambara's fiction presents introspective spiritual growth as a key component of social change. Lewis, "Black People."

193. Bambara, *Deep Sightings*, 143.

194. The Women's Community Revitalization Project, "Women Housing Women."

195. Women Against Abuse (Community Legal Service), "Peace at Home: Getting a Restraining Order."

196. Scribe Video Center, "Community Visions."

197. Byrd, "Feeling of Transport," 172.

198. See Benjamin, *Half in Shadow*, on McKay's legacy.

199. Byrd, "Feeling of Transport," 179.

200. Byrd, "Feeling of Transport," 179.

201. Byrd, "Feeling of Transport," 179.

202. Byrd, "Feeling of Transport," 179.

203. Byrd, "Feeling of Transport," 179.

204. Holmes, "Lessons in Boldness."

205. Holmes, "Lessons in Boldness," 154.

206. Murray, "1974 Graduate's Memories."

207. Finney, "Making of Paper."

208. Mixco, "So You Understand Once and For All."

Chapter Two. "This Class... Has Much to Teach America"

1. J. Jordan, introduction to "Tomorrow in English," 1967, box 76, folder 13, June Jordan Papers, Schlesinger Library, Radcliffe Institute, Harvard University, Cambridge, Massachusetts.
2. J. Jordan, introduction to "Tomorrow in English."
3. J. Jordan, introduction to "Tomorrow in English."
4. J. Jordan, "Notes toward a Black Balancing," 84.
5. One study by sociologist Doug McAdam found that in 1964 the Mississippi government spent, on average, $81.66 per year to educate a white student and $21.77 for a Black student. Hale, *Freedom Schools*, 83.
6. Ravitch, *Great School Wars*, 293, 310.
7. J. Jordan, "Merit Review Statement," 1993–94, University of California at Berkeley, box 78, folder 8, Jordan Papers.
8. Kinloch, *June Jordan*, 9.
9. Kinloch, *June Jordan*, 20.
10. J. Jordan, "For the Sake of People's Poetry," 242.
11. Kinloch, *June Jordan*, 27.
12. J. Jordan, "Notes of a Barnard Dropout," 98.
13. J. Jordan, "Notes of a Barnard Dropout," 100.
14. J. Jordan, "Notes of a Barnard Dropout," 99.
15. J. Meyer, "You Can't See," 11. June Meyer was Jordan's name during her marriage.
16. J. Meyer, "You Can't See," 11.
17. J. Meyer, "You Can't See," 11.
18. These figures assume that Jordan taught three courses per year, as was the requirement for part-time lecturers. Volpe, "Confessions," 775.
19. J. Jordan, "Black Studies," 50.
20. Erickson and Jordan, "After Identity," 141.
21. J. Jordan, introduction to "Tomorrow in English."
22. J. Jordan, introduction to "Tomorrow in English."
23. Whitehead, *Aims of Education*, 6.
24. Student essay in "Tomorrow in English."
25. J. Jordan, introduction to "Tomorrow in English."
26. J. Jordan, introduction to "Tomorrow in English."
27. J. Jordan, "Tomorrow in English."
28. J. Jordan, introduction to "Tomorrow in English."
29. J. Jordan, introduction to "Tomorrow in English."
30. J. Jordan, "Writing and Teaching," 480.
31. J. Jordan, "City and the City College," 46–47.
32. J. Jordan, "City and the City College," 47.
33. These essays appear in J. Jordan, "Tomorrow in English."
34. J. Jordan, "Instant Slum Clearance," 109.

35. As Conor Tomás Reed and Talia Shalev write, Jordan's "environmental analyses turn[ed] into pedagogical insights." Tomás Reed and Shalev, introduction to J. Jordan, *"Life Studies,"* 2.

36. June Jordan to Mina Shaughnessy, January 11, 1970, box 76, folder 14, Jordan Papers.

37. MacPhail, "June Jordan and the New Black Intellectuals."

38. J. Jordan, "Nicaragua," 110, 112.

39. Givens, *Fugitive Pedagogy*, 182.

40. Berlin, *Rhetoric and Reality*, 85–86.

41. Covington, "Oral History."

42. Covington, "Oral History."

43. J. Jordan to Mina Shaughnessy.

44. Covington, "Oral History."

45. Ferguson, *Reorder of Things*, 107.

46. Erickson and Jordan, "After Identity," 140.

47. J. Jordan, "Black Studies," 45–46.

48. Erickson and Jordan, "After Identity," 140.

49. Erickson and Jordan, "After Identity," 141.

50. J. Jordan, "Thinking about My Poetry," 129.

51. J. Jordan, "Black Studies," 46.

52. J. Jordan, "Black Studies," 46.

53. Ferguson, *Reorder of Things*, 89.

54. Erickson and Jordan, "After Identity," 141.

55. Tomás Reed, "Early Developments," 58.

56. J. Jordan, "Black Studies," 55.

57. Cooper argues that women should be given access to education because their perspectives are essential to our knowledge of art, economics, religion, and science. Cooper, "Higher Education of Women," 76.

58. Wagner, *End of Education*.

59. June Jordan to President Charles De Carlo, November 17, 1969, Sarah Lawrence College, box 76, folder 18, Jordan Papers.

60. R. Ghiradella, observation report on June Jordan, Eng. 60.11, March 11, 1976, City College, box 76, folder 14, Jordan Papers.

61. J. Jordan, "Old Stories," 137.

62. James J. Greene, observation report on June Jordan, Eng. 190.16B, March 11, 1976, City College, box 76, folder 14, Jordan Papers.

63. Greene, observation report.

64. Greene, observation report.

65. J. Jordan, 1969 course description for Literature and Social Change, Sarah Lawrence College, box 76, folder 18, Jordan Papers.

66. J. Jordan, "Ocean Hill Brownsville, I.S. 55 Graduation Speech," 31.

67. J. Jordan, "Ocean Hill Brownsville, I.S. 55 Graduation Speech," 34.

68. J. Jordan, "Black Studies," 51.

69. J. Jordan, "Statement at CUNY Board," 51.

70. Conference on College Composition and Communication, "Students' Rights," 1.

71. Gross, "How to Kill a College."

72. Gross, "How to Kill a College."

73. For more on Jordan and Black English, see Kinloch, "Revisiting the Promise"; Stalling, "Finding a Democratic Speech"; and Gumbs, "Nobody Mean More."

74. As Katherine McKittrick argues, Black feminist texts often present landscapes not as neutral backgrounds but as sites of power struggle that illuminate oppositional and subaltern geographies. McKittrick, *Demonic Grounds*.

75. J. Jordan, *His Own Where*, 3.

76. J. Jordan, *His Own Where*, 35.

77. J. Jordan, *His Own Where*, 84.

78. J. Jordan, *His Own Where*, 84.

79. J. Jordan, *His Own Where*, 20–21.

80. J. Jordan, *His Own Where*, 52.

81. J. Jordan, "White English/Black English," 59.

82. McGurl, *Program Era*, xi.

83. Lopate and New York Teachers and Writers Collaborative, *Living Experiment*, 9.

84. J. Jordan, "'Voice of the Children' Diaries," 135.

85. J. Jordan, "Voice of the Children," 32.

86. J. Jordan, "Voice of the Children," 32.

87. J. Jordan, "Voice of the Children," 29.

88. J. Jordan, "'Voice of the Children' Diaries," 137.

89. J. Jordan, "'Voice of the Children' Diaries," 135–36.

90. Flynn, "'Affirmative Acts,'" 163.

91. Blackwell, "Sands Junior High School."

92. Velez, "Children Are Slaves."

93. Goode, "April 4, 1968," 9.

94. Holt, introduction to Kohl, *Teaching the "Unteachable*," 5.

95. Holt, introduction to Kohl, *Teaching the "Unteachable*," 8.

96. J. Jordan, "Voice of the Children," 32.

97. J. Jordan, "'Voice of the Children' Diaries," 151.

98. Conrad, "'We Speak,'" 135.

99. Howard, "Ghetto."

100. Conrad, "'We Speak,'" 143–44.

101. J. Jordan, "'Voice of the Children' Diaries," 150.

102. J. Jordan, "Children and the Hungering For," 29.

103. J. Jordan, afterword to *Voice of the Children*, 96.

104. June Jordan to Milton Meltzer, January 28, 1969, box 53, folder 10, Jordan Papers.
105. J. Jordan to Meltzer.
106. Review of *Soulscript*, April 1, 1970, box 53, folder 14, Jordan Papers; and Tarver, review of *Soulscript*.
107. Review of *Soulscript*, April 1, 1970.
108. Fred Hullet, "The Voices," *Courier Post*, December 31, 1970, folder 11, box 54, Jordan Papers.
109. Conrad, "'We Speak,'" 150.
110. Kohl, *36 Children*, 3. As Conrad argues, Koch similarly "elevated his role as teacher." Conrad, "'We Speak,'" 140.
111. Hoffman, "Wishes, Feelings, Dreams," 3600.
112. *Midwife, gardener*, and *maestro* come from Weimer, *Learner-Centered Teaching*, 20.
113. Anna Julia Cooper, for instance "steward[ed] into print the work of other Black women." Moody-Turner, *Portable Anna Julia Cooper*, xxxii.
114. Hurston, "What White Publishers Won't Print."
115. In 1970 Morrison joined the editorial staff at Random House, where she published the work of writers including Bambara, Jordan, Lucille Clifton, and Gayl Jones and "helped to define two decades of African American literary history." Wall, "Toni Morrison," 139.
116. Warren, "Problem of Anthologies."
117. J. Jordan, "Merit Review Statement."
118. J. Jordan, "Finding the Haystack," 90.
119. J. Jordan, "Old Stories," 137.
120. J. Jordan, "Old Stories," 137.
121. J. Jordan, "Notes toward a Black Balancing," 84.
122. J. Jordan, "Writing and Teaching," 480–81.
123. June Jordan to Professor Cogan, May 6, 1969, box 76, folder 18, Jordan Papers.
124. J. Jordan to Cogan.
125. J. Jordan to Cogan.
126. J. Jordan, "Writing and Teaching," 481.
127. J. Jordan, "Writing and Teaching," 482.
128. J. Jordan to President De Carlo.
129. Jordan, "Notes toward a Black Balancing," 84.
130. *Daily News (NY)*, October 30, 1975.
131. Brier and Fabricant, *Austerity Blues*, 87.
132. The end of open admissions at CUNY was an early instance of the neoliberal reforms that would come to exacerbate inequality around the globe. Harvey, *Neoliberalism*, 45.
133. Mahabeer, "13 Black Profs Call Hunger Strike."
134. J. Jordan, "Statement at CUNY Board," 53.

135. J. Jordan, "Statement at CUNY Board," 53.
136. J. Jordan, "Black Studies," 50.
137. This was by 1980. Brier and Fabricant, *Austerity Blues*, 88.
138. J. Jordan, review of *Gorilla*.
139. Bambara, "Chosen Weapons," 41.
140. Toni Cade Bambara to June Jordan, March 25, 1981, box 28, folder 12, Jordan Papers.
141. J. Jordan, quoted in Scandaglia, "Lebanon Crisis."
142. J. Jordan, quoted in Scandaglia, "Lebanon Crisis."
143. J. Jordan, "Nobody Mean More," 168.
144. J. Jordan, "Nobody Mean More," 169.
145. J. Jordan, "Nobody Mean More," 170.
146. J. Jordan, "Nobody Mean More," 170.
147. Gumbs, "Nobody Mean More."
148. Karabel et al., "Freshman Admissions at Berkeley," 47.
149. J. Jordan, "Merit Review Statement."
150. J. Jordan, "Merit Review Statement."
151. J. Jordan, "Merit Review Statement."
152. J. Jordan, "Merit Review Statement."
153. J. Jordan, introduction to Muller, *Revolutionary Blueprint*, 5.
154. "Trial of the American Conscience."
155. Lehrman, "Off Course."
156. J. Jordan, *Life as Activism*, 129.
157. J. Jordan, *Life as Activism*, 129.
158. Givens, Fugitive Pedagogy.
159. Risam, "Academic Generosity, Academic Insurgency." See also Risam's forthcoming book *Insurgent Academics: A Radical Account of Public Humanities*.
160. Sharif, "Role of the Poet."
161. J. Jordan, "Merit Review Statement."
162. J. Jordan, "Merit Review Statement."
163. Leslie Simon created a program by the same name in 1975 at the City College of San Francisco that combined "analysis of poems from multiple traditions across time with a focus on community and social justice." Peckens, "Students Find Voice."
164. J. Jordan, *Life as Activism*, 82.
165. Muller, *Revolutionary Blueprint*, 106–9.
166. J. Jordan, *Life as Activism*, 82.
167. Bright, "Crouching," 29.
168. Navies, "Poet Is on the Front Lines," 22.
169. Villalobos, "Poetry as Revelation," 19.
170. Villalobos, "Poetry as Revelation," 19.
171. E. Meyer, "Margaret Hiller," 25–27.
172. Bright, "Crouching."

173. Bright, "Crouching," 30.

174. Ortega, "June Jordan's Radical Pedagogy," 193. See also Jocson, "'Taking It to the Mic.'"

175. J. Jordan, Poetry for the People Proposal, 1986, box 77, folder 9, Jordan Papers.

176. See Lee and McCabe, "Who Speaks"; Harwood et al., "Racial Microaggressions"; and Howard et al., "Students' Race and Participation."

177. J. Jordan, "Ground Rules."

178. J. Jordan, "Ground Rules."

179. J. Jordan, "Ground Rules."

180. J. Jordan, "Merit Review Statement."

181. Davidson and Katopodis, *The New College Classroom*, 103–9; and Savonick, "Community Guidelines."

182. "Technical Checklist," Poetry for the People, Fall 2000, Berkeley High School, 3, box 81, folder 9, Jordan Papers.

183. "Helpful Reading Tips," 1995–1996?, Poetry for the People, box 81, folder 9, Jordan Papers.

184. See "Research Evidence that Learner-Centered Approaches Work" in Weimer, *Learner-Centered Teaching*.

185. de Leon, "Publishing for the People."

186. Jordan, introduction to Muller, *Revolutionary Blueprint*, 8.

187. Bright, "Crouching," 29.

188. "Profiles in Conflict" anthology, 2002, box 81, folder 9, Jordan Papers.

189. Harney and Moten, *Undercommons*, 112.

190. Bambara, interviewed in Tate, *Black Women Writers*, 38.

191. Toni Cade Bambara, "Short Story Workshop: Midterm Assignment," 1987, box 5, Bambara Papers, Spelman College Archives.

192. Gumbs, "Your Mother"; and Thorsson in Jones et al., "Creation Is Everything."

193. Smith, "Press of Our Own," 11. Though the 1970s saw the birth of Women's Press, the Feminist Press, Diana Press, and Daughters, Inc., women writers of color experienced racism from these new presses led by middle- and upper-class white women.

194. Smith, "Press of Our Own," 11.

195. Moraga and Anzaldúa, *This Bridge*, xlv.

196. Tired of rejection from mainstream publishers, they utilized "the latest developments in desktop publishing and online communication," as well as radio appearances and direct sales to publish and market their work. Nishikawa, "Driven by the Market," 336.

197. See Thorsson, *Sisterhood*.

198. See "Bilingual Education and Home Language" and "Affirmative Acts: Language, Power, Information."

199. J. Jordan, "Finding the Haystack," 96. See also Hamilton and Nielsen, *Broke*

200. Moten and Harney, *Undercommons*, 26. Black women have long engaged in such forms of educational activism. Mary McLeod Bethune, for instance, "utilized school resources to teach community members who fell outside the traditional definition of college student." Evans, *Black Women in the Ivory Tower*, 143–44.

201. Muller, *Revolutionary Blueprint*, 161.
202. Muller, *Revolutionary Blueprint*, 161.
203. Jordan Winer, memo, n.d., box 81, folder 2, Jordan Papers.
204. Muller, *Revolutionary Blueprint*, 143.
205. Wisher, "Writing w/Strangers."
206. Chavez, *Anti-racist Writing Workshop*.
207. J. Jordan, "Merit Review Statement."
208. Jennie Portonoff, quoted in Theresa Tensuan, "Notes from the Workshop Poetry for the People, 26 August 1991," box 78, folder 7, Jordan Papers.
209. Navies, "A Poet is on the Front Lines," 22.
210. Michael Datcher, quoted in Tensuan, "Notes."
211. Michael Datcher, quoted in Tensuan, "Notes."
212. Kinloch, *June Jordan*, 124.
213. Taylor-Hachoose, "Kelly Elaine Navies."

Chapter Three. Of Parallels and Intersections

1. Rich, "Teaching Language," 55.
2. Gelpi and Gelpi, *Adrienne Rich's Poetry*, xi.
3. Rich, "Teaching Language," 63.
4. Exceptions include the prefatory materials in the collections published by Lost and Found: The CUNY Poetics Document Initiative; Tomás Reed, "'Treasures That Prevail'" and Streim, "Teaching the Unteachable."
5. Adrienne Rich to Crawford, c. 1975–78, folder 395, Rich Papers.
6. Holladay, *Power of Adrienne Rich*, 3, 5, 6.
7. Rich, quoted in Holladay, *Power of Adrienne Rich*, 9.
8. Rich, "Taking Women Students Seriously," 237.
9. Holladay, *Power of Adrienne Rich*, 77.
10. Rich, "Taking Women Students Seriously," 238.
11. Holladay, *Power of Adrienne Rich*, 48.
12. Rich, quoted in Holladay, *Power of Adrienne Rich*, 71.
13. Rich, "When We Dead Awaken," 44.
14. See Ostriker, *Stealing the Language*, 3–4.
15. Dean, "Adrienne Rich's Feminist Awakening."
16. Gold, "Adrienne Rich's Persistent Survival."
17. Arnold, preface to *Culture and Anarchy*, viii.
18. Adrienne Rich, reading list for Poetry Workshop, first semester, 1966–67, Columbia University, folder 381, Rich Papers.

19. Adrienne Rich, assignment for Spring 1968 Poetry Workshop, folder 381, Rich Papers.

20. Adrienne Rich, YWHA workshop description, 1967, folder 384, Rich Papers.

21. Holladay, *Power of Adrienne Rich*, 174–75.

22. Holladay, *Power of Adrienne Rich*, 175.

23. Holladay, *Power of Adrienne Rich*, 169.

24. Adrienne Rich to Jean Stafford, 1968, folder 383, Rich Papers.

25. Rich to Stafford.

26. Holladay, *Power of Adrienne Rich*, 184.

27. Rich, "Teaching Language," 52.

28. Rich, "Teaching Language," 52.

29. Rich, "Teaching Language," 53.

30. Byron, in "Report on the Summer Seminar, Pre-baccalaureate Program, City College,"1968, folder 385, Rich Papers.

31. Christian, in "Report on Summer Seminar."

32. Rich to Crawford, c. 1975–78.

33. Bambara, in "Report on Summer Seminar."

34. Rich, "Teaching Language," 55.

35. Rich, "Teaching Language," 63.

36. Rich, syllabus for English 1-H (Fall 1971), 2:22.

37. Rich, "SEEK English Course 1.8 (April 1969)," 2:14.

38. Rich, "English 1-H," 2:22.

39. Rich, "English 1-H," 2:22.

40. Rich, "SEEK English Course 1.8 (April 1969)," 2:13.

41. Rich, "SEEK English Course 1.8 (April 1969)," 13.

42. Rich, "Teaching Language," 65.

43. Rich, "Teaching Language," 65.

44. Rich, "Writing Exercises," 2:9–10.

45. Adrienne Rich, memo, c. 1968–73, folder 386, Rich Papers.

46. Adrienne Rich, writing assignment for Eng. 1.8, c. 1969–72, City College, folder 388, Rich Papers.

47. Rich, "Notes, Statements and Memos," 1:20.

48. Rich, memo.

49. At least since the 1920s, Black educators have formed "insurgent academic networks"—teachers' associations, communities, and organizations like the Association for the Study of Negro Life and History—and utilized venues like Carter Woodson's *Journal of Negro History* to share instructional materials. Givens, *Fugitive Pedagogy*, 179.

50. Rich, "Notes, Statements and Memos," 1:20–21.

51. Rich, "Writing Exercises," 2:10.

52. Rich, "Student Passes—Education Fails."

53. Rich, "Writing Exercises," 2:8.

54. Rich, *What Is Found There*, 169.

55. See Megan Behrent's forthcoming book on Lorde and Rich.

56. Rich, in A. Griffin and Parkerson, *Litany for Survival*.

57. Keller and Levi, "Dear June, Dear Adrienne," 298.

58. J. Jordan, "Introduction of Adrienne Rich," May 5, 1987, Guggenheim Museum, box 58, folder 20, Jordan Papers.

59. Rich's 1974 endorsement of Jordan's *New Days: Poems of Exile and Return*, 1974–75, box 46, folder 16, Jordan Papers.

60. Holladay, *Power of Adrienne Rich*, 201.

61. Biondi, *Black Revolution on Campus*, 124.

62. David Henderson, quoted in Tomás Reed, "'Treasures That Prevail,'" 44.

63. Rich, "Statement to CCNY Faculty."

64. Rich, "Statement to CCNY Faculty."

65. Traub, *City on a Hill*, 112.

66. Traub, *City on a Hill*, 112.

67. This era led to innovative approaches to writing instruction: from Kenneth Bruffee's experiments with peer tutoring and collaborative learning at Brooklyn College to the development of Writing across the Curriculum at Hunter College and the birth of basic (what is now sometimes called "developmental") writing. Otte and Mylnarczyk, *Basic Writing*, 8–9.

68. Adrienne Rich, assignment sequence for ENG 1-G 11, 1971, City College, folder 388, Rich Papers.

69. Adrienne Rich, "Assignment One: Description of a Place," September 25, ENG 1-G 11, 1971, City College, folder 388, Rich Papers.

70. Rich, "When We Dead Awaken," 41.

71. In 1976 David Wood, Jerome S. Bruner, and Gail Ross introduced the term into educational and development science, though its origins can be traced back to the earlier work of Nikolai Bernstein, Alexander Luria, and Lev Vygotsky. Shvarts and Bakker, "Early History." Sean Molloy notes that Rich's assignments were often "scaffolded with different prewriting steps." "Convenient Myopia," 265.

72. Rich, "Notes, Statements and Memos," 1:20. According to erica kaufman, Rich's early teaching materials "predate many of the texts that later become central to composition studies." kaufman, introduction, 7.

73. See Rich, "Hints on Revision," 2:12.

74. Elbow, "High Stakes and Low Stakes," 7.

75. Rich, syllabus for English 1-T, Fall 1970, 2:21; and Rich, syllabus for Images of Women in Poetry by Men, English 13.3 W, c. 1974–75, 2:25.

76. Rich, syllabus for English 1-T, Fall 1970, 2:21.

77. Molloy, "Convenient Myopia," 205, 210, 239, 264.

78. Rich, "Teaching Language," 64.

79. Rich, "Final Comments on the Interdisciplinary Program," 1:34.

80. Rich, "Final Comments on the Interdisciplinary Program," 1:34.
81. Rich, syllabus for SEEK English Course 1.8, April 1969, 2:15.
82. Rich, "Memo to Mina Shaughnessy (September 3, 1971)," 31; and Rich, "Final Comments on the Interdisciplinary Program (Spring 1972)," 35.
83. Rich, "Memo to Mina Shaughnessy," 1:32.
84. Elizabeth Cleaners Street School, *Starting Your Own High School*.
85. Rich, "Teaching Language," 68.
86. Rich, "Notes, Statements and Memos," 1:21.
87. Rich, "Taking Women Students Seriously," 238–39.
88. Rich, "Notes for English 1.8," 2:18–19.
89. Rich, "Teaching Language," 57.
90. Rich, "Burning of Paper," 18.
91. Rich, "What Country Is This?"
92. Holladay, *Power of Adrienne Rich*, 283.
93. While "Diving into the Wreck" is often read as an allegory for the women's movement, Tomás Reed reads it as a meditation on Rich and her students' experiences exploring the depths of a "previously submerged culture" while learning to navigate "the post-strike and Open Admissions conditions of City College." Tomás Reed, "'Treasures That Prevail,'" 62.
94. See Kalstone, review of *The Will to Change: Poems 1968–1970*; and Riley, *Understanding Adrienne Rich*, 37.
95. Rich, "Burning of Paper," 16.
96. Montenegro, "Adrienne Rich," 16.
97. Rich, quoted in Montenegro, "Adrienne Rich," 16.
98. Rich, "Teaching Language," 55–56.
99. Rich, "Notes, Statements and Memos," 1:15.
100. Lorde, "Teacher."
101. Rich, "Teaching Language," 53.
102. Rich, "Notes, Statements and Memos," 1:15.
103. Whelchel, "'Mining the Earth-Deposits,'" 52.
104. Whelchel, "'Mining the Earth-Deposits,'" 52.
105. Rich, "Teaching Language," 60–61.
106. Rich, "Teaching Language," 60–61.
107. Rich, "Teaching Language," 60, 63.
108. Rich, "Towards a Woman-Centered University," 132–33.
109. Rich, "Towards a Woman-Centered University," 127.
110. Rich, syllabus for Images of Women in Poetry by Men English 13.3 W, 2:25.
111. Rich, syllabus for Faces of Woman in the Poetry of Men, English 167A, 1972, Brandeis University, folder 394, Rich Papers.
112. Rich, "Notes on Eng. 13.3 W," 2:30.
113. Rich, "Notes on Eng. 13.3 W," 2:32.

114. Adrienne Rich, first speech delivered as A. D. White Professor at Large, n.d., folder 399, Rich Papers.

115. Rich, quoted in Holladay, *Power of Adrienne Rich*, 71.

116. Rich, quoted in Holladay, *Power of Adrienne Rich*, 71.

117. Rich, "Towards a Woman-Centered University," 152.

118. Rich, "Towards a Woman-Centered University," 141.

119. Rich, "Towards a Woman-Centered University," 145.

120. V. Franklin, "Hidden in Plain View"; and Boxer, *When Women Ask*.

121. Rich, "Towards a Woman-Centered University," 152.

122. Rich, "Towards a Woman-Centered University," 152.

123. Adrienne Rich to Prof. Edward Quinn, March 2, 1975, folder 389, Rich Papers.

124. Rich, "Taking Women Students Seriously," 238; and Rich, interviewed in Moyers, "Heart of Things."

125. Rich, "Teaching Language," 67.

126. Rich, "Taking Women Students Seriously," 238.

127. Rich, "Teaching Language," 52.

128. Rich to Quinn.

129. Rich to Quinn.

130. Denda, Hawkesworth, and Perrone, *Douglass Century*, 159.

131. Rich, "Taking Women Students Seriously," 240.

132. Adrienne Rich, observation, English 110 course, October 1, 1976, Douglass College, folder 395, Rich Papers.

133. Adrienne Rich, syllabus for American Women Poets: Anne Bradstreet to the Present, Eng. 350: 235, 1976, Douglass College, folder 397, Rich Papers.

134. See, for example, Tobias, "Female Studies Conference."

135. Rich, "Towards a Woman-Centered University," 145.

136. Rich, syllabus for American Women Poets.

137. Rich, syllabus for American Women Poets.

138. Leary, "Composing the Anthology."

139. Greenberg, "By Woman Taught," 93.

140. Holladay, *Power of Adrienne Rich*, 281.

141. Rich, observation.

142. Rich, "Taking Women Students Seriously," 245.

143. Rich, quoted in Greenberg, "By Woman Taught," 96.

144. Greenberg, "By Woman Taught," 96.

145. Greenberg, "By Woman Taught," 99.

146. Greenberg, "By Woman Taught," 96.

147. Rich, "Towards a Woman-Centered University," 133.

148. Student letter, August 9, 1977, folder 395, Rich Papers. In some instances, like this one, I have chosen not to include the names of student authors, though they appear on archival documents. As much as I want to give them credit for

their work, I have chosen to preserve their privacy because such documents were submitted to their instructor, and these students never consented to having their words made public.

149. Anonymous student, quoted in student letter, August 9, 1977.
150. Student reflection, June 19, n.d., folder 395, Rich Papers.
151. Student reflection, June 19, n.d.
152. Adrienne Rich, response to Tom Edwards, April 5, 1977, folder 398, Rich Papers.
153. Rich, "Taking Women Students Seriously," 239.
154. Rich, "Taking Women Students Seriously," 244.
155. Rich, "Taking Women Students Seriously," 239.
156. Adrienne Rich, syllabus for Woman to Woman Relationships in Literature, English 352/427: 02, Fall 1977, folder 398, Rich Papers.
157. Rich, syllabus for Woman to Woman Relationships in Literature.
158. It was originally written in 1978 for the "Sexuality" issues of *Signs*, published there in 1980.
159. Rich, "Compulsory Heterosexuality," 54.
160. Rust, "Making Emends," 97.
161. Lorde, quoted in DeVaux, *Warrior Poet*, 303.
162. Holladay, *Power of Adrienne Rich*, 255. Technically, they rejected the "patriarchal competition" and tokenism the prize encouraged and instead accepted the award in the name of all women.
163. Lorde, "Interview," 104.
164. Rich, in Lorde, "Interview," 104.
165. Rich, "Hunger."
166. Rust, "Making Emends," 100.
167. J. Jordan, "Sonnet for Adrienne Rich," 1998–2001, box 67, folder 4, Jordan Papers.
168. In "An Atlas of the Difficult World," Rich adapts Jordan's strategy of excluding violence and "the question of when to speak" into the question of what she will "allow to enter the self's record of place." Partridge, "'Where Do We See,'" 164.
169. J. Jordan, "Thinking about My Poetry," 126.
170. Holladay, *Power of Adrienne Rich*, 267.
171. Gumbs, "Your Mother."
172. Rich, "Disloyal to Civilization," 280.
173. J. Jordan, in Erickson and Jordan, "After Identity," 141.
174. Rich, "Wholeness Is No Trifling Matter," pt. 1, 10.
175. Rich, "Wholeness Is No Trifling Matter," pt. 2, 20, 24.
176. hooks, *Feminist Theory*, 51; hooks, *Teaching to Transgress*, 102; and Joseph, "Incompatible Ménage à Trois," 105.
177. Behrent, "'Way of Knowing,'" 22–23.

178. Rich, Quoted in Holladay, *Power of Adrienne Rich*, 354.
179. Woolf, quoted in Rich, "Blood, Bread, and Poetry," 183.
180. See Kaplan, *Questions of Travel*, 164.
181. Rich, "'Going There,'" 159.
182. Rich, "Notes towards a Politics of Location."
183. Kaplan, "Politics of Location," 141–43.
184. Kaplan, *Questions of Travel*, 167–68.
185. Kaplan, "Politics of Location," 142.
186. Adrienne Rich to Mary Lou Lewandowski, January 8, 1986, folder 406, Rich Papers.
187. Rich to Lewandowski.
188. Rich, "Resisting Amnesia," 148.
189. Adrienne Rich, syllabus for Woman Novelist as Historian, 159F, 1985, San Jose State University, folder 404, Rich Papers.
190. Student evaluations of Woman Novelist as Historian, ENG159H, San Jose State University, Fall 1985, folder 406, Rich Papers.
191. Student evaluations.
192. Rich, syllabus for Woman Novelist.
193. Student evaluations.
194. Student evaluations.
195. Student evaluations.
196. Rich, syllabus for Woman Novelist.
197. Freedman, "Small Group Pedagogy," 118.
198. Adrienne Rich, "Family Project," Feminist Studies 103/203, Fall 1988, Stanford University, folder 413, Rich Papers.
199. Similar situated, positional, and intersectional pedagogies were also emerging in Black studies (Neville and Cha-Jua, "Kufundisha," 463) and women's studies (Boxer, *When Women Ask*, 100–107).
200. Adrienne Rich, "Final Paper," The Activist Roots of Feminist Theory, Fall 1989, Stanford University, folder 413, Rich Papers.
201. Streim, "Teaching the Unteachable," 69.
202. Behrent, "'Way of Knowing,'" 28.
203. Rich, "Why I Refused," 100. Education trains artists in "the tools of their craft" and allows them to learn from other practitioners, past and present. It also generates audiences, "a literate citizenry." Rich, "Why I Refused," 103, 105.
204. Rich, "Arts of the Possible," 162.
205. Keller and Levi, *We're On*, 298.
206. Rich, untitled poem for June Jordan, June 3, 1996, 306.
207. Holladay, *Power of Adrienne Rich*, 401.
208. Rich, untitled poem for June Jordan, June 2, 1996, 303.
209. J. Jordan, untitled poem for Adrienne Rich, June 3–4, 1996, 308.
210. J. Jordan, "For the Poet: Adrienne Rich."
211. Rich, "For June."

212. Rich, foreword to J. Jordan, *Directed by Desire*, xvii.
213. Adrienne Rich and Michelle Cliff, reflections on English/Feminist Studies 160: Women and Difference: Marginality, Art, Politics, 1988, Stanford University, folder 422, Rich Papers.
214. Rich and Cliff, reflections on English/Feminist Studies 160: Women and Difference.
215. Freire, *Pedagogy of the Oppressed*.
216. Reinhold, quoted in Holladay, *Power of Adrienne Rich*, 359.
217. Holladay, *Power of Adrienne Rich*, 359.
218. Freedman, "Small Group Pedagogy," 119.
219. Freedman, "Small Group Pedagogy," 119.
220. Freedman, "Small Group Pedagogy," 121.

Chapter Four. Sharing the Illumination

1. Lorde, "Interview," 97.
2. Byrd, "Create Your Own Fire," 5, 21.
3. Crenshaw, "Demarginalizing."
4. Hong, *Death beyond Disavowal*; Ferguson, "Of Sensual Matters"; and Obourn, "Audre Lorde."
5. Khan-Cullors and Bandele, *Call You a Terrorist*, 72.
6. Lorde, "My Words," 161.
7. Lorde, *Zami*, 27.
8. DeVaux, *Warrior Poet*, 23, 27, 30.
9. Lorde, *Zami*, 82.
10. DeVaux, *Warrior Poet*, 26.
11. DeVaux, *Warrior Poet*, 26.
12. DeVaux, *Warrior Poet*, 27.
13. DeVaux, *Warrior Poet*, 32.
14. DeVaux, *Warrior Poet*, 38.
15. DeVaux, *Warrior Poet*, 68.
16. Randall, review of *The First Cities*, 13–14.
17. Atkin and Brown, introduction, 1.
18. Lorde, "Interview," 89.
19. Lorde, "Interview," 92.
20. Lorde and Rich, "Interview," 721.
21. Lorde, "Interview," 92.
22. Lorde, "Interview," 90.
23. Lorde, "Interview," 90.
24. DeVaux, *Warrior Poet*, 96.
25. Lorde, *Pound*.
26. DeVaux, *Warrior Poet*, 98.
27. P. Patterson, "Pound."

28. P. Patterson, "Pound."

29. Rushin, "Place to Grieve," 139.

30. Lorde, "Interview," 92.

31. Lorde, "Interview," 90.

32. Joseph, *Wind Is Spirit*, 23.

33. DeVaux, *Warrior Poet*, 100.

34. Lorde, "Interview," 93.

35. Lorde, "Interview," 93.

36. Lorde, "Interview," 94.

37. Lorde, "Interview," 94.

38. Lorde, "Interview," 94.

39. Mina Shaughnessy to Audre Lorde, July 29, 1968, box 8, folder 17A, Audre Lorde Papers, Spelman College Archives, Atlanta, Georgia.

40. Mayes, "Oral History."

41. Lorde, "Interview," 95.

42. Lorde, "Interview," 95.

43. Lorde, "Interview," 97.

44. DeVaux, *Warrior Poet*, 192.

45. Rich, "Hunger," 12.

46. See Rust, "Making Emends"; and Behrent, "'Way of Knowing.'"

47. J. Jordan, Donnell Library introduction, 1977, box 58, folder 16, Jordan Papers.

48. J. Jordan, reflections at memorial service.

49. DeVaux, *Warrior Poet*, 179.

50. Lorde, "Dear Toni . . ." 94.

51. Hill Collins, *Black Feminist Thought*, 205.

52. Gumbs, Martens, and Williams, *Revolutionary Mothering*. In "We Can Learn to Mother Ourselves," Gumbs writes of Black mothering as an act of queer pedagogy that involves "teaching a set of social values that challenge a social logic which believes that we, the children of black mothers, the queer, the deviant should not exist," 51.

53. Lorde, "Interview," 95.

54. Lorde, "Interview," 95.

55. DeVaux, *Warrior Poet*, 112.

56. Lorde, "Interview," 96.

57. Lorde, "Interview," 97.

58. Hanna, "Pedagogies in the Flesh," 238.

59. Alexis Pauline Gumbs, interview with Caleb Ward, Hamburg, Germany, 2023.

60. Lorde, "Race and the Urban Situation," 18–19. In the full version, there are discussion topics and assigned readings below each section. See also DeVaux, *Warrior Poet*, 117.

61. Lorde, "Race and the Urban Situation," 19.

62. Lorde, undated assignment, 31.

63. Audre Lorde, untitled assignment, Afro-American Literature, 1972, John Jay College, box 82, folder 27, Lorde Papers.

64. Lorde, "Race and the Urban Situation," 20.

65. Audre Lorde, Lesbian Literature notes, 1985, Hunter College, box 82, folder 50, Lorde Papers.

66. Audre Lorde, syllabus for Poetry Workshops I and II, n.d., Hunter College, box 82, folder 10, Lorde Papers.

67. Practitioners of feminist pedagogy used journal assignments to encourage critical introspection, reflection, and scrutiny of one's beliefs; the application of new ideas and information to previous knowledge; connections between personal experiences and structures of power; and the articulation of ideas students may not feel comfortable sharing in class. Some also saw it as a way to counter the silencing of women students in hierarchical classrooms and instead validate their ideas. O'Barr and Wyer, *Engaging Feminism*, 6; Mattingly, "Valuing the Personal," 155; and Boxer, *When Women Ask*, 88.

68. Student journal, Contemporary Black Women's Poetry, 1984, Free University of Berlin, box 82, folder 44, Lorde Papers.

69. Lorde, undated assignment, 31.

70. Atkin and Brown, introduction to Lorde, *"I Teach Myself,"* 4–5.

71. Lorde, "Assignment from 1972."

72. Audre Lorde, syllabus for Race and the Urban Situation, 1972, John Jay College, box 82, folder 25, Lorde Papers; and Lorde, "Assignment from 1972."

73. Oguntoye, "My Coming Out," 160.

74. DeVaux, *Warrior Poet*, 163. This figure may be a bit higher or lower depending on the exact year that this was her salary (likely 1974–76). It also seems that John Jay salaries failed to keep up with inflation, which could be another reason she eventually left for Hunter College.

75. See Tomás Reed, "Early Developments."

76. Audre Lorde and Blanche Wiesen Cook, syllabus for American Women in Black and White, Spring 1972, John Jay College, box 82, folder 20, Lorde Papers.

77. Cook, in "MOOC WHAW1.2x | 17.4.3 The Lesbian Movement."

78. "MOOC WHAW1.2x | 17.4.3 The Lesbian Movement."

79. Cook, in "MOOC WHAW1.2x | 17.4.3 The Lesbian Movement."

80. Hull and Smith, "The Politics of Black Women's Studies," xxiii–xxiv.

81. Student, "On Being Blue," English 101, John Jay College, box 82, folder 2, Lorde Papers.

82. See Molloy, "Convenient Myopia."

83. Student, "On Being Blue."

84. Lorde, "Interview," 98.

85. Lorde, "Poet as Teacher," 182.

86. Lorde, "Interview," 98.

87. See, for example, Haraway, "Situated Knowledges"; and hooks, *Feminist Theory*.

88. Lorde, "Poet as Teacher," 183.

89. Chinua Achebe, for example, celebrated the writer's role as an instructor of the people. Achebe valued how fiction could help heal the ravages wrought by a colonial school system and catalyze a kind of "re-education": instilling pride among readers and teaching a version of history that doesn't glorify colonialism. Achebe, "Novelist as Teacher," 45. In addition, members of the Black Arts Movement sought to use poetry and plays to, in Amiri Baraka's words, "instruct, inform—educate people so that they will then be able to transform society." Baraka, quoted in Bigsby, "The Theatre and the Coming Revolution," 135.

90. The women's health movement "called for women to liberate themselves from the masculine medical establishment by becoming knowledgeable about their own bodies." Jurecic, *Illness as Narrative*, 8.

91. Lorde, "Interview," 95.

92. Lorde, quoted in Joseph, *Wind Is Spirit*, 233.

93. Atkin and Brown, introduction to Lorde, *"I Teach Myself,"* 11. See also DeVaux, *Warrior Poet*, 120, 139.

94. Lorde, "Blackstudies," 52. Gumbs writes that Lorde used poetry to think "through the challenges of the institutional spaces she navigated." Gumbs, "17th Floor," 379.

95. "Blackstudies" combines Lorde's experiences teaching at Tougaloo and John Jay. See Angela Bowen's perceptive analysis of the ways they intertwine in this multi-layered poem. Bowen, "Diving into Audre Lorde's 'Blackstudies.'"

96. The poem "navigates the stereotypes, silences, and urgencies that shaped her experience as an educator." Gumbs, "17th Floor," 375.

97. On "Power," see DeVaux, *Warrior Poet*, 159–60; and Gumbs, "Nobody Mean More," 245–49.

98. Lorde, "Uses of Anger," 132.

99. Lorde, "Poetry is Not a Luxury."

100. Ferguson, "Of Sensual Matters."

101. Berrett, "The Day the Purpose of College Changed."

102. Ronald Reagan, press conference, February 21, 1967, Ronald Reagan Presidential Library Digital Collections.

103. Ronald Reagan, press conference, February 21, 1967, Ronald Reagan Presidential Library Digital Collections.

104. Clabaugh, "The Cutting Edge."

105. Lorde, "Audre Lorde Speaks!"

106. Lorde, "Audre Lorde Speaks!"

107. DeVaux, *Warrior Poet*, 163, 269.

108. Lorde, in A. Griffin and Parkerson, *Litany for Survival*.
109. Brown, quoted in Atkin and Brown, introduction to Lorde, *"I Teach Myself,"* 4.
110. Lorde, Lesbian Literature notes.
111. Lorde, Lesbian Literature notes.
112. Lorde, Lesbian Literature notes.
113. Lorde, *Cancer Journals*, 12.
114. Lorde, *Cancer Journals*, 12.
115. DeVaux, *Warrior Poet*, 230.
116. Audre Lorde, syllabus for The Other Woman: Lesbian Voices in 20th C. Lit, ENG 398.58–51, 1985, Hunter College, box 82, folder 49, Lorde Papers.
117. See also Atkin and Brown, introduction to Lorde, *"I Teach Myself,"* 9.
118. Lorde, syllabus for Lesbian Voices.
119. Lorde, Lesbian Literature notes.
120. Transcript of student conversation, December 11, 1985, ENG358.5751, Hunter College, box 82, folder 51, Lorde Papers.
121. Transcript of student conversation.
122. Transcript of student conversation.
123. Moraga, "Catching Fire," xxiv.
124. Melanie Kaye and Paula King, syllabus for Women as Creative Artists, WS199B, 1978, Portland State University, box 82, folder 34, Lorde Papers.
125. Kaye and King, syllabus for Women as Creative Artists.
126. Kaye and King, syllabus for Women as Creative Artists.
127. Lorde, proposal for faculty seminar, 42.
128. DeVaux, *Warrior Poet*, 347.
129. DeVaux, "Searching for Audre Lorde," 65.
130. As Jennifer C. Nash writes, Lorde, Jordan, and Bambara articulated a Black feminist love politics grounded in a shared utopian vision, rather than identity politics. Nash, "Practicing Love."
131. Lorde, *Cancer Journals*, 39.
132. Lorde, *Cancer Journals*, 39.
133. Lorde, *Cancer Journals*, 39.
134. Lorde, foreword to Ayim, Oguntoye, and Schultz, *Showing Our Colors*, vii.
135. Lorde, *Dream of Europe*, 72.
136. Student journal, Contemporary Black Women's Poetry, 1984, Free University of Berlin, box 82, folder 41, Lorde Papers.
137. Student journal, 1984, folder 44.
138. Lorde, *Dream of Europe*, 27.
139. Student journal, Contemporary Black Women's Poetry, 1984, Free University of Berlin, box 82, folder 40, Lorde Papers.
140. Lorde, *Dream of Europe*, 54.
141. Student journal, 1984, folder 40.

142. Student journal Contemporary Black Women's Poetry, 1984, Free University of Berlin, box 82, folder 39, Lorde Papers.

143. Student journal, Contemporary Black Women's Poetry, 1984, Free University of Berlin, box 82, folder 42, Lorde Papers.

144. Student journal, 1984, folder 40.

145. Lorde, "Power," 215.

146. Student journal 1984, folder 41.

147. Student journal, 1984, folder 39.

148. Student journal, 1984, folder 39.

149. Student journal, 1984, folder 40.

150. Lorde, "Interview," 106.

151. Ayim, Oguntoye, and Schultz, *Showing Our Colors*, xvi, xxii. See also Bolaki and Broeck, introduction to *Transnational Legacies*.

152. Kahina, "Elder Sister Audre Lorde," 201.

153. Kahina, "Elder Sister Audre Lorde," 201.

154. Lorde, "Litany for Survival," 255.

155. Lorde, "Interview," 108.

156. DeVaux, *Warrior Poet*, 229.

157. Lorde, in Tate, *Black Women Writers*, 116.

158. Lorde, *A Burst of Light*, 61. See also DeVaux, *Warrior Poet*, 327; Ahmed, *What's the Use?*, 223; and Reid-Pharr, "This Useful Death."

Conclusion

1. These assignments belong to Dan Radus and Teagan Bradway, respectively.

2. The video archive assignment is from Chandra Talpade Mohanty and Linda Carty (http://feministfreedomwarriors.org/);the anthology assignment is from Molly Appel (https://spinalcolumn.weebly.com/). Examples of networks include HASTAC, the *Journal of Interactive Technology and Pedagogy*, and the MLA's Humanities Commons.

3. Many thanks to Dr. Hobart (@hiokinai) for sharing this example and allowing me to include it here. Hiʻilei Julia Hobart, "As promised, I am showing off some of the decolonial postcards that my students produced this semester. They are really, really cool!!," Twitter, May 4, 2022, 2:55 p.m., https://twitter.com/hiokinai/status/1521941623898353666?s=20&t=62Y9_T_TU-WAQmx1MRVaMA.

4. Rachel, in Hobart, "As promised."

5. This tradition of activist teaching that involved expanding access to education extends back to women such as Anna Julia Cooper and Ida B. Wells. As Shirley Moody-Turner writes, Cooper's activist pedagogy involved expanding education access "to all people regardless of their race, gender, ability, age, color, class, or station in life." Moody-Turner, *Portable Anna Julia*

Cooper, 161. See also Omolade, "Black Feminist Pedagogy," 37–38; and Evans, *Black Women*.

6. For example, "in the early 1990s, California contributed 78 percent of the total cost per student, a number that had shrunk to 37 percent by the 2015–2016 academic year." Hamilton and Nielsen, "Our Broke Public Universities." See also Hamilton and Nielsen, *Broke*.

7. Chuh, *Difference Aesthetics Makes*, 28.

8. Mullen, *Degrees of Inequality*.

9. Brim, *Poor Queer Studies*, 196; and Brier and Fabricant, *Austerity Blues*, 27.

10. Cottom and Seamster, "Black and White Debt."

11. Hayot, "Sky Is Falling."

12. One recent study of the CUNY and SUNY systems found that students are more likely to interact with full-time professors if they're on a campus with relatively fewer Black and Hispanic students. Flaherty, "Full-Time Faculty Factor."

13. American Federation of Teachers, "Army of Temps," 1.

14. Flaherty, "Barely Getting By"; and Modern Language Association, "MLA Recommendation."

15. American Federation of Teachers, "Army of Temps," 4.

16. Flaherty, "Barely Getting By."

17. Scholars of abolitionist university studies have rightly pointed out that this supposed "golden era" of public higher education was funded by war, a slave economy, and Indigenous dispossession and genocide (Boggs et al., "Abolitionist University Studies"). We need to find ways of funding education without violence. This will involve policies that redistribute wealth of the 1 percent to public education.

18. Current programs like Accelerated Study in Associate Programs—piloted at CUNY and expanded to other community colleges—continue to demonstrate how students flourish when provided with free tuition, money for books, metro cards, dedicated advisors and tutors, peer mentors, and career counseling. P. Jordan, "Accelerated Study."

19. Things weren't perfect: at times, high teaching loads thwarted professors' efforts to provide personalized attention and feedback.

20. J. Jordan, "Black Studies," 48.

BIBLIOGRAPHY

Archival Collections

Bambara, Toni Cade. Papers. 1939–96. Spelman College Archives, Atlanta, Georgia.
Jordan, June. Papers. 1936–2002. Schlesinger Library, Radcliffe Institute, Harvard University, Cambridge, Massachusetts.
Lorde, Audre. Papers. 1950–2002. Spelman College Archives, Atlanta, Georgia.
Rich, Adrienne. Papers. 1927–99. Schlesinger Library, Radcliffe Institute, Harvard University, Cambridge, Massachusetts.

Other Sources

Achebe, Chinua. "The Novelist as Teacher." In *Morning Yet on Creation Day: Essays*, 55–60. Garden City, NY: Anchor Books, 1976.
Ahmed, Sara. *What's the Use? On the Uses of Use*. Durham, NC: Duke University Press, 2019.
American Federation of Teachers. "An Army of Temps." 2020. https://www.aft.org/sites/default/files/media/2020/adjuncts_qualityworklife2020.pdf.
Arnold, Matthew. Preface to *Culture and Anarchy*, v–xxxvii. London: Smith, Elder and Co., 1889.
Atkin, Miriam, and Iemanjá Brown. Introduction to Lorde, *"I Teach Myself in Outline,"* 1–14.
Attewell, Paul A., and David E. Lavin. *Passing the Torch: Does Higher Education for the Disadvantaged Pay Off across the Generations?* New York: Russell Sage Foundation, 2007.
Ayim, May, Katharina Oguntoye, and Dagmar Schultz, eds. *Showing Our Colors: Afro-German Women Speak Out*. Amherst: University of Massachusetts Press, 1992.

Backer, David I., Matthew Bissen, Jacques Laroche, Aleksandra Perisic, and Jason Wozniak. "What Is Horizontal Pedagogy? A Discussion on Dandelions." In *Out of the Ruins: The Emergence of Radical Informal Learning Spaces*, edited by Robert H. Haworth and John M. Elmore, 195–222. Oakland, CA: PM Press, 2017.

Bambara, Toni Cade. "The American Adolescent Apprentice Novel." Master's thesis, City College of New York, 1964.

Bambara, Toni Cade, ed. *The Black Woman: An Anthology*. New York: Washington Square, 1970.

Bambara, Toni Cade. "The Children Who Got Cheated." *Redbook*, January 1970, 64–65, 158–63.

Bambara, Toni Cade. "Chosen Weapons." *Ms.*, April 1981, 40–42.

Bambara, Toni Cade. *Deep Sightings and Rescue Missions: Fiction, Essays, and Conversations*. New York: Pantheon, 1996.

Bambara, Toni Cade. *Gorilla, My Love*. New York: Random House, 1972.

Bambara, Toni Cade. "The Lesson." In *Gorilla, My Love*, 85–96.

Bambara, Toni Cade. "Realizing the Dream of a Black University." *Observation Post*, February 14, 1969.

Bambara, Toni Cade. *Realizing the Dream of a Black University*. Edited by Makeba Lavan and Conor Tomás Reed. Lost and Found: The CUNY Poetics Document Initiative, ser. 7, no. 2. 2017. https://cuny.manifoldapp.org/read/realizing-the-dream-of-a-black-university-other-writings-part-ii/section/9e463fd4-f052-4200-b807-18eea9778acb.

Bambara, Toni Cade. *The Salt Eaters*. New York: Vintage, 1980.

Bambara, Toni Cade. *The Seabirds Are Still Alive: Collected Stories*. New York: Random House, 1977.

Bambara, Toni Cade, ed. *Tales and Stories for Black Folks*. Garden City, NY: Zenith Books, 1971.

Bambara, Toni Cade. *Those Bones Are Not My Child*. New York: Vintage, 2000.

Bambara, Toni Cade, and Geneva Powell. "The Three Little Panthers." In Bambara, *Tales and Stories*, 140–41.

Baraka, Amiri. *The Dead Lecturer: Poems*. New York: Grove, 1964.

Baraka, Amiri, and Larry Neal, eds. *Black Fire: An Anthology of Afro-American Writing*. New York: Morrow, 1968.

Beckman, Karen. "Black Media Matters: Remembering *The Bombing of Osage Avenue*." *Film Quarterly* 68, no. 1 (2015): 8–23.

Behrent, Megan. "'A Way of Knowing': Adrienne Rich's Marxism and the Poetics of Revolution." *Arizona Quarterly: A Journal of American Literature, Culture, and Theory* 78, no. 2 (2022): 13–42.

Benjamin, Shanna Greene. *Half in Shadow: The Life and Legacy of Nellie Y. McKay*. Chapel Hill: The University of North Carolina Press, 2021.

Berlin, James A. *Rhetoric and Reality: Writing Instruction in American Colleges, 1900–1985*. Carbondale: Southern Illinois University Press, 1987.

Bigsby, C. W. E. "The Theater and the Coming Revolution." In *Conversations with Amiri Baraka*, edited by Charles Reilly, 130–45. Jackson: University Press of Mississippi, 1994.

Biondi, Martha. *The Black Revolution on Campus*. Oakland: University of California Press, 2012.

Blackwell, Arlene. "Sands Junior High School." In J. Jordan and Bush, *Voice of the Children*, 31.

Blum, Susan D., ed. *Ungrading: Why Rating Students Undermines Learning (and What to Do Instead)*. Morgantown: West Virginia University Press, 2020.

Boggs, Abigail, Eli Meyerhoff, Nick Mitchell, and Zach Schwartz-Weinstein. "Abolitionist University Studies: An Invitation." Abolition University, August 2018. https://abolition.university/wp-content/uploads/2019/08/Abolitionist-University-Studies_-An-Invitation-Release-1-version.pdf.

Bolaki, Stella, and Sabine Broeck. Introduction to *Audre Lorde's Transnational Legacies*, edited by Stella Bolaki and Sabine Broeck, 1–19. Amherst: University of Massachusetts Press, 2015.

Bourdieu, Pierre, and Jean-Claude Passeron. *Reproduction in Education, Society and Culture*. Thousand Oaks, CA: Sage, 1990.

Bowen, Angela. "Diving into Audre Lorde's 'Blackstudies.'" *Meridians: Feminism, Race, Transnationalism* 4, no. 1 (2003): 109–29.

Bowles, Gloria, Maria Giulia Fabi, and Arlene R. Keizer. Introduction to *New Black Feminist Criticism, 1985–2000*, edited by Gloria Bowles, Maria Giulia Fabi, and Arlene R. Keizer, ix–xiii. Urbana: University of Illinois Press, 2007.

Boxer, Marilyn Jacoby. *When Women Ask the Questions: Creating Women's Studies in America*. Baltimore: Johns Hopkins University Press, 1998.

Brien, Shanti. *Almost Innocent: From Searching to Saved in America's Criminal Justice System*. Herndon, VA: Amplify, 2021.

Brier, Stephen. "It's Time to Revisit Community Control." In "Community Control and the 1968 Teacher Strikes in NYC at 50: A Roundtable." Gotham Center for New York City History, October 18, 2018. https://www.gothamcenter.org/blog/community-control-and-the-1968-teacher-strikes-in-nyc-at-50-a-roundtable.

Brier, Stephen, and Michael Fabricant. *Austerity Blues: Fighting for the Soul of Public Higher Education*. Baltimore: Johns Hopkins University Press, 2016.

Bright, Shanti. "Crouching in the Shadow of Columbus's Tomb." In Muller, *Revolutionary Blueprint*, 28–31.

Brim, Matt. *Poor Queer Studies: Confronting Elitism in the University*. Durham, NC: Duke University Press, 2020.

Bruffee, Kenneth A. "Collaborative Learning and the 'Conversation of Mankind.'" *College English* 46, no. 7 (1984): 635–52.

Bulkin, Elly. Introduction to *Lesbian Fiction: An Anthology*. Watertown, MA: Persephone Press, 1981.

Busia, Abena. "Teaching Toni Cade Bambara Teaching: Learning with the Children in Toni Cade Bambara's 'The Lesson.'" In Holmes and Wall, *Savoring the Salt*, 181–94.

Buurma, Rachel Sagner, and Laura Heffernan. *The Teaching Archive: A New History for Literary Study*. Chicago: University of Chicago Press, 2020.

Byrd, Rudolph P. "Create Your Own Fire: Audre Lorde and the Tradition of Black Radical Thought." In Byrd, Cole, and Guy-Sheftall, *I Am Your Sister*, 3–36.

Byrd, Rudolph P. "The Feeling of Transport." In Holmes and Wall, *Savoring the Salt*, 170–80.

Byrd, Rudolph P., Johnnetta Betsch Cole, and Beverly Guy-Sheftall, eds. *I Am Your Sister: Collected and Unpublished Writings of Audre Lorde*. New York: Oxford University Press, 2009.

Chandler, Zala. "Voices beyond the Veil: An Interview with Toni Cade Bambara and Sonia Sanchez." In *Wild Women in the Whirlwind: Afra-American Culture and the Contemporary Literary Renaissance*, edited by Joanne Braxton and Andree Nicola McLaughlin, 342–61. New Brunswick, NJ: Rutgers University Press, 1990.

Chatterjee, Piya, and Sunaina Maira, eds. *The Imperial University: Academic Repression and Scholarly Dissent*. Minneapolis: University of Minnesota Press, 2014.

Chavez, Felicia Rose. *The Anti-racist Writing Workshop: How to Decolonize the Creative Classroom*. Chicago: Haymarket, 2021.

Christian, Barbara. *Black Women Novelists: The Development of a Tradition, 1892–1976*. Westport, CT: Greenwood Press, 1980.

Christian, Barbara. "The Race for Theory." *Cultural Critique*, no. 6 (April 1987): 51–63.

Chuh, Kandice. *The Difference Aesthetics Makes*. Durham, NC: Duke University Press, 2019.

City College of New York. "Our History." April 17, 2023. https://www.ccny.cuny.edu/about/history.

Clabaugh, Gary K. "The Cutting Edge: The Educational Legacy of Ronald Reagan." *Educational Horizons* (2004): 256–59.

Clark, Joanna. "Motherhood." In Bambara, *Black Woman*, 63–72.

Cleaver, Eldridge. *Soul on Ice*. New York: McGraw-Hill, 1967.

Clemens, Paul G. E., and Carla Yanni. "The Early Years of Livingston College, 1964–1967." *Journal of the Rutgers University Libraries* 6, no. 2 (2016): 71–114.

Collins, Janelle. "Generating Power: Fission, Fusion, and Postmodern Politics in Bambara's *The Salt Eaters*." MELUS 21, no. 2 (1996): 35–47.

Conference on College Composition and Communication. "Students' Rights to Their Own Language." *College Composition and Communication* 25, no. 3 (1974): 1–32.

Conrad, Rachel. "'We Speak to Be Heard': June Jordan, Terri Bush, and the Voice of the Children." In *Time for Childhoods: Young Poets and Questions of Agency*, 125–58. Amherst: University of Massachusetts Press, 2019.

Cook, Blanche Wiesen. "MOOC WHAW1.2X | 17.4.3 The Lesbian Movement with Blanche Wiesen Cook." Interview by Alice Kessler-Harris. ColumbiaLearn, YouTube, July 5, 2017. https://www.youtube.com/watch?v=ewoolc4JwiA.

Cooper, Anna J. "The Higher Education of Women." In *A Voice from the South*, 72–87. New York: Oxford University Press, 1988.

Cooper, Jane R., ed. *Reading Adrienne Rich: Reviews and Re-visions, 1951–81*. Ann Arbor: University of Michigan Press, 1984.

Cornillon, Susan Koppelman, ed. *Images of Women in Fiction: Feminist Perspectives*. Bowling Green, OH: Bowling Green University Popular Press, 1972.

Cottom, Tressie McMillan, and Louise Seamster. "The Life Altering Differences between Black and White Debt." *New York Times*, November 2, 2021. https://www.nytimes.com/2021/11/02/opinion/ezra-klein-podcast-louise-seamster.html.

Covington, Francee. "Are the Revolutionary Techniques Employed in the Battle of Algiers Applicable in Harlem?" In Bambara, *Black Woman*, 244–51.

Covington, Francee. "An Oral History of the CCNY 1960s SEEK Program and the Paper." Interview by Sean Molloy. CUNY Digital History Archive, June 5, 2015. https://cdha.cuny.edu/items/show/7102.

Crenshaw, Kimberlé. "Demarginalizing the Intersection of Race and Sex: A Black Feminist Critique of Antidiscrimination Doctrine, Feminist Theory and Antiracist Politics." *University of Chicago Legal Forum* 140 (1989): 139–67.

Dash, Julie, dir. *Daughters of the Dust*. 1991. Geechee Girls / American Playhouse.

Datcher, Michael. *Raising Fences: A Black Man's Love Story*. New York: Diversion Books, 2015.

Davidson, Cathy N., and Christina Katopodis. *The New College Classroom*. Cambridge, MA: Harvard University Press, 2022.

Dean, Michelle. "Adrienne Rich's Feminist Awakening." *New Republic*, April 3, 2016.

de Leon, Aya. "June Jordan, Genre Fiction, and Publishing for the People." Feminist Wire, March 22, 2016. https://thefeministwire.com/2016/03/poetry-for-people/.

Denda, Kayo, M. E. Hawkesworth, and Fernanda Perrone. *The Douglass Century: Transformation of the Women's College at Rutgers University*. New Brunswick, NJ: Rutgers University Press, 2018.

DeVaux, Alexis. "Searching for Audre Lorde." *Callaloo* 23, no. 1 (2000): 64–67.

DeVaux, Alexis. *Warrior Poet: A Biography of Audre Lorde*. New York: Norton, 2004.

Dewey, John. *Democracy and Education*. New York: Macmillan, 1916.

Dewey, John. *Experience and Education*. New York: Kappa Delta Pi, 1938.

Du Bois, W. E. B. *Black Reconstruction in America, 1860–1880*. New York: Free Press, 1935.

Dunbar, Anthony. *The Will to Survive: A Study of a Mississippi Plantation Community, Based on the Words of Its Citizens*. Atlanta: Southern Regional Council, 1969.

Dunn, John J. "Do-It-Yourself: Writing a Novel in a Literature Class." *College English* 39, no. 3, (1977): 307–14.

Dyer, Conrad. "Protest and the Politics of Open Admissions: The Impact of the Black and Puerto Rican Students' Community (of City College)." PhD diss., CUNY, 1990.

Elbow, Peter. "High Stakes and Low Stakes in Assigning and Responding to Writing." *New Directions for Teaching and Learning*, no. 69 (1997): 5–13.

Elizabeth Cleaners Street School. *Starting Your Own High School*. New York: Random House, 1972.

Ellison, Ralph. *Invisible Man*. New York: Vintage, 1995.

Emanuel, James A., and Theodore L. Gross, eds. *Dark Symphony: Negro Literature in America*. New York: Free Press, 1968.

Erickson, Peter, and June Jordan. "After Identity." *Transition*, no. 63 (1994): 132–49.

Evans, Stephanie Y. *Black Women in the Ivory Tower, 1850–1954: An Intellectual History*. Gainesville: University Press of Florida, 2008.

Fanon, Frantz. *The Wretched of the Earth*. Translated by Richard Philcox. New York: Grove, 2021.

Ferguson, Roderick. "Of Sensual Matters: On Audre Lorde's 'Poetry Is Not a Luxury' and 'Uses of the Erotic.'" *Women's Studies Quarterly* 40, no. 3–4 (2012): 295–300.

Ferguson, Roderick. *The Reorder of Things: The University and Its Pedagogies of Minority Difference*. Minneapolis: University of Minnesota Press, 2012.

Finney, Nikkey. "The Making of Paper." *Meridians* 3, no. 2 (2003): 17–19.

"Five Demands." CUNY Digital History Archive. 1969, https://cdha.cuny.edu/items/show/6952.

Flaherty, Colleen. "Barely Getting By." Inside Higher Ed, April 20, 2020. https://www.insidehighered.com/news/2020/04/20/new-report-says-many-adjuncts-make-less-3500-course-and-25000-year.

Flaherty, Colleen. "The Full-Time Faculty Factor." Inside Higher Ed, December 2, 2021. https://www.insidehighered.com/news/2021/12/02/race-and-full-time-faculty-student-ratios-suny-cuny.

Flynn, Richard. "'Affirmative Acts': Language, Childhood, and Power in June Jordan's Cross-Writing." *Children's Literature* 30 (2002): 159–85.

Forman, Ruth. *Renaissance*. Boston: Beacon, 1998.

Foucault, Michel. "Two Lectures." In *Power/Knowledge: Selected Interviews and Other Writings, 1972–1977*, edited by Colin Gordon, 78–108. New York: Pantheon, 1980.

Franklin, Cynthia. *Writing Women's Communities: The Politics and Poetics of Contemporary Women's Anthologies*. Madison: University of Wisconsin Press, 1997.

Franklin, V. P. "Hidden in Plain View: African American Women, Radical Feminism, and the Origins of Women's Studies Programs, 1967–1974." *Journal of African American History* 87, no. 4 (Fall 2002): 433–45.

Freedman, Estelle B. "Small Group Pedagogy: Consciousness-Raising in Conservative Times." In *Feminist Pedagogy: Looking Back to Move Forward*, edited by Robbin D. Crabtree, David Alan Sapp, and Adela C. Licona, 117–37. Baltimore: Johns Hopkins University Press, 2009.

Freire, Paulo. *Pedagogy of the Oppressed*. Translated by Donald Macedo. New York: Continuum, 1970.

Gay, Geneva. *Culturally Responsive Teaching: Theory, Research, and Practice*. New York: Teachers College Press, 2018.

Gayle, Addison. *The Black Aesthetic*. New York: Doubleday, 1971.

Gayle, Addison, ed. *Black Expression: Essays by and about Black Americans in the Creative Arts*. New York: Weybright and Talley, 1969.

Gayle, Addison. "The Quiet Revolution: The Pre-baccalaureate Program of the City College." *Journal of Human Relations* 16, no.3 (1968): 301–14.

Gayle, Addison. "Racism and the American University." In *The Addison Gayle Jr. Reader*, edited by Nathaniel Norment, 50–59. Urbana: University of Illinois Press, 2009.

Gelpi, Barbara Charlesworth, and Albert Gelpi, eds. *Adrienne Rich's Poetry*. New York: W. W. Norton, 1975.

Giovanni, Nikki. "We Drove Together: Remembering Toni Cade Bambara." In Holmes and Wall, *Savoring the Salt*, 151–53.

Gilbert, Sandra M, and Susan Gubar. *The Madwoman in the Attic: The Woman Writer and the Nineteenth-Century Literary Imagination*. New Haven, CT: Yale University Press, 1979.

Givens, Jarvis R. "Fugitive Pedagogy: The Longer Roots of Antiracist Teaching." *Los Angeles Review of Books*, August 18, 2021. https://lareviewofbooks.org/article/fugitive-pedagogy-the-longer-roots-of-antiracist-teaching/.

Givens, Jarvis R. *Fugitive Pedagogy: Carter G. Woodson and the Art of Black Teaching*. Cambridge, MA: Harvard University Press, 2021.

Gold, Alexandra J. "Adrienne Rich's Persistent Survival." *Women's Studies* 46, no. 7 (2017): 610–27.

Goode, Michael. "April 4, 1968." In J. Jordan, *Soulscript*, 8–9.

Graff, Gerald. *Professing Literature: An Institutional History*. Chicago: University of Chicago Press, 1987.

Greenberg, Joyce. "By Woman Taught." *Parnassus* 7 (Fall/Winter 1979): 91–103.

Griffin, Ada Gay, and Michelle Parkerson, dirs. *A Litany for Survival: The Life and Work of Audre Lorde*. San Francisco: Independent Television Service, 1995. DVD.

Griffin, Farah Jasmine. "That the Mothers May Soar and the Daughters May Know Their Names: A Retrospective of Black Feminist Literary Criticism." *Signs* 32, no. 2 (2007): 483–507.

Gross, Theodore L. "How to Kill a College: The Private Papers of a Campus Dean." *Saturday Review*, February 4, 1978: 13–20.

Gumbs, Alexis Pauline. "Nobody Mean More: Black Feminist Pedagogy and Solidarity." In Chatterjee and Maira, *The Imperial University*, 237–59.

Gumbs, Alexis Pauline. "17th Floor: A Pedagogical Oracle from/with Audre Lorde." *Journal of Lesbian Studies* 21, no. 4 (October 2017): 375–90.

Gumbs, Alexis Pauline. "We Can Learn to Mother Ourselves: The Queer Survival of Black Feminism, 1968–1996." PhD diss., Duke University, 2010.

Gumbs, Alexis Pauline. "Your Mother: June Jordan and the Orchestration of Anger." *Littleblackbook* (blog), October 5, 2009. http://thatlittleblackbook.blogspot.com/2009/10/your-mother-june-jordan-and.html.

Gumbs, Alexis Pauline, China Martens, and Mai'a Williams, eds. *Revolutionary Mothering: Love on the Front Lines*. Oakland, CA: PM Press, 2016.

Hale, Jon N. *The Freedom Schools: Student Activists in the Mississippi Civil Rights Movement*. New York: Columbia University Press, 2016.

Hamilton, Laura T., and Kelly Nielsen. *Broke: The Racial Consequences of Underfunding Public Universities*. Chicago: University of Chicago Press, 2021.

Hamilton, Laura T., and Kelly Nielsen. "Our Broke Public Universities." *Chronicle of Higher Education*, June 1, 2021.

Hanna, Karen Buenavista. "Pedagogies in the Flesh: Building an Anti-racist Decolonized Classroom." *Frontiers: A Journal of Women Studies* 40, no. 1 (2019): 229–44.

Haraway, Donna. "Situated Knowledges: The Science Question in Feminism and the Privilege of Partial Perspective." *Feminist Studies* 14, no. 3 (1988): 575–99.

Harney, Stefano, and Fred Moten. *The Undercommons: Fugitive Planning and Black Study*. New York: Minor Compositions, 2013.

Hartman, Saidiya. "Venus in Two Acts." *Small Axe* 12, no. 2 (26) (2008): 1–14.

Harvey, David. *A Brief History of Neoliberalism*. Oxford: Oxford University Press, 2011.

Harwood, Stacy, Shinwoo Choi, Moises Orozco, Margaret Browne Huntt, and Ruby Mendenhall. *Racial Microaggressions at the University of Illinois at Urbana-Champaign: Voices of Students of Color in the Classroom*. University of Illinois at Urbana-Champaign and Center on Democracy in a Multiracial Society, 2015. https://inside.nku.edu/content/dam/inclusive/docs/U.%20ILLINIOIS.RMA-Classroom-Report.pdf.

Hayot, Eric. "The Sky Is Falling." MLA *Profession*, May 2018. https://profession.mla.org/the-sky-is-falling/.

Heller, Louis G. *The Death of the American University: With Special Reference to the Collapse of the City College of New York*. New Rochelle, NY: Arlington House, 1973.

Henry, Annette. "Black Feminist Pedagogy: Critiques and Contributions." In *Black Protest Thought and Education*, edited by William H. Watkins, 89–105. New York: Peter Lang, 2005.

Hershenson, Jay. "Second Chances: The CUNY and SEEK College Discovery Story." 2011. CUNY TV, YouTube, March 19, 2012. https://www.youtube.com/watch?t=21&v=TtGbYi4KtlE.

Hill Collins, Patricia. *Black Feminist Thought: Knowledge, Consciousness, and the Politics of Empowerment*. New York: Routledge, 2000.

Hines, Andy. *Outside Literary Studies: Black Criticism and the University*. Chicago: University of Chicago Press, 2022.

Hoffman, Marvin. "Wishes, Feelings, Dreams," *Library Journal* 15 (October 1970): 3599–601.

Holladay, Hilary. *The Power of Adrienne Rich: A Biography*. New York: Knopf, 2021.

Holleran, Samuel. "'Free as Air and Water,'" *Places Journal* (May 2019). https://placesjournal.org/article/cooper-union-free-as-air-and-water/#0.

Holmes, Linda Janet. *A Joyous Revolt: Toni Cade Bambara, Writer and Activist*. Santa Barbara, CA: Prager, 2014.

Holmes, Linda Janet. "Lessons in Boldness, 101." In Holmes and Wall, *Savoring the Salt*, 154–59.

Holmes, Linda Janet. Remarks at the School of Toni Cade Bambara event, Wendy's Subway, New York, December 15, 2020.

Holmes, Linda Janet, and Cheryl A. Wall, eds. *Savoring the Salt: The Legacy of Toni Cade Bambara*. Philadelphia: Temple University Press, 2007.

Holt, John. Introduction to *Teaching the "Unteachable,"* by Herbert R. Kohl, 5–10. New York: New York Review, 1967.

Hong, Grace Kyungwon. *Death beyond Disavowal: The Impossible Politics of Difference*. Minneapolis: University of Minnesota Press, 2015.

hooks, bell. *Feminist Theory: From Margin to Center*. New York: Routledge, 2015.

hooks, bell. *Teaching to Transgress: Education as the Practice of Freedom*. New York: Routledge, 1994.

Howard, Jay, et al. "Students' Race and Participation in Sociology Classroom Discussion: A Preliminary Investigation." *Journal of Scholarship of Teaching and Learning* 6, no. 1 (2006): 14–38.

Howard, Vanessa. "Ghetto." In J. Jordan and Bush, *Voice of the Children*, ix.

Hughes, Langston. "Theme for English B." In *The Collected Poems of Langston Hughes*, 409–10. New York: Vintage, 1951.

Hull, Gloria T., Patricia Bell-Scott, and Barbara Smith, eds. *All the Women Are White, All the Blacks Are Men, but Some of Us Are Brave: Black Women's Studies*. New York City: Feminist Press, 2015.

Hull, Gloria T., and Barbara Smith. "The Politics of Black Women's Studies." In Hull, Bell-Scott, and Smith, *All the Women Are White*, xvii–xxxii.

Hurston, Zora Neale. "What White Publishers Won't Print." In *I Love Myself When I am Laughing and Then Again When I Am Looking Mean and Impressive*, edited by Alice Walker, 169–73. New York: Feminist Press, 1979.

Inoue, Asao B. *Antiracist Writing Assessment Ecologies: Teaching and Assessing Writing for a Socially Just Future*. Fort Collins, CO: WAC Clearinghouse, 2015.

Jimenez, Lillian. "Puerto Ricans and Educational Civil Rights: a History of the 1969 City College Takeover (an interview with five participants)." *Centro Journal* 21, no. 2 (2009): 159–75.

Jocson, Korina M. "'Taking It to the Mic': Pedagogy of June Jordan's Poetry for the People and Partnership with an Urban High School." *English Education* 37, no. 2 (2005): 132–48.

Jones, LeRoi (Amiri Baraka). "Cuba Libre." In *Home: Social Essays*, 23–78.

Jones, LeRoi (Amiri Baraka). *Home: Social Essays*. Brooklyn, NY: Akashic Books, 2009.

Jones, Patricia Spears, Kimberly Springer, Mecca Jamilah Sullivan, and Courtney Thorsson. "Creation Is Everything You Do: Shange, the Sisterhood and Black Collectivity." Barnard College, YouTube, March 16, 2021. https://www.youtube.com/watch?v=tv322Y_qZgc.

Jordan, June. "Affirmative Acts: Language, Information, and Power." In J. Jordan, *Affirmative Acts*, 247–62.

Jordan, June. *Affirmative Acts: Political Essays*. New York: Anchor Books, 1998.

Jordan, June. Afterword to J. Jordan and Bush, *Voice of the Children*, 93–98.

Jordan, June. "Bilingual Education and Home Language." In J. Jordan, *Affirmative Acts*, 263.

Jordan, June. "Black Studies: Bringing Back the Person." In J. Jordan, *Civil Wars*, 45–58.

Jordan, June. "Children and the Hungering For." In J. Jordan, *"Life Studies,"* 21–29.

Jordan, June. "The City and the City College: An Off-Campus, Off Camera Perspective." In J. Jordan *"Life Studies,"* 45–50.

Jordan, June. *Civil Wars*. Boston: Beacon, 1981.

Jordan, June. *Directed by Desire: The Collected Poems of June Jordan*. Port Townsend, WA: Copper Canyon, 2007.

Jordan, June. "Finding the Haystack in the Needle, or, the Whole World of America and the Challenge of Higher Education." In *Technical Difficulties: African American Notes on the State of the Union*, 89–101. New York: Pantheon, 1992.

Jordan, June. "For the Poet: Adrienne Rich." In *Directed by Desire*, 245.

Jordan, June. "For the Sake of People's Poetry: Walt Whitman and the Rest of Us." In *Some of Us Did Not Die: New and Selected Essays of June Jordan*, 242–56. New York: Basic/Civitas Books, 2002.

Jordan, June. "Ground Rules for Poetry for the People." In Muller, *Revolutionary Blueprint*, 16.

Jordan, June. *His Own Where*. New York: Feminist Press, 2010.
Jordan, June. "Instant Slum Clearance." *Esquire*, April 1965, 108–11.
Jordan, June. Introduction to Muller, *Revolutionary Blueprint*, 1–9.
Jordan, June. *Life as Activism: June Jordan's Writings from the Progressive*. Edited by Stacy Russo. Sacramento, CA: Litwin Books, 2014.
Jordan, June. *"Life Studies": 1966–1976*. Edited by Conor Tomás Reed and Talia Shalev. Lost and Found: The CUNY Poetics Document Initiative, ser. 7, no. 3. 2017. https://cuny.manifoldapp.org/projects/june-jordan-life-studies-cuny-lf.
Jordan, June. *New Days: Poems of Exile and Return*. New York: Emerson Hall, 1974.
Jordan, June. "Nicaragua: Why I Had to Go There." *Essence*, January 1984, 77–78, 107–10, 112.
Jordan, June. "Nobody Mean More to Me Than You and the Future Life of Willie Jordan." In J. Jordan, *Some of Us Did Not Die*, 157–73.
Jordan, June. "Notes of a Barnard Dropout." In J. Jordan, *Civil Wars*, 96–102.
Jordan, June. "Notes toward a Black Balancing of Love and Hatred." In J. Jordan, *Civil Wars*, 84–89.
Jordan, June. "Ocean Hill Brownsville, I.S. 55 Graduation Speech." In J. Jordan, *"Life Studies,"* 30–35.
Jordan, June. "Old Stories: New Lives." In J. Jordan, *Civil Wars*, 130–39.
Jordan, June. *On Call: Political Essays*. Boston: South End, 1985.
Jordan, June. Review of *Gorilla My Love* by Toni Cade Bambara. *Black World* 22 (July 1973): 80.
Jordan, June. *Some of Us Did Not Die: New and Selected Essays of June Jordan*. New York: Basic Books, 2002.
Jordan, June, ed. *Soulscript: A Collection of Classic African American Poetry*. New York: Doubleday, 1970.
Jordan, June. "Statement at CUNY Board of Higher Education Tuition Hearing." In J. Jordan, *"Life Studies,"* 51–54.
Jordan, June. "Thinking about My Poetry." In J. Jordan, *Civil Wars*, 122–29.
Jordan, June. Untitled poem for Adrienne Rich, June 3–4, 1996. In Keller and Levi, *We're On*, 307–8.
Jordan, June. "The Voice of the Children." In J. Jordan, *Civil Wars*, 29–38.
Jordan, June. "'The Voice of the Children' Diaries." In *Journal of a Living Experiment*, edited by Phillip Lopate, 134–57. New York: Teachers and Writers Collaborative, 1979.
Jordan, June. "White English/Black English: The Politics of Translation." In J. Jordan, *Civil Wars*, 59–73.
Jordan, June. "Writing and Teaching." *Partisan Review* 36, no. 3 (1969): 478–82.
Jordan, June, and Terri Bush, eds. *The Voice of the Children*. New York: Holt, Rinehart and Winston, 1970.

Jordan, Philip. "Accelerated Study in Associate Programs, City University of New York." Harvard Kennedy School, January 2022. https://ash.harvard.edu/files/ash/files/311850_hks_policy_brief_asap_v2.pdf?m=1641569133.

Joseph, Gloria. "Black Feminist Pedagogy and Schooling in Capitalist White America." In *Words of Fire*, edited by Beverly Guy-Sheftall, 462–72. New York: New Press, 1995.

Joseph, Gloria. "The Incompatible Ménage à Trois: Marxism, Feminism and Racism." In *Women and Revolution*, edited by Lydia Sargent, 91–108. Boston: South End, 1981.

Joseph, Gloria, ed. *The Wind Is Spirit: The Life, Love and Legacy of Audre Lorde*. New York: Villarosa Media, 2016.

Jurecic, Ann. *Illness as Narrative*. Pittsburgh: University of Pittsburgh Press, 2012.

Kahina, Chenzira Davis. "Chats with Elder Sister Audre Lorde in St. Croix." In Joseph, *Wind Is Spirit*, 199–201.

Kalstone, David. Review of *The Will to Change: Poems 1968–1970*. In J. Cooper, *Reading Adrienne Rich*, 221–25.

Kaplan, Caren. "The Politics of Location as Transnational Feminist Practice." In *Scattered Hegemonies: Postmodernity and Transnational Feminist Practice*, edited by Inderpal Grewal and Caren Kaplan, 137–52. Minneapolis: University of Minnesota Press, 1994.

Kaplan, Caren. *Questions of Travel: Postmodern Discourses of Displacement*. Durham, NC: Duke University Press, 1996.

Karabel, Jerome, Ernest Koenigsberg, Dave Lin, Kenneth K. Mei, Leonard S. Miller, Roger Montgomery, Guillermo Rodriguez, Margaret B. Wilkerson, and Robert L. Bailey. "Freshman Admissions at Berkeley: A Policy for the 1990s and Beyond." The Committee on Admissions and Enrollment Berkeley Division, Academic Senate, University of California, 1989. https://academic-senate.berkeley.edu/sites/default/files/karabel_report.pdf.

kaufman, erica. Introduction to Rich, "What We Are Part Of," 1:1–8.

Keller, Christoph, and Jan Heller Levi. "Dear June, Dear Adrienne." In Keller and Levi, *We're On*, 298–308.

Keller, Christoph, and Jan Heller Levi, eds. *We're On: A June Jordan Reader*. Farmington, ME: Alice James Books, 2017.

Kelley, Robin D. G. "Black Study, Black Struggle." *Boston Review*, March 7, 2016. https://bostonreview.net/forum/robin-d-g-kelley-black-study-black-struggle.

Kelley, Robin D. G. *Freedom Dreams: The Black Radical Imagination*. Boston: Beacon, 2002.

Kendi, Ibram X. *The Black Campus Movement: Black Students and the Racial Reconstitution of Higher Education, 1965–1972*. New York: Palgrave Macmillan, 2012.

Khan-Cullors, Patrisse, and Asha Bandele. *When They Call You a Terrorist: A Black Lives Matter Memoir*. New York: St. Martin's, 2017.

Kingston, Maxine Hong. *The Woman Warrior: Memoirs of a Girlhood among Ghosts*. New York: Vintage, 1976.

Kinloch, Valerie. *June Jordan: Her Life and Letters*. Westport, CT: Praeger, 2006.

Kinloch, Valerie. "Revisiting the Promise of 'Students' Right to Their Own Language': Pedagogical Strategies." *College Composition and Communication* 57, no. 1 (2005): 83–113.

Kinloch, Valerie, and Margaret Grebowicz, eds. *Still Seeking an Attitude: Critical Reflections on the Work of June Jordan*. Lanham, MD: Lexington Books, 2005.

Kirkus Reviews. "*Tales and Stories for Black Folks*, edited by Toni Cade Bambara." January 1, 1971.

Kishimoto, Kyoko. "Anti-racist Pedagogy: From Faculty's Self-Reflection to Organizing within and beyond the Classroom." *Race Ethnicity and Education* 21, no. 4 (July 2018): 540–54.

Kohl, Herbert R. *Teaching the "Unteachable."* New York: New York Review, 1967.

Kohl, Herbert R. *36 Children*. New York: Signet, 1967.

Kriegel, Leonard. "Surviving the Apocalypse: Teaching at City College." *Change* 4, no. 6 (1972): 54–62.

Kynard, Carmen. *Vernacular Insurrections: Race, Black Protest, and the New Century in Composition-Literacies Studies*. Albany: State University of New York Press, 2013.

Ladson-Billings, Gloria. "Toward a Theory of Culturally Relevant Pedagogy." *American Educational Research Journal* 32, no. 3 (1995): 465–91.

Lavan, Makeba, and Conor Tomás Reed. Introduction to Bambara, *Realizing the Dream of a Black University*, 1–10.

Lavin, David E., Richard D. Alba, and Richard A. Silberstein. *Right versus Privilege: The Open-Admissions Experiment at the City University of New York*. New York: Free Press, 1981.

Lavin, David E., and David Hyllegard. *Changing the Odds: Open Admissions and the Life Chances of the Disadvantaged*. New Haven, CT: Yale University Press, 1996.

Leary, Christopher. "Composing the Anthology: An Exercise in Patchwriting." In *Writing Spaces: Readings on Writing*, edited by Charlie Lowe and Pavel Zemliansky, 225–34. Minneapolis: Open Textbook Library, 2010.

Lee, Jennifer, and Janice M. McCabe. "Who Speaks and Who Listens: Revisiting the Chilly Climate in College Classrooms." *Gender and Society* 35, no. 1 (2021): 32–60.

Lehrman, Karen. "Off Course." *Mother Jones*, September/October 1993. https://www.motherjones.com/politics/1993/09/motherjones-so93-course/.

Lewis, Heather. *New York City Public Schools from Brownsville to Bloomberg: Community Control and Its Legacy*. New York: Teachers College Press, 2013.

Lewis, Thabiti. *"Black People Are My Business": Toni Cade Bambara's Practices of Liberation*. Detroit: Wayne State University Press, 2020.

Lopate, Phillip, and New York Teachers and Writers Collaborative. *Journal of a Living Experiment: A Documentary History of the First Ten Years of Teachers and Writers Collaborative*. New York: Teachers and Writers Collaborative, 1979.

Lorde, Audre. "Age, Race, Class, and Sex: Women Redefining Difference." In Lorde, *Sister Outsider*, 114–23.

Lorde, Audre. "Assignment from 1972." In Lorde, *"I Teach Myself in Outline,"* 32.

Lorde, Audre. "Audre Lorde Speaks! March for Lesbian and Gay Rights Washington D.C. 1979." October 14, 1979, YouTube. https://www.youtube.com/watch?v=bQK8yawGQXE.

Lorde, Audre. "The Bees." In Lorde, *The Collected Poems of Audre Lorde*, 146.

Lorde, Audre. "Blackstudies." In *New York Head Shop and Museum*, 52. Detroit: Broadside, 1974.

Lorde, Audre. *The Black Unicorn*. New York: W. W. Norton, 1978.

Lorde, Audre. *A Burst of Light: Essays*. Ithaca, NY: Firebrand Books, 1988.

Lorde, Audre. *Cables to Rage*. London: Paul Breman, 1973.

Lorde, Audre. *The Cancer Journals*. San Francisco: Aunt Lute Books, 2007.

Lorde, Audre. "The Classrooms." In Lorde, *"I Teach Myself in Outline,"* 17.

Lorde, Audre. *Coal*. New York: W. W. Norton, 1976.

Lorde, Audre. *The Collected Poems of Audre Lorde*. New York: W. W. Norton, 1997.

Lorde, Audre. "Dear Toni…" In Lorde, *The Collected Poems of Audre Lorde*, 93–95.

Lorde, Audre. *Dream of Europe: Selected Seminars and Interviews, 1984–1992*. Edited by Mayra Rodríguez Castro. Chicago: Kenning Editions, 2020.

Lorde, Audre. "Excerpt from Deotha." In Lorde, *"I Teach Myself in Outline,"* 43–65.

Lorde, Audre. "Eye to Eye: Black Women, Hatred, and Anger." In Lorde, *Sister Outsider*, 145–75.

Lorde, Audre. *The First Cities*. New York: Poets Press, 1968.

Lorde, Audre. Foreword to Ayim, Oguntoye, and Schultz, *Showing Our Colors*, vii–xiv.

Lorde, Audre. "An Interview: Audre Lorde and Adrienne Rich." In Lorde, *Sister Outsider*, 81–109.

Lorde, Audre. *"I Teach Myself in Outline": Notes, Journals, and an Excerpt from Deotha*. Edited by Miriam Atkin and Iemanjá Brown. Lost and Found: The CUNY Poetics Documents Initiative, ser. 7, no. 1, 2017. https://cuny.manifoldapp.org/projects/audre-lorde-i-teach-myself-in-outline-cuny-lf.

Lorde, Audre. "A Litany for Survival." In Lorde, *The Collected Poems of Audre Lorde*, 255–56.

Lorde, Audre. "Love Poem." In Lorde, *The Collected Poems of Audre Lorde*, 127.

Lorde, Audre. "The Master's Tools Will Never Dismantle the Master's House." In Lorde, *Sister Outsider*, 110–13.

Lorde, Audre. "My Words Will Be There." In Byrd, Cole, and Guy-Sheftall, *I Am Your Sister*, 160–69.
Lorde, Audre. "Poet as Teacher—Human as Poet—Teacher as Human." In Byrd, Cole, and Guy-Sheftall, *I Am Your Sister*, 182–83.
Lorde, Audre. "Poetry Is Not a Luxury." In Lorde, *Sister Outsider*, 36–39.
Lorde, Audre. "Power." In Lorde, *The Collected Poems of Audre Lorde*, 215.
Lorde, Audre. Proposal for faculty seminar at Hunter on race. In Lorde, *"I Teach Myself in Outline,"* 40–42.
Lorde, Audre. "Race and the Urban Situation Syllabus." In Lorde, *"I Teach Myself in Outline,"* 18–20.
Lorde, Audre. "The Same Death Over and Over or Lullabies Are for Children." In Lorde, *The Collected Poems of Audre Lorde*, 282.
Lorde, Audre. *Sister Outsider: Essays and Speeches*. Freedom, CA: Crossing, 1984.
Lorde, Audre. "Teacher." In *From a Land Where Other People Live*, 20.
Lorde, Audre. "The Transformation of Silence into Language and Action." In Lorde, *Sister Outsider*, 40–44.
Lorde, Audre. Undated assignment. In Lorde, *"I Teach Myself in Outline,"* 31.
Lorde, Audre. "The Uses of Anger." In Lorde, *Sister Outsider*, 124–33.
Lorde, Audre. "A Woman/Dirge for Wasted Children." In Lorde, *The Collected Poems of Audre Lorde*, 228.
Lorde, Audre. *Zami: a New Spelling of My Name*. Watertown, MA: Persephone Press, 1982.
Lorde, Audre, and Adrienne Rich. "An Interview with Audre Lorde." *Signs* 6, no. 4 (1981): 713–36.
Lurie, Ellen. *How to Change the Schools*. New York: Random House, 1970.
MacPhail, Scott. "June Jordan and the New Black Intellectuals." *African American Review* 33, no. 1 (1999): 57–71.
Mahabeer, Pamela. "13 Black Profs Call Hunger Strike to Protest City U 'Resegregation.'" *The Campus* 138, no. 12 (May 7, 1976): 1.
Massiah, Louis (dir.), and Toni Cade Bambara. *The Bombing of Osage Avenue*. 1986. WHYY and Scribe Video Center.
Mattingly, Carol. "Valuing the Personal: Feminist Concerns for the Writing Classroom." In *Gender and Academe: Feminist Pedagogy and Politics*, edited by Sara Munson Deats and Lagretta Tallent Lenker, 153–66. Lanham, MD: Rowman and Littlefield, 1994.
Mayes, Janet. "An Oral History of the SEEK Program." CUNY Digital History Archive, June 29, 2016. https://cdha.cuny.edu/items/show/7052.
McCormick, Richard P. *The Black Student Protest Movement at Rutgers*. New Brunswick, NJ: Rutgers University Press, 1990.
McGurl, Mark. *The Program Era: Postwar Fiction and the Rise of Creative Writing*. Cambridge, MA: Harvard University Press, 2011.
McKittrick, Katherine. *Demonic Grounds: Black Women and the Cartographies of Struggle*. Minneapolis: University of Minnesota Press, 2006.

McWorter, Gerald, and Ronald Bailey. "Black Studies Curriculum Development in the 1980s: Its Patterns and History." *Black Scholar* 15, no. 2 (1984): 18–31.

Mendelsohn, Sue, and Clarissa Walker. "Agents of Change: African American Contributions to Writing Centers." *Writing Center Journal* 39, no. 1–2 (2021): 21–54.

Meyer, Elizabeth Riva. "Margaret Hiller: A Poet in Her Own Right." In Muller, *Revolutionary Blueprint*, 25–27.

Meyer, June (June Jordan). "You Can't See the Trees for the School." *Urban Review* 2, no. 3 (1967): 11–16.

Mirikitani, Janice, ed. *Third World Women*. San Francisco, CA: Third World Communications, 1972.

Mixco, Miguel Huezo. "So You Understand Once and For All." In *On The Front Line Guerilla Poems of El Salvador*, edited and translated by Claribel Alegría and Darwin J. Flakoll, 51. Willimantic, CT: Curbstone Books, 1995.

Modern Language Association. "MLA Recommendation on Minimum Per-Course Compensation for Part-Time Faculty Members." January 2023. https://www.mla.org/Resources/Guidelines-and-Data/Reports-and-Professional-Guidelines/Salaries-and-Working-Conditions/MLA-Recommendation-on-Minimum-Per-Course-Compensation-for-Part-Time-Faculty-Members.

Molloy, Sean. "A Convenient Myopia: SEEK, Shaughnessy, and the Rise of High-Stakes Testing at CUNY." PhD diss., CUNY, 2016.

Molloy, Sean. "'Human Beings Engaging with Ideas': The 1960s SEEK Program as a Precursor Model of Ecological and Sociocultural Writing Pedagogy and Assessment." In *Writing Assessment, Social Justice, and the Advancement of Opportunity*, edited by Mya Poe, Asao B. Inoue, and Norbert Elliot, 71–104. Fort Collins, CO: WAC Clearinghouse, 2018.

Molloy, Sean. "SEEK's Fight for Racial and Social Justice at CUNY (1965–1969)." CUNY Digital History Archive, June 23, 2017. https://cdha.cuny.edu/secondary-sources/seek.

Montenegro, David. "Adrienne Rich." In *Points of Departure: International Writers on Writing and Politics*, 5–21. Ann Arbor: University of Michigan Press, 1991.

Moody-Turner, Shirley, ed. *The Portable Anna Julia Cooper*. New York: Penguin Books, 2022.

Moraga, Cherríe. "Catching Fire." In Moraga and Anzaldúa, *This Bridge Called My Back*, xv–xxvi.

Moraga, Cherríe. *Loving in the War Years*. Cambridge, MA: South End Press, 2000.

Moraga, Cherríe, and Gloria Anzaldúa, eds. *This Bridge Called My Back*. New York: Kitchen Table: Women of Color Press, 1981.

Morrison, Toni. Preface to *Deep Sightings and Rescue Missions*, by Toni Cade Bambara, vii–xi.

Moyers, Bill. "The Heart of Things: Adrienne Rich, Michael Harper and Victor Hernández Cruz." Billmoyers.com. July 28, 1995. https://billmoyers.com/content/language-of-life-adrienne-rich-michael-harper-victor-hernandez-cruz/.

Mullen, Ann L. *Degrees of Inequality: Culture, Class, and Gender in American Higher Education*. Baltimore: Johns Hopkins University Press, 2010.

Muller, Lauren, ed. *June Jordan's Poetry for the People: A Revolutionary Blueprint*. New York: Routledge, 1995.

Murch, Donna Jean. *Living for the City: Migration, Education, and the Rise of the Black Panther Party in Oakland, California*. Chapel Hill: University of North Carolina Press, 2010.

Murray, Marian. "A 1974 Graduate's Memories of a Groundbreaking College on a Diverse Campus." Livingston Alumni Association, March 19, 2016. https://livingstonalumni.org/1974-graduates-memories-groundbreaking-college-diverse-campus.

Nash, Jennifer C. "Practicing Love: Black Feminism, Love-Politics, and Post-intersectionality." *Meridians* 11, no. 2 (2011): 1–24.

National Center for Education Statistics. "Race/Ethnicity of College Faculty." October 15, 2023. https://nces.ed.gov/fastfacts/display.asp?id=61.

National Council of Teachers of English. "Position Statement on Multimodal Literacies." November 17, 2005, http://www.ncte.org/positions/statements/multimodalliteracies.

Navies, Kelly Elaine. "A Poet Is on the Front Lines." In Muller, *Revolutionary Blueprint*, 22–24.

Neville, Helen A., and Sundiata K. Cha-Jua. "Kufundisha: Toward a Pedagogy for Black Studies." *Journal of Black Studies* 28, no. 4 (1998): 447–70.

Newfield, Christopher. *The Great Mistake: How We Wrecked Public Universities and How We Can Fix Them*. Baltimore: Johns Hopkins University Press, 2016.

Nishikawa, Kinohi. "Driven by the Market: African American Literature after Urban Fiction." *American Literary History* 33, no. 2 (2021): 320–49.

O'Barr, Jean F., and Mary Wyer. *Engaging Feminism: Students Speak Up and Speak Out*. Charlottesville: University of Virginia Press, 1992.

Obourn, Megan. "Audre Lorde: Trauma Theory and Liberal Multiculturalism." *MELUS* 30, no. 3 (2005): 219–45.

Oguntoye, Katharina. "My Coming Out as a Black Lesbian in Germany." In Joseph, *Wind Is Spirit*, 157–61.

Oguntoye, Katharina, and May Opitz. Introduction to Ayim, Oguntoye, and Schultz, *Showing Our Colors*, xxi–xxiii.

Omolade, Barbara. "A Black Feminist Pedagogy." *Women's Studies Quarterly* 15, no. 3/4 (1987): 32–39.

Ortega, Kirsten Bartholomew. "June Jordan's Radical Pedagogy: Activist Poetry in Public Education." In Kinloch and Grebowicz, *Still Seeking an Attitude*, 189–208.

Orwell, George. *Such, Such Were the Joys*. New York: Harcourt Brace, 1953.
Ostriker, Alicia. *Stealing the Language: The Emergence of Women's Poetry in America*. Boston: Beacon, 2002.
Otte, George, and Rebecca Mlynarczyk. *Basic Writing*. West Lafayette, IN: Parlor, 2010.
Palmeri, Jason. *Remixing Composition: A History of Multimodal Writing Pedagogy*. Carbondale: Southern Illinois University Press, 2012.
Parker, Pat. "Where Will You Be?" In Smith, *Home Girls*, 202–6.
Partridge, Kate. "'Where Do We See It From': Revising Documentary Perspective in Adrienne Rich's 'An Atlas of the Difficult World.'" *Arizona Quarterly: A Journal of American Literature, Culture, and Theory* 78, no. 2 (2022): 145–72.
Patterson, Martha. "Bambara Teaches from a Different Perspective." *Carletonian*, May 13, 1988, 9, 13.
Peckens, Sadie. "Students Find Voice and Share It in Poetry for the People." *Guardsman*, September 4, 2020. http://theguardsman.com/1_culture_idst36_peckens/.
Perlow, Olivia N., Durene I. Wheeler, Sharon L. Bethea, and BarBara M. Scott, eds. *Black Women's Liberatory Pedagogies: Resistance, Transformation, and Healing within and beyond the Academy*. London: Palgrave, 2018.
Pontecorvo, Gillo, dir. *The Battle of Algiers*. Criterion Collection, 1966.
Randall, Dudley. Review of *The First Cities* by Audre Lorde. *Negro Digest* 17, nos. 11–12, (September/October 1968): 13–14.
Ravitch, Diane. *The Great School Wars: A History of the New York City Public Schools*. Baltimore: Johns Hopkins University Press, 2000.
Reagan, Ronald. "National SEEK and College Discovery Day, 1986." Proclamation 5583, December 2, 1986. https://www.govinfo.gov/content/pkg/STATUTE-101/pdf/STATUTE-101-Pg2047.pdf.
Reeves, LaVona L. "Mina Shaughnessy and Open Admissions at New York's City College." *Thought and Action* 17, no. 2 (2001–2): 117–28.
Reid-Pharr, Robert. "This Useful Death." *Feminist Wire*, February 25, 2014, http://www.thefeministwire.com/2014/02/this-useful-death-audre-lorde/.
Rich, Adrienne. *A Change of World*. Yale Series of Younger Poets 48. New York: AMS Press, 1971.
Rich, Adrienne. "A Long Conversation." In Rich, *Collected Poems (1950–2012)*, 837–47.
Rich, Adrienne. "An Atlas of the Difficult World." In Rich, *Collected Poems (1950–2012)*, 709–728.
Rich, Adrienne. "Arts of the Possible." In Rich, *Arts of the Possible*, 146–67.
Rich, Adrienne. *Arts of the Possible: Essays and Conversations*. New York: W. W. Norton, 2001.
Rich, Adrienne. *Blood, Bread, and Poetry: Selected Prose, 1979–1985*. New York: W. W. Norton, 1986.

Rich, Adrienne. "Blood, Bread, and Poetry: The Location of the Poet." In Rich, *Blood, Bread, and Poetry*, 167–87.

Rich, Adrienne. "The Burning of Paper Instead of Children." In *The Will to Change: Poems, 1968–1970*, 15–18. New York: W. W. Norton, 1971.

Rich, Adrienne. "Claiming an Education." In Rich, *On Lies, Secrets, and Silence*, 231–35.

Rich, Adrienne. *Collected Poems: 1950–2012*. New York: W. W. Norton, 2016.

Rich, Adrienne. "Compulsory Heterosexuality and Lesbian Existence." In Rich, *Blood, Bread, and Poetry*, 23–75.

Rich, Adrienne. "Disloyal to Civilization: Feminism, Racism, Gynephobia." In Rich, *On Lies, Secrets, and Silence*, 275–310.

Rich, Adrienne. *Diving into the Wreck: Poems, 1971–1972*. New York: W. W. Norton, 1973.

Rich, Adrienne. "Final Comments on the Interdisciplinary Program (Spring 1972)." In Rich, *"What We Are Part Of,"* 1:33–40.

Rich, Adrienne. Foreword to J. Jordan, *Directed by Desire*, xxi–xxviii.

Rich, Adrienne. "For June, in the Year 2001." In Rich, *Collected Poems (1950–2012)*, 898–99.

Rich, Adrienne. "'Going There' and Being Here." In Rich, *Blood, Bread, and Poetry*, 156–59.

Rich, Adrienne. "Hints on Revision." In Rich, *"What We Are Part Of,"* 2:11–13.

Rich, Adrienne. "Hunger." In *Dream of a Common Language*, 12–14. New York: W. W. Norton, 1978.

Rich, Adrienne. "Invisibility in Academe." In Rich, *Blood, Bread, and Poetry*, 198–201.

Rich, Adrienne. "Memo to Mina Shaughnessy (September 3, 1971)." In Rich, *"What We Are Part Of,"* 1:29–32.

Rich, Adrienne. "Notes for English 1.8." In Rich, *"What We Are Part Of,"* 2:18–20.

Rich, Adrienne. "Notes on Eng. 13.3 W." In Rich, *"What We Are Part Of,"* 2:29–35.

Rich, Adrienne. "Notes, Statements and Memos on SEEK, Basic Writing and the Interdisciplinary Program (1969–1972)." In Rich, *"What We Are Part Of,"* 1:15–40.

Rich, Adrienne. "Notes towards a Politics of Location." In Rich, *Blood, Bread, and Poetry*, 210–31.

Rich, Adrienne. *Of Woman Born: Motherhood as Experience and Institution*. New York: W. W. Norton, 1986.

Rich, Adrienne. *On Lies, Secrets, and Silence: Selected Prose, 1966–1978*. New York: W. W. Norton, 1979.

Rich, Adrienne. "Poem for Jordan." June 3, 1996. In Keller and Levi, *We're On*, 305–7.

Rich, Adrienne. "Resisting Amnesia." In Rich, *Blood, Bread, and Poetry*, 136–55.

Rich, Adrienne. "The School Among the Ruins." In Rich, *Collected Poems (1950–2012)*, 900–903.

Rich, Adrienne. *Snapshots of a Daughter-in-Law: Poems, 1954–1962.* New York: W. W. Norton, 1967.

Rich, Adrienne. "The Soul of a Woman's College." In Rich, *Blood, Bread, and Poetry*, 188–97.

Rich, Adrienne. "Statement to CCNY Faculty Meeting (April 23)." In Rich, *"What We Are Part Of,"* 1:22–23.

Rich, Adrienne. "Student Passes—Education Fails." In Rich, *"What We Are Part Of,"* 1:25–28.

Rich, Adrienne. Syllabus for English 1-H (Fall 1971). In Rich, *"What We Are Part Of,"* 2:22.

Rich, Adrienne. Syllabus for English 1-T. In Rich, *"What We Are Part Of,"* 2:21–23.

Rich, Adrienne. Syllabus for English 13.3w: Images of Women in Poetry by Men. In Rich, *"What We Are Part Of,"* 2:25.

Rich, Adrienne. Syllabus for SEEK English Course 1.8 (April 1969). In Rich, *"What We Are Part Of,"* 2:13–15.

Rich, Adrienne. "Taking Women Students Seriously." In Rich, *On Lies, Secrets, and Silence*, 237–46.

Rich, Adrienne. "Teaching Language in Open Admissions." In Rich, *On Lies, Secrets, and Silence*, 51–68.

Rich, Adrienne. "Towards a Woman-Centered University." In Rich, *On Lies, Secrets, and Silence*, 125–56.

Rich, Adrienne. Untitled poem for June Jordan, June 2, 1996. In Keller and Levi, *We're On*, 303–4.

Rich, Adrienne. Untitled poem for June Jordan, June 3, 1996. In Keller and Levi, *We're On*, 305–7.

Rich, Adrienne. "What Country Is This?" *Boston Review*, March 1, 2009. https://bostonreview.net/what-country-is-this-rereading-leroi-jones-adrienne-rich.

Rich, Adrienne. *What Is Found There: Notebooks on Poetry and Politics.* New York: W. W. Norton, 1993.

Rich, Adrienne. *"What We Are Part Of": Teaching at CUNY, 1968–1974.* Edited by Iemanjá Brown, Stefania Heim, erica kaufman, Kristin Moriah, Conor Tomás Reed, Talia Shalev, Wendy Tronrud, Ammiel Alcalay. 2 vols. New York: Lost and Found: The CUNY Poetics Document Initiative, ser. 4, no. 3, 2013.

Rich, Adrienne. "When We Dead Awaken: Writing as Revision." In Rich, *On Lies, Secrets, and Silence*, 33–50.

Rich, Adrienne. "Wholeness Is No Trifling Matter: Some Fiction by Black Women." *New Women's Times Feminist Review*, December 1980–January 1981, 10–13; and February–March 1981, 12–13, 20–24.

Rich, Adrienne. "Why I Refused the National Medal for the Arts." In Rich, *Arts of the Possible*, 98–105.

Rich, Adrienne. *The Will to Change: Poems 1968–1970.* New York: W. W. Norton, 1971.

Rich, Adrienne. "Writing Exercises." In Rich, *"What We Are Part Of,"* 2:7–11.

Rickford, Russell. *We Are an African People: Independent Education, Black Power, and the Radical Imagination*. New York: Oxford University Press, 2016.

Riley, Jeannette E. *Understanding Adrienne Rich*. Columbia: The University of South Carolina Press, 2016.

Risam, Roopika. "Academic Generosity, Academic Insurgency." Public Books, November 27, 2019. https://www.publicbooks.org/academic-generosity-academic-insurgency/.

Rushin, Kate. "A Place to Grieve." In Joseph, *Wind Is Spirit*, 137–40.

Rust, Marion. "Making Emends: Adrienne Rich, Audre Lorde, Anne Bradstreet." *American Literature* 88, no. 1 (2016): 93–126.

Savonick, Danica. "Community Guidelines: Fostering Inclusive Discussions of Difference." HASTAC, August 28, 2017, https://teaching-learning.hastac.hcommons.org/2017/08/28/community-guidelines-fostering-inclusive-discussions-of-difference/.

Scandaglia, Gregory. "June Jordan on Lebanon Crisis." *Stony Brook Press*, December 9, 1982, 7.

Schumach, Murray. "50% of Freshmen to Come from Slums without Need to Qualify on Grades." *New York Times*, May 24, 1969.

Scribe Video Center. "Community Visions." October 15, 2023. https://www.scribe.org/community-visions.

Scribe Video Center. "The Mission and History of Scribe." October 15, 2023. https://www.scribe.org/mission-and-history-scribe.

Sharif, Solmaz. "The Role of the Poet: An Interview with Solmaz Sharif." Interview by Zinzi Clemmons. *Paris Review*, July 27, 2016. https://www.theparisreview.org/blog/2016/07/27/the-role-of-the-poet-an-interview-with-solmaz-sharif/.

Shesgreen, Sean. "Canonizing the Canonizer: A Short History of *The Norton Anthology of English Literature*." *Critical Inquiry* 35, no. 2 (2009): 293–318.

Shipka, Jody. *Toward a Composition Made Whole*. Pittsburgh: University of Pittsburgh Press, 2011.

Shvarts, Anna, and Arthur Bakker. "The Early History of the Scaffolding Metaphor: Bernstein, Luria, Vygotsky, and Before." *Mind, Culture, and Activity* 26, no. 1 (2019): 4–23.

Silko, Leslie Marmon. *Ceremony*. New York: Penguin, 1986.

Smith, Barbara, ed. *Home Girls: A Black Feminist Anthology*. New York: Kitchen Table: Women of Color Press, 1983.

Smith, Barbara. "A Press of Our Own: Kitchen Table: Women of Color Press." *Frontiers: A Journal of Women's Studies* 10, no. 3 (1989): 11–13.

Smith, Barbara. "Toward a Black Feminist Criticism." *The Radical Teacher*, no. 7 (1978): 20–27.

Spacks, Patricia Meyer. *The Female Imagination*. New York: Knopf, 1975.

Stalling, Jonathan. "Finding a Democratic Speech: The Intercultural Poetics and Pedagogy of June Jordan's Poetry for the People." In Kinloch and Grebowicz, *Still Seeking an Attitude*, 209–32.

Streim, Alex. "Teaching the Unteachable: Adrienne Rich and the Limits of Pedagogy." *Arizona Quarterly: A Journal of American Literature, Culture, and Theory* 78, no. 2 (2022): 69–97.

Tarver, Ingrid. Review of *Soulscript*, edited by June Jordan. *Alabama News*, October 4, 1970.

Tate, Claudia, ed. *Black Women Writers at Work*. New York: Continuum, 1983.

Taylor-Hachoose, Yvette. "Kelly Elaine Navies: A Legacy of an Oral Historian Sharing Her Story." *What's Your Legacy?* (podcast), March 25, 2021. https://whatsyourlegacy.libsyn.com/kelly-elaine-navies-a-legacy-of-an-oral-historian-sharing-her-story.

Thorsson, Courtney. *The Sisterhood: How a Network of Black Women Writers Changed American Culture*. New York: Columbia University Press, 2023.

Tobias, Sheila. "Report of Female Studies Conference." *Cornell Chronicle*, May 21, 1970. https://files.eric.ed.gov/fulltext/ED063910.pdf.

Tomás Reed, Conor. "The Early Developments of Black Women's Studies in the Lives of Toni Cade Bambara, June Jordan, and Audre Lorde." *Anuario de la Escuela de Historia*, no. 30 (2018): 46–77.

Tomás Reed, Conor. *New York Liberation School: Study and Movement for the People's University*. Brooklyn, NY: Common Notions, 2023.

Tomás Reed, Conor. "'Treasures That Prevail': Adrienne Rich, the SEEK Program, and Social Movements at the City College of New York, 1968–1972." In Rich, *"What We Are Part Of,"* 2:37–65.

Tomás Reed, Conor, and Talia Shalev. Introduction to J. Jordan, *"Life Studies,"* 1–10.

Traub, James. *City on a Hill: Testing the American Dream at City College*. Boston: Addison-Wesley, 1994.

Traylor, Eleanor. "ReCalling the Black Woman." In Bambara, *Black Woman*, ix–xviii.

"A Trial of the American Conscience." Pacifica Radio Archives, July 15, 1993. https://www.pacificaradioarchives.org/recording/pz0218.

Vazquez, Alexandra T. *Listening in Detail: Performances of Cuban Music*. Durham, NC: Duke University Press, 2014.

Velez, Isabel. "Children Are Slaves." In J. Jordan and Bush, *Voice of the Children*, 32.

Villalobos, Ruben Antonio. "Poetry as Revelation." In Muller, *Revolutionary Blueprint*, 18–21.

Volpe, Edmond L. "The Confessions of a Fallen Man: Ascent to the D. A." *College English* 33, no. 7 (1972): 765–79.

Wagner, Geoffrey. *The End of Education*. South Brunswick, NJ: A. S. Barnes, 1976.

Walker, Alice. "In Search of Our Mothers' Gardens." In *In Search of Our Mothers' Gardens: Womanist Prose*, 231–43. New York: Harcourt Brace Jovanovich, 1983.

Wall, Cheryl E. "Toni Morrison, Editor and Teacher." In *The Cambridge Companion to Toni Morrison*, edited by Justine Tally, 139–48. Cambridge: Cambridge University Press, 2007.

Waller-Peterson, Belinda. "'Are You Sure, Sweetheart, That You Want to Be Well?': The Politics of Mental Health and Long-Suffering in Toni Cade Bambara's *The Salt Eaters*." *Religions* 10, vol. 4 (2019): 263. https://www.mdpi.com/2077-1444/10/4/263.

Warren, Kenneth. "The Problem of Anthologies, or Making the Dead Wince." *American Literature* 65, no. 2 (1993): 338–42.

Weimer, Maryellen. *Learner-Centered Teaching: Five Key Changes to Practice*. San Francisco: Jossey-Bass, 2013.

Wheeler, Lesley, and Chris Gavaler. "Imposters and Chameleons: Marianne Moore and the Carlisle Indian School." *Paideuma* 33, no. 2–3 (2004): 53–82.

Whelchel, Marianne. "'Mining the Earth-Deposits': Women's History in Adrienne Rich's Poetry." In J. Cooper, *Reading Adrienne Rich*, 51–71.

White, Marvina. "An Oral History of the CCNY 1960'S SEEK Program." CUNY Composition Community, January 27, 2015. https://compcomm.commons.gc.cuny.edu/marvina-white-an-oral-history-of-the-ccny-1960s-seek-program/.

Whitehead, Alfred North. *Aims of Education*. New York: Macmillan, 1929.

Williams, Emlyn. *The Corn Is Green*. New York: Random House, 1941.

Winslow, Barbara. "Shirley Chisholm, CUNY and U.S. History." Professional Staff Congress, CUNY, June 2012. https://psc-cuny.org/clarion/2012/june/shirley-chisholm-cuny-and-us-history/.

Wisher, Yolanda. "Writing w/Strangers: A Poetry for the People in Philadelphia." Poetry Foundation, April 14, 2015. https://www.poetryfoundation.org/harriet-books/2015/04/writing-w-strangers-a-poetry-foR-the-people-in-philadelphia.

Women Against Abuse (Community Legal Service). "Peace at Home: Getting a Restraining Order in PA." Scribe Video Center, 1991. https://scribe.org/catalogue/peace-home-getting-restraining-order-pa.

The Women's Community Revitalization Project, "Women Housing Women." Scribe Video Center, 1992. https://www.scribe.org/catalogue/women-housing-women.

Woolf, Virginia. *A Room of One's Own*. New York: Harcourt, 2005.

Yancey, Kathleen Blake. "Made Not Only in Words: Composition in a New Key." *College Composition and Communication* 56, no. 2 (2004): 297–328.

Zimmerman, Jonathan. *The Amateur Hour: A History of College Teaching in America*. Baltimore: Johns Hopkins University Press, 2020.

INDEX

abolitionist university studies, 18, 212n17
academic insurgency, 89
academic salaries. *See* compensation (for postsecondary teachers)
Achebe, Chinua, 37, 210n89
activist teaching, 12, 100, 104–5, 169, 212n5
additive emendation, 128
Adnan, Etel: *Sitt Marie Rose*, 131
affirmative action, 48, 55, 87, 95, 135–36
Africa, 31, 50
African American literature, 7, 23, 44, 57, 81, 105, 197n115. *See also* Black literature
African American studies, 87. *See also* Black studies
Afrocentric teaching, 27, 29
Afro-German movement, 173
Ahmad, Aijaz, 49
Alamac Hotel, 1, 26, 30
Albuquerque, NM, 80
Algeria, 31, 41
Allport, Gordon: *Nature of Prejudice, The*, 139
All the Women Are White, All the Blacks Are Men, but Some of Us Are Brave (anthology), 44
alternative education, 53, 132
American Book Award, 19
American literature, 3, 8, 17, 19, 22, 61, 139–40
American Poetry Review, 128
American Sign Language, 96
anthologies of student writing, 16–17, 44–51, 61, 65, 76–82, 92–94, 96–97, 123, 143, 173–75. *See also individual titles*
antihierarchical teaching, 123, 133
anti-Semitism, 6

Anzaldúa, Gloria: *This Bridge Called My Back*, 94–95
apartheid, 31, 61, 77, 96, 131, 175
Arab Americans, 93
Arnold, Matthew, 102
assessment. *See* evaluation (of students)
Association for the Study of Negro Life and History, 201n49
Atkin, Miriam, 11, 154
Atlanta, GA, 17, 41, 52, 55, 163
Atwood, Margaret: *Handmaid's Tale, The*, 87
Auden, W. H., 101
autobiography, 42, 113, 131. *See also* memoirs
Ayim, May: *Showing Our Colors*, 173–75

Baldwin, James, 113, 190n103
Ballard, Allen B., 39, 184n19, 184nn27–28
Bambara, Toni Cade: and academia, 54–55, 58, 180; and anthologies of student writing, 17, 44–51, 65, 78, 155, 174–75; and community-controlled pedagogy, 12, 27–34; early life of, 20–22; and feminist pedagogy, 14; and film workshops, 56–57, 98; and Jordan, 2, 16–17, 35, 61, 64, 69–72, 81–82, 85, 89, 92–95; and Lorde, 16, 70, 143, 147–49, 153, 158, 161, 169–70, 175; and Morrison, 35, 197n115; and multimodal pedagogy, 17, 40–44, 88; and Rich, 35, 92, 104–7, 111–12, 119–21, 129, 132; and the SEEK program, 7, 9, 15, 20, 22–27, 38–39, 177; teaching materials of, 11, 59; and transgressive teaching, 4; writings of, 19, 34–38, 52–53
Bambara, Toni Cade (courses of): Colonialism, Neocolonialism, and Liberation (Alamac Hotel), 30–34, 36, 38; Contemporary Black

Bambara, Toni Cade (courses of) (*continued*)
Women Writers (Carleton), 58; Introduction to Third World Literature (Duke), 52; Text as a Rite of Recovery, The (Delaware), 52–54, 132, 170

Bambara, Toni Cade (teaching career): at Alamac Hotel, 1, 26, 30; at Carleton College, 20, 57–58; at City College of New York, 2, 16, 20, 22–42, 44–45, 47–49, 51–52, 54, 56, 59, 78, 179; at Duke University, 20, 52; at Livingston College, 48–51, 50–52, 58, 121; at Scribe Video Center, 20, 55–57, 59, 98; at University of Delaware, 20, 52–54, 94, 132, 170

Bambara, Toni Cade (works of): "American Adolescent Apprentice Novel, The," 22; *Black Woman, The*, 16–17, 20, 44–47, 50–51, 78, 119, 148–49, 155; *Bombing of Osage Avenue, The* (film), 55–56; "Children Who Got Cheated, The," 30; "Geraldine Moore," 190n78; *Gorilla, My Love*, 19, 85; "Lesson, The," 34–35; "Realizing the Dream of a Black University," 36–39, 119–21, 129; review of *Civil Wars*, 85; *Salt Eaters, The*, 19, 29, 43–44, 53, 129, 191n120; *Sea Birds Are Still Alive, The*, 19; short story in *Massachusetts Review*, 34; *Tales and Stories for Black Folks*, 50–51, 65; *These Bones Are Not My Child*, 85; "Three Little Panthers, The," 51

Baraka, Amiri, 25, 36, 97, 210n89; *Black Fire*, 47; "Cuba Libre," 24, 105; *Dead Lecturer, The*, 113; *Home*, 24, 151

Barnard College, 62, 92, 120–21

Bashir, Samiya, 98

Beauvoir, Simone de, 119

Behrent, Megan, 130, 134

Benjamin, Shanna, 44

Bennet, Lerone, Jr.: *Before the Mayflower*, 152

Berger, Leslie, 184nn27–28

Berlin, James A., 25, 68

Bernstein, Nikolai, 202n71

Berrett, Dan: "Day the Purpose of College Changed, The," 162–63

Bethune, Mary McLeod, 4, 200n200

Biafra, 83

Biondi, Martha, 39

Black Arts Movement, 16, 19, 24, 35, 49, 143, 210n89

Black Arts Repertory Theater/School, 24

Black English, 73–74, 86, 95, 114–15, 146

Black feminism, 19–20, 37, 42, 44, 94–95, 127, 129–30, 179, 196n74, 211n130. *See also* feminism

Black feminist pedagogy, 14, 42–43

Black Fire (anthology), 47

Black liberation movements, 29, 55, 61, 69, 120, 139, 146, 154, 165. *See also* civil rights movement

Black literary criticism, 47–48

Black literature, ix, 45–48, 52–53, 106, 113. *See also* African American literature

Black Lives Matter, xi, 140, 150

Black Panther Party, 37, 45, 139, 152

Black Power movement, 5, 24, 29, 31, 33, 69, 144, 184n14

Black Scholar, 170; "Black Culture," 151; "Black Psychology," 151

Black students, 2–8, 25, 31, 36–40, 48–51, 61, 66, 85, 109, 140–43, 147, 149–50, 170, 184n14

Black Student Union, 38

Black studies, 18, 70, 140, 155, 179. *See also* African American studies

Black teachers, 26, 48, 68–69, 85, 89, 100, 106, 119, 155

Blackwell, Arlene: "Sands Junior High School," 77

Black Woman, The (anthology), 16–17, 20, 44–47, 50–51, 78, 119, 148–49, 155

Black Women's Health Project, 56

Black women's literature, 94, 129. *See also* women's literature

Black women's studies, 12, 14, 44, 58. *See also* women's studies

Black women writers, 54, 81, 94–95, 126, 129, 131, 170

Black World, 85

Blake, William, 100

Boggs, James: "Uprooting Racism and Racists," 151

Bosnia, 92–93

Bourdieu, Pierre, 4

Bowen, Angela, 210n95

Boxer, Marilyn Jacoby, 120

Bradstreet, Anne, 100

Brandeis University, 118

Braxton, Toni, 90

Brier, Stephen, 30

Bright Brien, Shanti: *Almost Innocent*, 98; "Crouching in the Shadow of Columbus's Tomb," 90

Brim, Matt, 15, 46

Britton, James, 42

Brooklyn, NY, 63, 75–76, 86; Bedford-Stuyvesant, 62; Ocean Hill–Brownsville, 72

Brooklyn College, 202n67

Brooks, Gwendolyn, 77

Brown, Iemanjá, 11, 154

Brown, Jacqueline, 164

Brown v. Board of Education, 61
Bruffee, Kenneth A., 28, 188n40, 202n67
Bruner, Jerome S., 202n71
Bulkin, Elly: introduction to *Lesbian Fiction*, 167
Bush, Terri, 76–78; *Voice of the Children, The*, 47, 78–81, 92
Busia, Abena, 12, 29, 35
Buurma, Rachel Sagner, 13, 15, 46
Byrd, Rudolph P., 57–58, 140
Byron, Fred, 103

Cade, Helen, 21
Cambodia, 83
campus essays, 16, 37–38, 70–71, 116, 120, 134–35
campus novels, 16
Camus, Albert: *Plague, The*, 105
capitalism: and Black women, 168; and education, 18, 57, 149, 174; and film, 55; and knowledge, 46; in literature, 19, 24, 26, 43, 147; racial, 181
Carew, Jan, 49
Carleton College, 20, 57–58
Carlisle Indian School, 15
Carroll, Lewis: *Alice in Wonderland*, 72
Catlett, Elizabeth, 15
Catonsville Nine, 114
Chad School, 27, 29
Chaucer, Geoffrey, 40
Chavez, Felicia Rose, 97
Cheever, John, 16
Chicago, IL, 139, 144
Chicago, Judy, 169
children's stories, 50–51, 71–74
Chisholm, Shirley, 6, 9
Christian, Barbara: *Black Women Novelists*, 192n146; and Black women's studies, 10, 58; at City College, 7, 103; at Columbia, 22–23, 48; and journal assignments, 111, 153; on literary theory, 192n147; "Race for Theory, The," 42; and the SEEK program, 17, 20, 25–26, 35, 48
Chrysalis, 69, 94, 128, 162
Citizenship and Freedom Schools, 5
City College of New York: admissions at, 184n19, 184n22; Bambara at, 2, 16, 20, 22–42, 44–45, 47–49, 51–52, 54, 56, 59, 78, 179; Cohen Library, 27; English Department, 15, 25–26, 85, 160; history of, 3, 5–9; Jordan at, 2, 17, 60–61, 63–76, 82–87, 93, 179; Lorde at, 2, 17, 139–40, 145–50, 155, 161, 169–70, 179; Rich at, 2, 17, 99–100, 103–24, 126, 129–31, 133–34, 136, 179; student protests at, 31, 36, 47, 69–70. *See also* Search for Education, Elevation, and Knowledge (SEEK) program

City College of San Francisco, 198n163
City University of New York (CUNY): Accelerated Study in Associate Programs, 213n18; classrooms at, 12, 16–18, 141, 159; faculty of, 15, 156, 213n12; funding of, 6, 84; open admissions at, 3, 5–9, 39, 145, 162–63, 177, 197n132; opening of, 75, 109; Poetics Documents Initiative, 11; student population of, 71, 163; tuition at, xi. *See also* City College of New York; Hunter College; John Jay College of Criminal Justice; Lehman College; Queens College
Civil Rights Act (1875), 152
civil rights movement, 5, 7, 23, 39, 60, 66, 69, 101, 113, 137, 144. *See also* Black liberation movements
Claremont, CA, 131
Clark, Joanna: "Motherhood," 45–46
Clark, Kenneth, 61
classroom lyrics, 16, 115–16, 134, 161–62
Cleaver, Eldridge: "Eyes," 106; *Soul on Ice*, 31, 105
Cleveland, OH, 144
Cliff, Michelle, 136–37, 169; *Abeng*, 131
Clifford, James, 130
Clifton, Lucille, 197n115
Cold War, 120
College Discovery, 185n40
College of the Virgin Islands, 169
Collins, Janelle, 43
Collins, Patricia Hill, 149
colonialism, 12, 30–31, 51–53, 115, 167, 174, 178, 210n89
Columbia University: Christian at, 22–23, 48; discrimination at, 6, 21; Lorde at, 142; protests at, 144; Rich at, 2, 99, 102, 105, 117–18, 133
Combahee River Collective, 130
communism, 4, 21, 31, 134
communist labor schools, 5, 183–84n14
community-controlled teaching movement, 17, 20, 27–34, 39, 49, 52, 72, 93, 189n53, 190n104
compensation (for postsecondary teachers), 23, 63, 104, 145, 154, 180–81, 209n74
compulsory heterosexuality, 100
Computer Academy (Oakland), 96
Conference on College Composition and Communication, 73
Congress of Racial Equality (CORE), 6, 45, 60
Connecticut University, 82–83
Conrad, Alfred, 108–9
Conrad, Joseph, 37
Conrad, Rachel, 78–79

consciousness-raising groups, 137–38, 168
consciousness-raising teaching, 5, 35
Cook, Blanche Wiesen, 154–55
Cooper, Anna Julia, 4, 13, 195n57, 212n5; "Higher Education of Women, The," 71
Cooper, Peter, x–xi
Coppin, Fanny Jackson, 4, 13
Cornell University, 2, 131, 185n30
Cornillon, Susan Koppelman: *Images of Women in Fiction*, 118–19
Costa Rica, 90
Courier Post, 80
Covington, Francee, 26, 68; "Are the Revolutionary Techniques Employed . . . ," 45
creative mimicry assignments, 24–25, 64, 77, 90, 105–6, 168, 174
Crenshaw, Kimberlé, 140
critical fabulation, 12
critical pedagogy, 13, 111, 186n58
Cruz, Victor Hernández, 24, 77
Cuba, 112, 170

Daly, Mary, 119
Dark Symphony (anthology), 47
Dash, Julie: *Daughters of the Dust*, 55
Datcher, Michael: *Raising Fences*, 98
Deaf poetry, 96
de Leon, Aya, 92
DeVaux, Alexis, 141, 143, 166, 170
developmental writing, 202n67
Dewey, John, 13; *Democracy and Education*, 10, 186n54; *Experience and Education*, 186n54
Dickinson, Emily, 69, 100, 117
Dinkins, David, 6
diPrima, Diane, 141
Disch, Robert: *White Racism*, 151
Dostoevsky, Fyodor, 37
Douglass, Frederick: *Narrative of the Life of Frederick Douglass*, 113
Douglass College, 100, 121, 124–27, 131, 133–34
Dublin Women's Prison, 96
Du Bois, W. E. B., 81, 185n37
Duke University, 20, 52
Dunbar, Anthony: *Will to Survive, The*, 66–67
Dunbar, Paul Laurence, 62, 79
Dyer, Conrad, 8

education (theories of), 3–5
educational activism, 14–15, 61, 108–9, 169, 200n200
educational racism, 2, 6, 23, 44, 61, 99
Elbow, Peter, 42, 111

Elizabeth Cleaners Street School, 112–13
Ellington, Duke, 144
Ellison, Ralph: *Invisible Man*, 24, 48
Emanuel, James: *Dark Symphony*, 47
Emig, Janet, 42
engaged pedagogy, 13–14
English (language). *See* Black English; Standard English
Essence magazine, 67
ethnic studies, 18, 87, 95, 179
evaluation (of courses), 150
evaluation (of students), xi, 20, 25, 32–33, 52, 64, 112, 189n66
Evans, Mari, 171; "Vive Noir!," 172
Evans, Stephanie Y., 4, 9
Evergreen Review, 70
experiential knowledge, 14, 16, 35, 49, 131
experiential learning, 29, 37

Fanon, Frantz, 24, 36, 83, 136; *Black Skin, White Masks*, 155; *Wretched of the Earth, The*, 31
Fauset, Jessie, 81
feminism: anti-, 173; antiracist, 113–14; consciousness-raising, 137, 168; courses on, ix, 133; intersectional, 3, 100, 126, 130–31, 140; lesbian, 16, 130–31, 150, 158, 175; Lorde and, 140, 147, 160; poetry, 162; and publishing, 46–47, 69, 95, 128; Rich and, 17, 99, 101, 117, 119; second-wave, 100, 127, 138; and the SEEK program, 35–36; and teaching, 121–23, 138, 166, 169, 179; white, 100, 129; woman-of-color, 94. *See also* Black feminism
feminist criticism, 3, 8, 16–17, 20, 42, 44, 46–47, 99, 130, 140, 158, 168
feminist historiography, 12
feminist literature, 11, 16–17, 99, 129
feminist pedagogy, 14, 57, 81, 120, 135, 153, 209n67
Ferguson, Roderick, 27, 68, 70, 140, 162
Finney, Nikkey, 59
Flynn, Richard, 77
Ford, Gerald, 84
Forman, Ruth: *Renaissance*, 98
Foucault, Michel, 186n51
Franklin, V. P., 120
Free Academy. *See* City College of New York
Freedman, Estelle B.: Introduction to Feminist Studies course, 137; "Small Group Pedagogy," 138
Freedom Library Day School, 29
Free University of Berlin, 17, 170–75
Freire, Paulo, 13, 31, 52, 113, 136–37, 146; *Pedagogy of the Oppressed*, 4–5, 10, 13, 63

Frost, Robert, 102
fugitive pedagogy, 4, 89
Fuller, R. Buckminster, 66
funding (of universities), 18, 39, 55, 71, 82, 95, 162–63, 179–80, 184n21, 213n17

Gavaler, Chris, 15
Gay and Lesbian March on Washington, 164
gay and lesbian movements, 139, 164–65
Gayle, Addison, 7–8, 17, 20, 22–23, 26, 35, 45, 48, 50; *Black Aesthetic, The*, 47; *Black Expression*, 47
Georgia Writers Hall of Fame, 19
Germany, 171–74, 178
Get Out (film), 178
Gilbert, Sandra: *Madwoman in the Attic, The*, 47
Giovanni, Nikki, 49, 171
Giroux, Henry, 13
Givens, Jarvis R., 4, 28, 68, 89, 106, 188n46
Glide Memorial Church, 96
Gloster, Hugh M., 42
Glover, Clifford, 160–61, 172
Gold, Alexandra J., 101
Goode, Michael: "April 4, 1968," 77
Gorbanevskaya, Natalya, 117
Gordimer, Nadine: *Burger's Daughter*, 131
Gossett, Hattie, 49
Gossett, Thomas: *Race: The History of an Idea*, 151
grading. *See* evaluation (of students)
Graff, Gerald, 190n103
grammatical correctness, 25. *See also* Black English; Standard English
Great Depression, 26, 68, 84
Greenberg, Joyce, 124–25
Greer Academy, 21
Grimms' Fairy Tales, 72
Gross, Theodore L.: *Dark Symphony*, 47; "How to Kill a College," 15, 40, 73
Gubar, Susan: *Madwoman in the Attic, The*, 47
Guggenheim Fellowship, 99
Gumbs, Alexis Pauline, 7, 12, 86, 149, 151, 208n52

Hale, Jon N., 5, 184n14
Hall, Radclyffe: *Well of Loneliness, The*, 167
Hamer, Fannie Lou, 73
Hamilton, Edith: *Mythology*, 63
Hampshire College, 169–70
Hampton College, 42
Hanley, Lynn, 123
Hanna, Karen Buenavista, 150
Hansberry, Lorraine, 100; *Raising in the Sun, A*, 182

Harlem, NY: activism in, 45, 60, 102, 120, 147; Bambara in, 1, 20–22, 27–28; City College in, 2, 5–6, 24; Jordan in, 66, 70, 74, 135; Lorde in, 169; Rich in, 100, 135; school districts in, 30; Spanish, 68
Harlem Community Resource Center, 76
Harlem Opera House, 21
Harlem Riots of 1964, 66
Harlem University, 39, 70, 146
Harlem Writers Guild, 143
Harney, Stefano, 7, 93, 95
Hartman, Saidiya, 12
Harvard University, 3, 6, 101, 120; Schlesinger Library at Radcliffe Institute for Advanced Study, 10–11, 65. *See also* Radcliffe College
Heffernan, Laura, 13, 15, 46
Heidegger, Martin, 102–3
Heller, Louis G.: *Death of the American University*, 15
Henderson, David, 7, 35, 109, 111, 153
Herald Tribune, 60
Herschel, Caroline, 117
heterosexism, 172
heterosexuality, 100, 110, 118, 123, 134, 148, 167
Highland Elementary School, 96
Highsmith, Patricia: *Price of Salt, The*, 167
Hijuelos, Oscar, 44
Hines, Andy, 5, 183–84n14
historically Black colleges and universities (HBCUs), 7–8, 37, 142, 185n37
Hobart, Hiʻilei Julia, 212n3; Race and Indigeneity in the Pacific course, 178–79
Hoffman, Marvin, 81
Holiday, Billie, 137
Holladay, Hilary, 108, 113, 135, 137
Holmes, Linda Janet, 12, 21, 32, 35, 40, 46, 51, 56, 58–59, 190n78
Home Girls (anthology), 44
homophobia, 55, 87, 130, 147, 154, 160–61, 164, 168
Hong, Grace Kyungwon, 140
hooks, bell, 4, 9, 13–14, 129–30
horizontal pedagogy, x
Housman, A. E., 102
Howard, Mary, 121
Howard, Vanessa: "Ghetto," 78–80
Howe, Florence, 119
Hughes, Langston, 51, 77, 79, 97; "Theme of English B," 21
Hull, Gloria T., 155
humanities, 15, 17, 21, 162–63, 174, 179
Hunter College, 142, 158, 164, 169–70, 202n67

Hunter High School, 141
Hurston, Zora Neale, 81, 85

Images of Women in Fiction (anthology), 118–19
Indiana University, 47
individualism, 44, 68, 76, 93, 117, 131, 177
Inoue, Asao B.: *Antiracist Writing Assessment Ecologies*, 32
institutional racism, 150–53, 170
insurgent academic networks, 201n49
insurgent knowledge, 12, 90
intellectual imperialism, 30
intersectional feminism, 3, 100, 126, 130–31, 140
Israel, 135
Ivanhoe, Granville, 62

Jackson, MS, 142
Jamaica, 131
Jersey City, NJ, 20
Jewish people, x, 6, 12, 36
Jim Crow, 4, 68, 152
John Jay College of Criminal Justice, 140, 150–51, 153, 155, 158, 161–62, 164, 209n74
Johnson, Lyndon B., 151, 184n21
Jones, Gayl, 197n115
Jones, LeRoi. *See* Baraka, Amiri
Jordan, June: and academia, 82–85, 95–96, 180, 182; and anthologies of student writing, 47, 65, 76–82, 92–95, 143, 173–75; and Bambara, 2, 16–17, 35, 61, 64, 69–72, 81–82, 85, 89, 92–95; and counter-poetic pedagogy, 12; early life of, 61–63; and feminist pedagogy, 14; and Lorde, 16, 69–70, 94, 147–48, 170; and Morrison, 197n115; and Poetry for the People, 89–92, 135; and project-based pedagogy, 17, 86–89; and Rich, 16, 69, 104, 108–12, 120, 128–29, 135–36; and the SEEK program, 7, 9, 15, 66–72, 177; teaching materials of, 11, 97; and transgressive teaching, 4; writings of, 60–61, 72–76
Jordan, June (courses of): The Art of Black English (Stony Brook), 86–87; Coming into the World Female (Berkeley), 88; Contemporary Global Issues for Women (Berkeley), 87–88; Freshman Composition (City College), 64–65; Literature and Social Change (Sarah Lawrence), 83–84; Martin and Malcolm (Berkeley), 88; Poetry for the People (Berkeley), 89–92, 96–98, 135; Politics of Childhood, The (Berkeley), 88; Teaching and Writing of Poetry (Berkeley), 91–92, 96
Jordan, June (teaching career): at City College of New York, 2, 17, 60–61, 63–76, 82–87, 93, 179; at Connecticut College, 82–83; at Sarah Lawrence College, 82–83; at SUNY Stony Brook, 85–86, 95–96; at Teachers and Writers Collaborative, 76–82; at University of California, Berkeley, 87–96, 110; at Yale University, 82–83
Jordan, June (works of): "Black Studies: Bringing Back the Person," 70; *Civil Wars*, 85; *Directed by Desire: The Collected Poems*, 136; "Finding the Haystack in the Needle," 95; "For the Poet: Adrienne Rich," 136; *His Own Where*, 73–75; "Merit Review Statement," 97; *New Days*, 108; "Nicaragua: Why I Had to Go There," 67–68; "Poem about My Rights," 87; *Poetry in a Time of Genocide*, 92–93; "Profiles in Conflict," 93; review of *Gorilla, My Love*, 85; *Revolutionary Blueprint, A*, 97; "Skyrise for Harlem," 66–67, 74; "Sonnet for Adrienne Rich" (unpublished), 128; *Soulscript*, 47, 79–80, 92; "Tomorrow in English" (unpublished), 65; *Voice of the Children, The*, 47, 78–81, 92; "White English/Black English," 73; *Whose Country Is This, Anyway*, 92; "Writing and Teaching," 11; "You Can't See the Trees for the School," 63
Jordan, Reggie, 86
Jordan, Willie, 86
Joseph, Gloria, 14, 129, 143–44, 169; Insurgent Sisters course, 170
Joseph, Steven: *Me Nobody Knows, The*, 80
journal assignments, 13, 111, 141, 152–54, 158–59, 171–72, 174, 209n67
Joyce, James, 97
June Jordan's Poetry for the People (anthology), 97. *See also* Poetry for the People

Kahina, Chenzira Davis, 175
Kahlo, Frida, 137
Kaplan, Caren, 130
Katherine Dunham School, 21
Katz, Cindi, 130
kaufman, erica, 11
Kaye, Melanie: Women as Creative Artists course, 168–69
Keats, John, 100, 119
Kendi, Ibram X., 37
Kenya, 87
Khan-Cullors, Patrisse, 140
Killens, Oliver, 15
King, Martin Luther, Jr., 1, 61, 77, 99, 144–45
King, Paula: Women as Creative Artists course, 168–69
Kingston, Maxine Hong: *Woman Warrior, The*, 53

Kinloch, Valerie, 12
Kitchen Table: Women of Color Press, 94
Koch, Kenneth: *Wishes, Lies, and Dreams*, 80
Kohl, Herbert R., 60; *36 Children*, 80; *Teaching the "Unteachable,"* 80
Kovel, Joel: *White Racism*, 139
Kriegel, Leonard: "Surviving the Apocalypse," 109
Ku Klux Klan, 142
Kynard, Carmen, 8, 185n37

Laney, Lucy, 4
Larsen, Nella: *Quicksand*, 151
Lavan, Makeba, 11, 37, 46
Lavin, David E., 39, 185n43
Lawrence, D. H., 102; *Sons and Lovers*, 105
Leary, Christopher, 123
Lebanon, 61, 131, 135
Lehman College, 149–50, 160
Lerner, Gerda: *Woman in American History, The*, 155
lesbian continuum, 100, 127
lesbian literature, 166
lesbians: and feminism, 16, 130–31, 150, 158, 175; and Lorde, 131, 140, 143–44, 147, 150, 155, 158, 160–61, 164–67, 170, 175; and publishing, 94; and Rich, 36, 99–100, 119, 123, 127, 130, 134, 137
lesbian separatism, 119
Levertov, Denise, 102
Lewis, Heather, 189n53
Lewis, Thabiti, 35, 43
liberal individualism, 44, 46–47, 93, 117, 131, 177
liberalism, 24, 48, 51, 105, 115, 140, 161, 174
liberatory pedagogy, 5, 111
Litany for Survival, A (documentary), 108, 164
literary criticism, 15, 47–48, 100
literary theory, 192n147
literature. *See* American literature; Black literature; feminist literature; lesbian literature; women's literature
Livingston College, 48–51, 58, 121
Locke, Alain, 81
Lorde, Audre: and academia, 149–52, 180; and Bambara, 16, 35, 70, 143, 147–49, 153, 158, 161, 169–70, 175; and counter-poetic pedagogy, 12; early life of, 141–44; and feminist pedagogy, 14, 155–57; in Germany, 170–75; and Jordan, 16, 69–70, 94, 147–48, 170; and journal assignments, 152–54; and pedagogy of difference, 17–18, 141, 163–70; and Rich, 16, 69, 104, 107–8, 111, 115–16, 127–29, 146–47, 162, 169–70; and the SEEK program, 2, 7, 9, 15, 145–46, 177; teaching materials of, 11; and transgressive teaching, 4; writings of, 15, 139–40, 157–63

Lorde, Audre (courses of): Afro-American Literature (John Jay), 163; American Women in Black and White (John Jay), 154–55, 159, 163; Contemporary Black Women's Poetry (Free University), 171–73; English 101 (John Jay), 156; Lesbian Voices (Hunter College), 166–68; Poet as Outsider (Hunter College), 165; Race and the Urban Situation (John Jay), 16, 139, 150–54, 157, 159–61, 164, 166, 172

Lorde, Audre (teaching career): at City College of New York, 2, 17, 139–40, 145–50, 155, 161, 169–70, 179; at Free University of Berlin, 170–75; at Hunter College, 164–69; at John Jay College of Criminal Justice, 140, 150–164, 210n95; at Lehman College, 149–50, 160; at Tougaloo College, 2, 142–45, 150, 173, 210n95

Lorde, Audre (works of): "Age, Race, Class, and Sex," 159; "Bees, The," 157–58; "Blackstudies," 157, 160–62, 210n95; *Black Unicorn, The*, 147; *Burst of Light, A*, 159, 175; *Cables to Rage*, 144; *Cancer Journals, The*, 158–59, 175; "Classrooms, The," 157, 159; *Coal*, 147; "Dear Toni," 148–49, 157, 161, 169, 174; "Eye to Eye," 167–68; *First Cities, The*, 108, 142; introduction to *Showing Our Colors*, 173; "Love Poem," 160; "Master's Tools Will Never Dismantle the Master's House, The," 15–16; "Poet as Teacher," 156; "Poetry Is Not a Luxury," 159, 162–63; *Pound*, 143, 173; "Power," 161, 172; "Same Death Over and Over, The," 161; *Sister Outsider*, 140; "Teacher," 116; "Transformation of Silence into Language and Action, The," 147; "Woman/Dirge for Wasted Children, A," 161; *Zami*, 131, 140

Luria, Alexander, 202n71
Lurie, Ellen: *How to Change the Schools*, 113

MacPhail, Scott, 67
Malcolm X, 60–61, 113, 152
Malraux, André: *Man's Fate*, 31
Martens, China, 149
Marxism, ix, 57, 130
Massachusetts Review, 34
Massiah, Louis, 45; *Bombing of Osage Avenue, The* (film), 55–56
Matthiessen, F. O., 101
Mayes, Janet, 145–46
McGurl, Mark, 16, 76
McKay, Claude, 81
McKay, Nellie Y., 44, 58

McKittrick, Katherine, 196n74
McLaren, Peter, 13
medical-industrial complex, 158–59
Meltzer, Milton, 79
memoirs, 31, 80, 98, 105, 140, 158–59, 167. *See also* autobiography
memorization, 13, 64, 76, 152
Me Nobody Knows, The (anthology), 80
Meyer, Elizabeth Riva, 90, 98
MFA programs, 16, 76, 99, 102, 125
Milne, A. A.: *Winnie the Pooh*, 72
Milton, John, 113
Mississippi Freedom Schools, 184n14
Mixco, Miguel Huezo, 59
Mobilization for Youth, 60
Modern Language Association (MLA), 108, 180
Mohanty, Chandra Talpade, 130
Molloy, Sean, 25–26, 48, 189n66
Montenegro, David, 114
Moody-Turner, Shirley, 212n5
Moore, Marianne, 15
Moraga, Cherríe, 168; *Loving in the War Years*, 167; *This Bridge Called My Back*, 94–95
Morrison, Toni, 35, 81–82, 197n115; *Sula*, 58
Moten, Fred, 7, 93, 95
motherhood, 44–46, 99, 101, 108, 118, 124–25, 149, 162, 208n52
Mother Jones, 88
MOVE (organization), 55–56
Ms. magazine, 67, 69
Muller, Laura: *Revolutionary Blueprint, A*, 97
multiculturalism, 58, 140
multicultural literacy, 54
multimedia pedagogy. *See* multimodal pedagogy
multimodal pedagogy, 20, 41–43, 51, 58, 88, 111, 177
Murch, Donna Jean, 5
Murray, Marian, 49, 59

NAACP (National Association for the Advancement of Colored People), 37
Nabokov, Vladimir, 2
Nairobi Schools, 29
National Advisory Commission on Civil Disorders, 151
National Book Award, 59, 89, 98, 127–28, 147
National Council of Teachers of English (NCTE), 41–42
National Higher Education Act, 184n21
National Institute of Arts and Letters Award, 99
National SEEK and College Discovery Day, 9

National Women's Studies Association (NWSA), 108
Native Americans, 4, 53, 87, 105, 165, 177–78
Navies, Kelly Elaine, 90, 97–98
Neighborhood Arts Center (Atlanta), 17, 55
neocolonialism, 31
neoliberalism, 18, 55, 57, 134, 162–63, 179–80, 197n132
Newark, NJ, 27, 29, 41, 144
Newfield, Christopher, 184n21
New Jersey College and University Coalition on Women's Education, 126
New Republic, 67
Newsday, 86
New Women's Times, 129
New York City, NY: Bambara in, 49, 143; Black communities in, 9, 45, 149, 163; Board of Education, 30, 72; education funding in, 6, 18, 21, 39, 61, 84; Latinx communities in, 9; in literature, 74; Lorde in, 142, 164; Police Department, 102, 139; poverty in, 61, 184n28; Rich in, 101; sanitation worker strike (1968), 144. *See also* Brooklyn, NY; Harlem, NY; Queens, NY
New York Times, 14–15, 24, 60, 80, 87
New Zealand, 178
Nicaragua, 61, 67, 130
9/11 terrorist attacks, 93
Nishikawa, Kinohi, 95, 199n196
Northfield School for Girls, 62

Oakland, CA, 96
Oakland Community School, 29
Obourn, Megan, 140
Occupy Wall Street, x, 37
Oguntoye, Katharina: *Showing Our Colors*, 173–75
O'Keeffe, Georgia, 96
Omolade, Barbara, 14
open admissions (genres of). *See* anthologies of student writing; campus essays; classroom lyrics
open admissions era (definition of), 3
Ortega, Kirsten Bartholomew, 12, 90
Orwell, George, 190n103; "Such, Such Were the Joys," 106–7

Pacifica National Radio, 87
Palestine, 61
Pan-Africanism, 5, 21, 27, 29, 184n14
Panama, 90

Parker, Pat, 171; "Where Will You Be?," 172
Partridge, Kate, 128
Passeron, Jean-Claude, 4
Paton, Alan: *Cry, the Beloved Country*, 31
Patterson, Raymond, 7, 35
pedagogy: activist, 67, 212n5; Black feminist, 14, 42–43; collectivist, 44; community-controlled, 32–34, 52; counter-poetic, 12; and creative mimicry, 77; critical, 13, 111, 186n58; definition of, 9–11; despisal, 76; of difference, 18, 141, 145, 161, 165–66, 168; engaged, 13; feminist, 14, 57, 81, 120, 135, 153, 209n67; in film, 56; fugitive, 4, 89; of gathering, 49; grassroots, 46; horizontal, x; liberatory, 5, 111; in literature, 74–75, 158; of location, 17, 100, 106, 118, 130–38; multimodal, 17, 20, 41–43, 51, 58, 88, 111, 177; nonexperiment, 62; progressive, 29; project-based, 61, 87, 97; public, 154; publishing, 65, 78, 81–82, 85, 90, 93–95; queer, 167, 208n52; social justice, 3, 136, 179; student-centered, 14, 25, 27, 33, 35, 80, 100, 141, 186n55; of student knowledge, 174
peer review, 10, 28
Penale, Anthony, 22
Perlow, Olivia N., 9
Petry, Ann, 25; *Darkness and Confusion*, 106
Philadelphia, PA, 20, 29, 53, 55–56, 97, 102
Philadelphia Unemployment Project, 56
Piscataway, NJ, 48
placemaking, 75, 91
Plath, Sylvia, 102
Plato: *Republic*, 105
Plessy v. Ferguson, 152
Poe, Edgar Allan, 62
Poetry for the People, 89, 91–92, 96–98, 135
Poetry in a Time of Genocide, 92–93
police: teaching, 140, 150–51, 153–57, 160–61; violence, xi, 56, 61, 86, 139, 154, 156, 160, 172
politics of location, 130–31
Pontecorvo, Gillo: *Battle of Algiers, The*, 31, 41
Poor People's Campaign, 1, 83–84
Portland State University, 168–69
Pound (anthology), 143, 173
Pound, Ezra, 102
Powell, Geneva: "Three Little Panthers, The," 51
praxis, 10, 57, 153, 169
prison-industrial complex, 116
problem papers, 61, 66–68, 87
process pedagogy, 111
publishing industry, 81, 94–95, 128, 147, 165, 197n115, 199n196
Puerto Rican literature, 24, 26–27, 47, 52

Puerto Rican students, 2–3, 6, 22, 25, 38–40, 48, 53, 66, 76, 104, 150, 184n28
Puerto Rican studies, 36, 160
Puerto Rico, 53, 61
Pulitzer Prize for Fiction, 44
Pynchon, Thomas, 16

Queen Latifah, 90
Queens, NY, 20, 61, 160–61, 172
Queens College, xi, 22, 44
queer theory, 15–16, 100, 140

racial exclusion, 5–7, 11, 39, 61, 63, 91, 183n14, 184n21, 185n37, 185n46. *See also* segregation
racism. *See* educational racism; institutional racism; racial exclusion; white supremacy
Radcliffe College, 99, 101, 119–20
Random House, 197n115
Reagan, Ronald, 9, 163
Reconstruction, 185n37
Redbook magazine, 30
Reinhold, Sue, 137
revolutionary mothering, 149
Rich, Adrienne: and academia, 118–21, 134–35, 180; and antihierarchical teaching, 123–24; and Bambara, 16, 35, 143, 147–49, 153, 158, 161, 169–70, 175; early life of, 100–103; educational activism of, 108–9; and feminism, 12, 14, 99–100, 117–18; and Jordan, 16, 69, 92, 104, 108–12, 120, 128–29, 135–36; and Lorde, 16, 104, 107–8, 111, 115–16, 127–29, 146–47, 162, 169–70; and pedagogy of location, 17, 130–34; and pedagogy of student knowledge, 174; and the SEEK program, 2, 7, 9, 15, 103–7, 121–22, 177; and student-centered teaching, 112; teaching materials of, 11, 125; teaching with Cliff, 136–38; and transgressive teaching, 4; writing classes of, 110–11; writings of, 113–17, 126–29, 161–62
Rich, Adrienne (courses of): Activist Roots of Feminist Theory, The (Stanford), 133–34; American Women Poets (Douglass), 121–23; ENG 1-G11 (City College), 110–11; English 1.8 (City College), 104–5; English 1-H (City College), 105; English 1-T (City College), 104–5; Feminist Studies 102/203 (Stanford), 133; Images of Women in Poetry by Men (City College), 118–19, 137; Woman Novelist as Historian (SJSU), 131–32; Woman to Woman Relationships in Literature (Douglass), 127; Women and Difference (Stanford), 136–37; Writing out of Female Experience (Douglass), 123–25

Rich, Adrienne (teaching career): at City College of New York, 2, 17, 99–100, 103–24, 126, 129–31, 133–34, 136, 179; at Columbia University, 2, 99, 102, 105, 117–18, 133; at Cornell University, 131; at Douglass College, 100, 121–27, 131, 133–34; at San Jose State University, 131–33; at Scripps College, 131, 134; at Stanford University, 133–34, 136–37

Rich, Adrienne (works of): "Arts of the Possible," 134; "Atlas of the Difficult World, An," 205n168; "Burning of Paper Instead of Children, The," 114–15, 161–62; *Change of World, The*, 101; "Claiming an Education," 126; "Compulsory Heterosexuality and Lesbian Existence," 118, 127; "Disloyal to Civilization," 129; *Diving into the Wreck*, 99–100, 203n93; "For June, in the Year 2001," 136; "Hunger," 147; introduction to *Directed by Desire*, 136; "Invisibility in Academe," 134; "Long Conversation, A," 134; "Resisting Amnesia," 131; "School among the Ruins, The," 134; *Snapshots of a Daughter in Law*, 101; "Soul of a Woman's College, The," 134; "Student Passes—Education Fails," 107; "Taking Women Students Seriously," 126; "Teaching Language in Open Admissions," 11, 115, 117–18; "Towards a Woman-Centered University," 119–21; "Wholeness Is No Trifling Matter," 129; "Why I Refused the National Medal for the Arts," 134; *Will to Change, The*, 113; *Of Woman Born*, 118

Rickford, Russell, 5, 184n14
Risam, Roopika, 89
Rivera, Louis Reyes, 39
Rockefeller, Nelson, 39
Roland Park Country School, 100–101
Ross, Gail, 202n71
Rushin, Kate, 143
Rust, Marion, 127–28
Rutgers University, 17; Douglass College, 100, 121, 124–27, 131, 133–34; Livingston College, 48–51, 58, 121

Sacramento, CA, 163
Sanchez, Sonia, 49, 69, 171
San Francisco State, 38
San Jose State University (SJSU), 131–33
Sarah Lawrence College, 82–84, 142
Sartre, Jean-Paul: *No Exit*, 105
scaffolding, 110–11, 202n71
Schomburg Center for Research in Black Culture, 27
Schultz, Dagmar, 170–71; *Showing Our Colors*, 173–74

Schwartz, Barry N.: *White Racism*, 151
Scribe Video Center (Philadelphia), 20, 55, 59, 98; Community Visions project, 56–57; Video for Social Change, 56
Scripps College, 131, 134
Search for Education, Elevation, and Knowledge (SEEK) program: admissions to, 184n28, 185n40; Bambara and, 2, 16, 20, 22–42, 44–45, 47–49, 51–52, 54, 56, 59; funding of, 187n13, 188n44; history of, 3, 6–9, 181, 184n27; Jordan and, 66–73, 82; legacy of, 12, 179, 185n30; Lorde and, 145–50, 153, 166; Rich and, 17, 92, 100, 103–17, 121–22, 126
segregation, 6, 26, 85, 102, 185n37. *See also* racial exclusion
Servicemen's Readjustment Act (GI Bill), 184n21
sexism: in academia, 18, 52, 54, 160–61; in Black liberation movements, 154; and the gay and lesbian movement, 164; in literature, 19, 43, 45, 60; in the New Left, 130; and pedagogy, 14, 72, 87, 149, 168, 172, 175; in publishing, 94, 128
Sexton, Anne, 102
sexual harassment, 133–34
Shakespeare, William, 24, 62, 117, 169
Shalev, Talia, 11, 195n35
Shange, Ntozake, 92
Sharif, Solmaz, 89, 98
Shaughnessy, Mina, 7, 26, 66–68, 103, 111, 145, 153
Shea, Thomas J., 160–61
Shelley, Percy Bysshe: *The Masque of Anarchy*, 83
Shipka, Jody, 41
Shor, Ira, 13
Showalter, Elaine, 121
Showing Our Colors (anthology), 173–75
Signs, 128
Silberstein, Richard A., 185n43
Silko, Leslie Marmon: *Ceremony*, 53
Simon, Leslie, 198n163
Sisterhood (Black women writers group), 94, 148
situated knowledge, 158
16th Street Baptist Church bombing, 158
slavery, 36, 50, 113, 129, 170
Smith, Barbara, 94, 155, 166, 169; *Homegirls*, 167; Invisible Woman in Literature course, 166; "Towards a Black Feminist Criticism," 167
Smith, Holly, 11
Smith, Neil, 130
Soulscript (anthology), 79–80, 92
South Africa, 96, 131, 175
Spacks, Patricia Meyer: *Female Imagination, The*, 47
Speaker's Corner (Harlem), 21, 28

Spellman, A. B., 49
Spelman College, 20, 52; Archives, 10–11
Stafford, Jean, 102–3
Standard English, 41, 114–15, 146
standpoint theory, 158
Stanford University, 17, 133–34, 136–37
Stanley, Julia, 166
State University of New York (SUNY), 12, 185n30, 213n12; Stony Brook, 85–86, 95–96
St. Croix, 175
St. Croix Women Writers Symposium, 169
Steinbeck, John: *Grapes of Wrath*, 83
Stevens, Wallace, 102
St. Mark's Academy, 141
Streim, Alex, 134
student activism, 8, 31, 36–39, 48–49, 87, 102, 144, 146, 164, 179
student anthologies. *See* anthologies of student writing
student assignments. *See* creative mimicry assignments; journal assignments; problem papers
student-centered pedagogy, 14, 25, 27, 33, 35, 80, 100, 141, 186n55
student-centered teaching, 13, 17, 20, 104, 112, 123, 181, 186n56
student debt, x, 18, 179–80
Student Nonviolent Coordinating Committee (SNCC), 45
student-teacher poets (STPS), 91–93, 96
Sundiata, Sekou, 44
Sutton, Percy, 6
Swarthmore College, 102
Swift, Jonathan: *Modest Proposal, A*, 83

Tales and Stories for Black Folks (anthology), 50–51, 65
Tallahassee, FL, 136
Teachers and Writers Collaborative (TWC), 76–78, 80, 83
teaching materials (archives), 2, 10–14, 17, 35–36, 59, 65, 68, 116, 131–33
teaching methods. *See* activist teaching; Afrocentric teaching; antihierarchical teaching; community-controlled teaching; consciousness-raising teaching; student-centered teaching; transgressive teaching
theory in the flesh, 168
Third Cinema, 55
Third World Women (anthology), 44
This Bridge Called My Back (anthology), 44, 94–95, 178

Thoreau, Henry David, 190n103
Thorsson, Courtney, 95
Tomás Reed, Conor, 11–12, 37, 46, 70, 195n35, 203n93
"Tomorrow in English" (anthology), 65
Toomer, Jean, 79
Tougaloo College, 2, 142–45, 150, 173
transgressive teaching, 4–5, 8, 10, 68, 87, 89, 150, 177–78, 181
Traub, James, 109
Traylor, Eleanor, 46, 49
Trenton, NJ, 41

Ulanov, Barry, 63–64, 92
ungrading, 33, 111
United Nations, 87
United States: citizenship in, 130; education in, 4–5, 42, 134; free university in, 5, 9; imperialism of, 53, 61, 67; racism in, 31, 151; student debt in, x, 18, 179–80; student movements in, 70, 102, 144; women in, 130, 154
University of California, 95, 98; Board of Regents, 135–36
University of California, Berkeley, 48, 87, 93, 95–97, 110, 135
University of California San Diego, 37
University of Chicago, 62
University of Delaware, 20, 52–54, 94, 132, 170
University of Nebraska, 166
University of Texas at Austin, 178
Upward Bound, 83

Valéry, Paul, 102
Vazquez, Alexandra T., 51
Velez, Isabel, 77
Vietnam War, 1, 31, 83, 99, 101–2, 114, 144, 163
Village Voice, 80
Villalobos, Ruben Antonio, 98; "Tio Juancho," 90
Voice of the Children, The (anthology), 47, 78–80, 92
Volpe, Edmond, 26
Vonnegut, Kurt, 16
Vygotsky, Lev, 202n71

Wagner, Geoffrey, 40, 71; *End of Education, The*, 15
Walker, Alice, 51, 69, 94, 127, 148; "In Search of Our Mothers' Gardens," 42
Wallace, Michele, 130
Waller-Patterson, Belinda 43
Ware, Kassandra, 11
Warren, Kenneth, 82

Washington, Booker T., 152
Webster, Horace, 5
welfare state, 180
Wellesley University, 47
Wells, Ida B., 212n5
West India, 62
West Virginia University, 163
Wheeler, Lesley, 15
White, Marvina, 25
White Citizens Council, 142–43
Whitehead, Alfred North, 25; *Aims of Education*, 63–64
white privilege, ix, 113, 119
white students, 6, 20, 26, 36, 61, 82, 95, 149–50, 152, 181, 185n43, 194n5
white supremacy, xi, 5, 50, 61, 79, 89, 106, 119, 143, 161, 177
white teachers, 10, 23, 32, 80
white women, 106, 127, 129, 147, 150, 159, 171, 180
Whitman, Walt, 119, 135
Whose Country Is This, Anyway, 92
Wilcox, Preston, 61
Williams, Emlyn: *Corn Is Green, The*, 103
Williams, Mai'a, 149
Williams, Shirley Anne, 92
Wilson, Edmund, 2
Wisher, Yolanda, 97
Wishes, Lies, and Dreams (anthology), 80

Wittgenstein, Ludwig, 102–3
Women against Abuse, 56
women's colleges, 119–21, 131, 134–35
Women's Community Revitalization Project, 57
women's health movement, 158, 210n90
women's literature, 47, 121, 129. *See also* Black women's literature
women's movement, 44, 69, 100, 112, 118–22, 127, 129, 137–38, 144, 154, 165–66, 203n93
women's studies, 5, 14, 16, 87–88, 100, 120–22, 135, 153–55, 168, 174. *See* Black women's studies
Wood, David, 202n71
Woodson, Carter, 4, 29; *Journal of Negro History*, 201n49
Woolf, Virginia, 25, 130, 137; "Room of One's Own, A," 168–69
Wordsworth, William, 40, 105
Wright, Richard, 25, 83; "Man Who Lived Underground, The," 106; *Native Son*, 48
W. W. Norton, 47, 147

Yale University, 3, 6, 82–83
Yale Younger Poets Award, 99
Yancey, Kathleen Blake, 41
Yeats, W. B., 102, 119
Yerba Buena Center for the Arts, 96

Zimmerman, Jonathan, 13